AF752327

AGRICULTURE ISSUES AND POLICIES

THE FARM BILL

REVIEW, BACKGROUND, AND THE WTO

AGRICULTURE ISSUES AND POLICIES

Additional books and e-books in this series can be found on Nova's website under the Series tab.

CONGRESSIONAL POLICIES, PRACTICES AND PROCEDURES

Additional books and e-books in this series can be found on Nova's website under the Series tab.

AGRICULTURE ISSUES AND POLICIES

THE FARM BILL

REVIEW, BACKGROUND, AND THE WTO

KATIE M. HARRISON
EDITOR

snova
New York

Copyright © 2019 by Nova Science Publishers, Inc.

All rights reserved. No part of this book may be reproduced, stored in a retrieval system or transmitted in any form or by any means: electronic, electrostatic, magnetic, tape, mechanical photocopying, recording or otherwise without the written permission of the Publisher.

We have partnered with Copyright Clearance Center to make it easy for you to obtain permissions to reuse content from this publication. Simply navigate to this publication's page on Nova's website and locate the "Get Permission" button below the title description. This button is linked directly to the title's permission page on copyright.com. Alternatively, you can visit copyright.com and search by title, ISBN, or ISSN.

For further questions about using the service on copyright.com, please contact:
Copyright Clearance Center
Phone: +1-(978) 750-8400 Fax: +1-(978) 750-4470 E-mail: info@copyright.com.

NOTICE TO THE READER

The Publisher has taken reasonable care in the preparation of this book, but makes no expressed or implied warranty of any kind and assumes no responsibility for any errors or omissions. No liability is assumed for incidental or consequential damages in connection with or arising out of information contained in this book. The Publisher shall not be liable for any special, consequential, or exemplary damages resulting, in whole or in part, from the readers' use of, or reliance upon, this material. Any parts of this book based on government reports are so indicated and copyright is claimed for those parts to the extent applicable to compilations of such works.

Independent verification should be sought for any data, advice or recommendations contained in this book. In addition, no responsibility is assumed by the Publisher for any injury and/or damage to persons or property arising from any methods, products, instructions, ideas or otherwise contained in this publication.

This publication is designed to provide accurate and authoritative information with regard to the subject matter covered herein. It is sold with the clear understanding that the Publisher is not engaged in rendering legal or any other professional services. If legal or any other expert assistance is required, the services of a competent person should be sought. FROM A DECLARATION OF PARTICIPANTS JOINTLY ADOPTED BY A COMMITTEE OF THE AMERICAN BAR ASSOCIATION AND A COMMITTEE OF PUBLISHERS.

Additional color graphics may be available in the e-book version of this book.

Library of Congress Cataloging-in-Publication Data

ISBN: 978-1-53615-272-2

Published by Nova Science Publishers, Inc. † New York

Contents

PREFACE

The farm bill is an omnibus, multi-year law that governs an array of agricultural and food programs. Although agricultural policies are sometimes created and changed by freestanding legislation or as part of other major laws, the farm bill provides a predictable opportunity for policymakers to comprehensively and periodically address agricultural and food issues. Chapter 1 reviews our current farm programs and discuss solutions for the upcoming 2018 bill.

Chapter 2 provides background on each of the major titles of the current farm bill and previews of some of the potential issues that could factor into the debate.

Every new farm bill involves some modification or replacement of existing farm programs. A key question likely to be asked of every new program is how it will affect U.S. commitments under the World Trade Organization's (WTO's) Agreement on Agriculture (AoA) and its Agreement on Subsidies and Countervailing Measures (SCM) as described in chapter 3.

Chapter 1 - This is an edited, reformatted and augmented version of Field Hearing before the Committee on Agriculture, Nutrition, and Forestry United States Senate, One Hundred Fifteenth Congress, First Session, Publication No. S. HRG. 115–168, dated February 23, 2017.

Chapter 2 - Congress periodically establishes agricultural and food policy in an omnibus farm bill. The 115th Congress faces reauthorization of the 2014 farm bill—the Agricultural Act of 2014 (P.L. 113-79, H.Rept. 113-333)—because many of its provisions expire in 2018. The 2014 farm bill is the most recent omnibus farm bill. It was enacted in February 2014 and succeeded the Food, Conservation, and Energy Act of 2008 (P.L. 110-246, "2008 farm bill"). In recent decades, the breadth of farm bills has steadily grown to include new and expanding food and agricultural interests. The 2014 farm bill contains 12 titles encompassing farm commodity revenue supports, farm credit, trade, agricultural conservation, research, rural development, energy, and foreign and domestic food programs, among other programs. Provisions in the 2014 farm bill reshaped the structure of farm commodity support, expanded crop insurance coverage, consolidated conservation programs, reauthorized and revised nutrition assistance, and extended authority to appropriate funds for many U.S. Department of Agriculture (USDA) discretionary programs through FY2018. When the 2014 farm bill was enacted, the Congressional Budget Office (CBO) estimated that the total cost of mandatory programs would be $489 billion over the five years FY2014-FY2018. Four titles accounted for 99% ($483.8 billion) of anticipated farm bill mandatory program outlays: nutrition, crop insurance, conservation, and farm commodity support. The nutrition title, which includes the Supplemental Nutrition Assistance Program (SNAP), comprised 80% of the total, with the remaining 20% mostly geared toward agricultural production across other titles. Traditionally, a primary focus of omnibus farm bills has been commodity-based revenue support policy—namely, the methods and levels of federal support provided to agricultural producers. The 2014 farm bill amended U.S. farm safety net programs by expanding crop insurance provisions and modifying counter-cyclical support while eliminating direct payments to growers of grains, cotton, and peanuts. Upland cotton was removed from eligibility for participation in the new revenue support programs as part of compliance with a World Trade Organization dispute settlement case with Brazil. Instead, cotton producers were offered an insurance-like support program that protects against within-season revenue shortfalls. Another major change involved dairy: Previous support programs were replaced with a new insurance-like margin program that insures against shortfalls in the difference between milk prices and feed costs. Most farm program proponents agree that the new cotton and dairy programs have performed ineffectively and are likely to see proposals for change. Other farm interest groups, however, continue to point to competing policy priorities—covering a range of equity concerns across the entire farm sector—and call for enhanced support for small and medium-sized farms, specialty crops, organic agriculture, local and regional food systems, healthy and nutritious foods, research, conservation, and rural development, among others. One of the principal drivers of a new farm bill debate will be the federal budget. According to CBO estimates, if ongoing programs were to continue under current law, mandatory farm bill spending by the four largest titles—nutrition, crop insurance, farm commodity programs, and conservation—is projected to be about $435 billion over the next five years (FY2018-FY2022), with domestic nutrition assistance accounting for nearly 77% of the total. This compares with actual costs for the first three years of the 2014 farm bill and projections for its last two years, which suggest that these four titles may cost $456 billion over FY2014-FY2018.

Chapter 3 - Omnibus U.S. farm legislation—referred to as the farm bill—has typically been renewed every five or six years. Farm income and commodity price support programs have been a part of U.S. farm bills since the 1930s. Each successive farm bill usually involves some modification or replacement of existing farm programs. A key question likely to be asked of every new farm proposal or program is how it will affect

U.S. commitments under the World Trade Organization's (WTO's) Agreement on Agriculture (AoA) and its Agreement on Subsidies and Countervailing Measures (SCM). The United States is currently committed, under the AoA, to spend no more than $19.1 billion annually on those domestic farm support programs most likely to distort trade—referred to as amber box programs and measured by the Aggregate Measure of Support (AMS). The AoA spells out the rules for countries to determine whether their policies—for any given year—are potentially trade distorting and how to calculate the costs. The most recent U.S. notification to the WTO of domestic support outlays (made on May 1, 2018) is for the 2015 crop year. To date, the United States has never exceeded its $19.1 billion amber box spending limit. However, this has been achieved in some years (1999, 2000, and 2001) through judicious use of the *de minimis* exclusion described below. An additional consideration for WTO compliance—the SCM rules governing adverse market effects resulting from a farm program—comes into play when a domestic farm policy effect spills over into international markets. The SCM details rules for determining when a subsidy is "prohibited" (e.g., certain export- and import-substitution subsidies) and when it is "actionable" (e.g., certain domestic support policies that incentivize overproduction and result in significant market distortion—whether as lower market prices or altered trade patterns). Because the United States is a major producer, consumer, exporter, and/or importer of most major agricultural commodities, the SCM is relevant for most major U.S. agricultural products. As a result, if a particular U.S. farm program is deemed to result in market distortion that adversely affects other WTO members—even if it is within agreed-upon AoA spending limits—then that program may be subject to challenge under the WTO dispute settlement procedures. Designing farm programs that comply with WTO rules can avoid potential trade disputes. Based on AoA and SCM rules, U.S. domestic agricultural support can be evaluated against five specific successive questions to determine how it is classified under the WTO rules, whether total support is within WTO limits, and whether a specific program fully complies with WTO rules:

- Can a program's support outlays be excluded from the AMS total by being placed in the green box of minimally distorting programs?
- Can a program's support outlays be excluded from the AMS total by being placed in the blue box of production-limiting programs?
- If amber, will support be less than 5% of production value (either product-specific or non-product-specific) thus qualifying for the *de minimis* exclusion?
- Does the total, remaining annual AMS exceed the $19.1 billion amber box limit?

- Even if a program is found to be fully compliant with the AoA rules and limits, does its support result in price or trade distortion in international markets? If so, then it may be subject to challenge under SCM rules.

In: The Farm Bill: Review, Background, and the WTO
Editor: Katie M. Harrison
ISBN: 978-1-53615-272-2
© 2019 Nova Science Publishers, Inc.

Chapter 1

HEARING FROM THE HEARTLAND: PERSPECTIVES ON THE 2018 FARM BILL FROM KANSAS*

Committee on Agriculture, Nutrition, and Forestry, United States Senate

Thursday, February 23, 2017

McCain Auditorium, Kansas State University, *Manhattan, KS*

The Committee met, pursuant to notice, at 2:02 p.m., McCain Auditorium at Kansas State University, 1501 Goldstein Circle, Manhattan, Kansas, Hon. Pat Roberts, Chairman of the Committee, presiding.

Present: Senators Roberts and Stabenow.

Chairman ROBERTS. Good afternoon. I call this hearing of the Senate Committee on Agriculture, Nutrition, and Forestry to order. I am privileged to convene this Committee as Chairman here in Manhattan, where I spent many years of learning as a student. I learned about journalism and a few other things. As your Senator, I continue to learn about how important agriculture is to our Nation's economy and our national security.

Kansas State University exemplifies higher education, especially when it comes to preparing young people for lives in agriculture, from conducting fundamental practical research and extension to advance production to providing critical policy analysis and development to address our challenges. I am humbled and honored to be your Chairman and to kick off the 2018 farm bill right here, right now, at home.

---

* This is an edited, reformatted and augmented version of Field Hearing before the Committee on Agriculture, Nutrition, and Forestry United States Senate, One Hundred Fifteenth Congress, First Session, Publication No. S. HRG. 115–168, dated February 23, 2017.

I am also very proud to welcome my partner, Senator and former Chairwoman Deborah Stabenow from Michigan, back to Kansas, this time to Manhattan—the first time in Wichita and now Manhattan. Together, we will blaze a trail to a new farm bill.

Before we offer our opening remarks, we will hear from our distinguished welcoming panel. I will introduce you all and then turn it over to you for your individual remarks.

First we have our host, president of Kansas State University, Retired U.S. Air Force General Richard Myers. After a decorated career where he rose to the rank of four-star general and Chairman of the Joint Chiefs of Staff, President Myers retired to his home State to serve as president of his alma mater. We are proud of him, and we are grateful for his leadership.

In 1863—I would remind my dear friend and colleague—Kansas State University became the first fully operational land-grant college in America. Since its founding, Kansas State has continued to serve its students, Kansas, the Nation, and the world by providing high-quality education, research, and extension services. President Myers, thank you for hosting us today.

Next is Congressman and Doctor Roger Marshall, the newest member of the Kansas delegation in the U.S. Congress. He represents the 1st Congressional District. We obviously call it the "Big First." Roger was recently appointed to serve on the House Agriculture Committee, and I am pleased to work with him on all the issues that we face.

Prior to being elected to the House, Dr. Marshall was a practicing OB/GYN from Great Bend. Dr. Marshall also served his country and earned the rank of captain in the United States Army Reserves, where he served 7 years. Dr. Marshall earned his undergraduate degree from, you guessed it, Kansas State University and his medical degree from that other university next to Baker.

[Laughter.]

Chairman ROBERTS. The University of Kansas. Thank you for your testimony today, Congressman Marshall.

I am also very proud to have Dr. Jackie McClaskey, our Kansas Secretary of Agriculture, join us this afternoon. Secretary McClaskey grew up on a diversified farm near Girard and is also a proud alumna of K–State. She understands Washington well as she was a staff member for then-Congressman Sam Brownback.

She earned a master's degree from Texas A&M.

[Laughter.]

Chairman ROBERTS. But came to her senses, returned to K–State for her Ph.D. in animal science, specializing in animal disease response policy.

Thank you to our distinguished welcoming panel, President Myers, Dr. Marshall, Congressman Marshall, Secretary McClaskey. Each panelist is recognized for 3 minutes for remarks. Sorry for that limit, but basically we are like King Tut. We are pressed for time.

[Laughter.]

Chairman ROBERTS. President Myers.

STATEMENT OF GENERAL RICHARD B. MYERS, PRESIDENT, KANSAS STATE UNIVERSITY, MANHATTAN, KANSAS

General MYERS. I do not know where to go with that, but, Chairman Roberts, it is indeed a pleasure to welcome you on behalf of Kansas State University to the campus of our great university and your alma mater. Welcome. All Kansans value your leadership on this important Committee. Senator Stabenow, thank you for wearing purple. You do us proud, and we very much appreciate that.

[Applause.]

General MYERS. We welcome you to Kansas State University as well, another great land-grant institution which you are well familiar with.

To my co-panelists up here for the introduction, Congressman Marshall, always good to be with you, and Secretary McClaskey. These are teammates as we try to make progress here in the State of Kansas, indeed the Nation and the world.

What an opportunity we have today to watch Government in action. This is a serious hearing, a very serious hearing, just like if it were held in one of the hearing rooms on Capitol Hill. This is the same deal. You get to watch it right here up close and personal. You get to see the effort and the intelligence and energy that is put into these hearings, and we just feel so privileged that you chose Kansas State University to hold your hearing here today.

Everybody in this room is going to be impacted by the policy that comes out of these deliberations, and so everybody has an interest, and I am glad you are all here.

Kansas State University, we are the land-grant institution of the State of Kansas, and, of course, research and extension is a big part of that. We provide trusted, practical education to help individuals, businesses, and communities solve problems and develop skills to build a better future. A couple of examples.

As many of you know, Senator Pat Roberts and many others on the Kansas delegation—Federal, our local legislators, the city of Manhattan, in fact, the whole State—were instrumental in getting the National Bio and Agro Defense Facility located here in Manhattan, Kansas. It is changing a lot of things for the way we view the world. Just recently last month, we had the Blue Ribbon Commission on Bio Ago Defense visit Kansas State University for 2 days. Both of these honorable folks here next to me were part of that as well.

Senator Daschle led the Blue Ribbon Commission, and he passed on in his remarks, by the way, about how much he enjoyed working with you in the Senate when he was in the Senate as well from South Dakota.

He said on the second day, in opening up a series of panels that were going to inform on bio-agro defense, he said, "From what I have seen the first day, Kansas State is the Silicon Valley of bio-agro defense." I think that is probably true in lots of ways, but particularly since we have the NBAF here, this is not something that Kansas State could do by ourselves. But we think we are probably maybe the epicenter of how we protect our food system from both natural-caused issues and those by terrorists. So it is an opportunity, I think, to put the importance of agriculture infrastructure on the front burner in Washington, DC, and that is why we did it. Senator Daschle has been a good friend in that work.

A few other brag points from research and extension. When it comes to wheat breeding, they say that the world's population is going to double by 2050, and how are we going to feed all these new mouths? Well, there are a lot of innovative practices that benefit Kansas, our Nation, and the world through cutting-edge research in areas such as genetics, disease prevention, and food security. We help agriculture—Kansas' largest employer—be more profitable, sustainable, and efficient.

With a name befitting its place at the summit of Kansas agriculture, the K–State-produced wheat variety called "Everest" just completed its fourth year as the top variety in the State and the fifth time out of the last 6 years that a K–State variety has held the top spot. Everest was first in the field in 2009.

Of course, we have a lot of interest in sorghum as well. As a global leader in sorghum research and promotion, K–State co-founded a unique coalition with industry leaders and producers. In early 2016, the Kansas Grain Sorghum Commission, United Sorghum Checkoff Program, the Kansas Department of Agriculture, and K–State formed the Collaborative Sorghum Investment Program. The program focuses on expanding markets for sorghum and increasing the average national sorghum yield from 62 bushels per acre to 100 bushels per acre by 2025 by funding research in such areas as plant breeding, genetics, and field-level management.

Then trying to tie a lot of things we do here in Kansas between the urban settings and the rural settings, 5 years ago it seemed like a simple idea: How do we find a way for our smallholder farmers in Kansas to sell the food they grow to more people? So K–State Research and Extension helps do this and helps farmers become more efficient, more profitable, and more self-sustaining. We also assist consumers and communities in developing their local food system, which adds a lot of vitality, of course, to the community.

This food hub is a producer cooperative that goes beyond just the farmers markets and finds ways to get their produce to the larger buyers, such as restaurants, hospitals, schools, and food companies. It has been a very successful program to date.

So, in closing, I could not be prouder that both you Senators are here holding this hearing with these number of constituents that are out there that will be very interested in everything we talk about today, and we are just as proud as we can be as Kansas State University to be hosting you. Thank you so much.

[The prepared statement of General Myers can be found on page 119 in the appendix.]

Chairman ROBERTS. Mr. President, thank you very much.

Congressman Marshall.

STATEMENT OF THE HON. ROGER MARSHALL, MD, A REPRESENTATIVE IN CONGRESS FROM THE STATE OF KANSAS

Dr. MARSHALL. Chairman Roberts and Ranking Member Stabenow, let me also be among the first to welcome you to the Big First Congressional District of Kansas, our Nation's largest ag-producing district.

You are now in the leading State for wheat and sorghum production, the largest district for beef sales, and home of the fastest growing dairy herd in the country. This is a fitting place to launch a review of our current farm programs and discuss solutions for the upcoming 2018 bill.

You are also at ground zero for the challenges facing America's farmers and ranchers. The hurt in farm country is real. I am confident that today you will hear from folks in the trenches of this current economic downturn. I am looking forward to hearing their ideas and solutions to take back to Washington.

For me, the downturn in the ag economy we all hear about becomes very real when I see the Kansas Farm Management Association reporting that net farm income in Kansas was less than $6,000 in 2015. I cannot imagine trying to raise a family on that income level. We know that these levels will fall in 2016, and unless something drastically different happens, they are going to fall even lower in 2017.

Today's hearing is focused on the 2018 farm bill, but I want to instill this: We cannot make farm policy in a vacuum. Monetary policy, trade policy, regulatory and economic policy all impact our producers' bottom lines just as much as the programs we will be discussing today—none perhaps more than trade. A robust agricultural trade agenda would work hand-in-hand with our safety net programs to provide revenue from the marketplace and opportunity for our producers to succeed.

I do not have all the answers on any of this current crisis, but I am committed to working with my colleagues across the aisle, down the aisle, and across the Capitol as we begin to write this 2018 farm bill. It is my hope that we can identify the areas where the 2014 bill fell short, correct them, and ensure we have farm, food, and nutrition policy that works for our farmers, ranchers, and consumers.

I am honored to be here. I am honored to represent Kansas State University in the Big First District of Kansas. Thank you for having me.

[The prepared statement of Mr. Marshall can be found on page 99 in the appendix.]

Chairman ROBERTS. Roger, thank you very much.

Secretary McClaskey.

STATEMENT OF THE HON. JACKIE MCCLASKEY, SECRETARY, KANSAS DEPARTMENT OF AGRICULTURE, MANHATTAN, KANSAS

Ms. MCCLASKEY. On behalf of the State of Kansas, Governor Sam Brownback, and the entire agricultural industry, it is also my honor to welcome you both here today—Chairman Roberts, to welcome you home, and, Senator Stabenow, to welcome you back. We are very pleased to have you here.

Obviously, agriculture is important to Kansas. It is our State's largest industry. Forty-three percent of our economy is dependent upon agriculture. It contributes nearly $65 billion to our State economy. We export nearly $5 billion in agricultural exports. When we think about the future of agricultural policy, we know how critical that is not just to agriculture but to our entire State economy. So we very much appreciate the opportunity to be here with you today and join with you.

When we think about that agricultural economy in our State, it is dependent on the farmers and the ranchers that you are going to meet today. You are going to meet some of the State's best and brightest agricultural leaders, and they are going to share with you their concerns. I will tell you that, without question, our economy is not where—it does not have the potential it is—agriculture is not as important to us without those individuals. They embody the same pioneer spirit of their forefathers. They show the values of family and faith and hard work and persistence and entrepreneurship and community and achievement every day in what they do. Because of those people and because of what they do, it is really interesting to me as I travel the State, and I was just thinking, as I sit here, in the last 48 hours I have been from Ulysses to Kansas City, Kansas, and then back here to Manhattan, and had the chance to see a lot of agricultural leaders. While, yes, everybody is concerned about commodity prices in a depressed farm economy, at the same time what I see is a positive attitude, an outlook to the future, a desire to grow and think about how we can do things better. It is because of those pioneer spirit values that they have that Kansas farmers and ranchers are able to continue to look forward and look to the future.

But we hear the same challenges that I am sure you are going to hear about today. They are looking for a stable and a predictable safety net. They are looking for policy that is going to allow us to have a reliable workforce to serve the agricultural industry. They want to make sure that there are conservation policies out there that allow us to balance the needs of natural resources and economics. They want to make sure that regulations are based off sound science, common sense, and a good business mind-set. Like I am sure you are going to hear over and over today, we need access to more and more international markets so that we have a place to move our product.

I sit here very confident that under your leadership, especially when you two talk about working together, that we can meet those challenges and we can do it together, whether that is State and Federal or the industries all working together. If you think about all the entities represented in this room, I am pretty sure there is nothing that we cannot accomplish.

It is National FFA Week, so I will do my shout out to FFA and know that I am not the only person, that you all share this, that I believe in the future of agriculture, and I know this room does, and I believe that we can reach solutions together.

Thank you for giving us the opportunity to be here.

[The prepared statement of Ms. McClaskey can be found on page 100 in the appendix.]

Chairman ROBERTS. Madam Secretary, thank you very much.

Congressman, thank you so much.

General Myers, President Myers, take care of your new knee, and do not do stupid things.

[Laughter.]

General MYERS. Yes, sir.

Chairman ROBERTS. I ask that our first panel of witnesses now take their seats. Senator Stabenow and I will then give our opening remarks. Thank you all. Would the first panel please come and take your seats?

[Applause.]

STATEMENT OF HON. PAT ROBERTS, U.S. SENATOR FROM THE STATE OF KANSAS, CHAIRMAN, COMMITTEE ON AGRICULTURE, NUTRITION, AND FORESTRY

Chairman ROBERTS. Thank you very much to all of you for coming, and we look forward to your testimony.

Senator Stabenow, ladies and gentlemen on the panel, others here in McCain Auditorium, where as a freshman member of a social fraternity, Pi Kappa Alpha, I used to sit right up there in those seats because every assembly was required. I will not tell you what we did up there, but then that is beside the point.

Welcome to the Senate Committee on Agriculture, Nutrition, and Forestry's first hearing on the 2018 farm bill. We start the journey to a successful and timely 2018 farm bill in the heartland because that is where it matters most. On our farms and ranches, businesses, and city and county halls all across the countryside, products, agribusiness, and our rural communities are the ones who sign up for the programs, comply with the regulations, and feel the burden firsthand of overburdensome or unsupported policies.

So it is only right that we start this conversation here with you. No one understands the impacts of farm bills or policies set in Washington like America's farmers and ranchers in rural communities. Your experience, your story is what we need to hear before we start writing a new farm bill. What a success story you have to tell. America's producers, the folks that Paul Harvey spoke about in his famed "So God Made a Farmer" speech, have overcome drought, disease, floods, tornadoes, embargoes, and even their own Government to produce the safest, most abundant, and affordable food and fiber supply the world has ever seen or known.

Your fight and perseverance yields results. According to the most recent census of agriculture, your hard work resulted in over $394 billion worth of ag products sold. In Kansas, that value is over $18 billion. More specifically to the Sunflower State, Kansas planted 23.2 million acres to crops in 2016. Livestock in Kansas includes 6.25 million cattle, 1.9 million hogs, and over 140,000 dairy cows. Those folks are growing pretty quick.

Our agriculture industry throughout the value chain must grow. Technology must advance to better service this growth. Critical to that growth is stability and an adequate safety net. That is why we need a good farm bill.

This farm bill journey will not be like the last one. The agriculture sector enjoyed high prices during the last debate. Now we face multiple years of low prices across the board. I am working to make Washington understand the differences between the economic conditions then and what you all are facing now. You all understand it. Washington needs to as well. Senator Stabenow understands it as well.

To those who say passing a farm bill in this environment is a daunting task, I say together we can get it done. We have done that. We can get it done again. We must embrace the attitude of our producers' optimism and ingenuity. A farmer does not plant the seed without the faith and optimism of harvesting a good crop.

But passing a new farm bill will not be easy. That is why with your help in crafting a bill that meets the needs of producers across all regions and all crops is absolutely necessary. Note that I said all regions and all crops. All of agriculture is struggling, not just one or two commodities. We must write a bill that works across our entire Nation.

At the same time our Government is spending money it does not have, our national debt exceeds $19 trillion, agriculture, and specifically the farm bill, has consistently answered to that call to do more with less. The last farm bill voluntarily cut spending. The previous crop insurance contract with the Department of Agriculture was cut $6 billion from the program. I could go on and on, on where ag gave at the store. Farmers and ranchers pulled themselves up from their bootstraps. They understand fiscal responsibility. Therefore, we must be judicious with the scarce resources that we have. We must ensure programs accomplish their fundamental purpose. We must ask relevant questions and reexamine programs to determine their effectiveness.

Are our conservation programs keeping farmland in operation or are they merely used to comply with overburdensome regulations? Are rural development programs helping to increase economic opportunities in farm country, or are they being used to build out infrastructure in urban areas?

Now is the time to examine the core mission of USDA programs to ensure they are operating as intended, and if they are not, then we must refocus them. We need bold thinking and new ideas to address today's challenges during tough economic times.

Let us not forget—it has been said before by our president, the president of Kansas State—that in a few short decades the global population will top 9 billion people, agricultural production will need to double—double—in the near future to meet demand. Accomplishing this task requires efficiency not just on the farm and ranch but also in our Government. Feeding an increasing global population is not simply an agriculture challenge. It is a national security challenge. Show me a country that cannot feed itself, and I will show you a nation in chaos. Look around the world.

This means we need to grow more and raise more with fewer resources. That will take research, new technology, lines of credit, proper risk management. It takes the Government providing an adequate safety net and then getting out of the producers' way and then, of course, a robust and aggressive and transparent trade policy, quickly—quickly. I know the President wants strong bilateral trade agreements. It is time. It is time. We need to get our Secretary of Agriculture on board.

Madam Senator—I do not think I have ever called you that before.

[Laughter.]

Chairman ROBERTS. To my colleague, but we need to get Sonny Perdue on board. We need a new Secretary. We need the Under Secretaries; they do the work. We need to implement a robust trade policy just as soon as possible.

So that is why we are here today, to hear from the entire value chain of agriculture on what is working, what is not, and how we can improve. Thank you to our witnesses for taking time to provide your advice and counsel and perspective. Thank you to those in the audience for being here as well.

Now, for those who want to provide advice and counsel on the farm bill, we have set up an email address on the Senate Ag Committee's website to collect your input into the farm bill discussion.

Please go to Ag.senate.gov. That is pretty simple, Ag—even I can get that—Ag.senate.gov, click on the farm bill hearing box on the left side of your screen. You can send us your own input for the Committee to consider as we write the next farm bill. That link will be open for 5 business days following today's hearing. We want to hear from you. We want to hear your advice, your counsel, and your suggestions.

I now recognize the distinguished Senator from Michigan, Senator Stabenow, for her opening remarks.

STATEMENT OF HON. DEBBIE STABENOW, U.S. SENATOR FROM THE STATE OF MICHIGAN

Senator STABENOW. Well, thank you, Mr. Chairman, and good afternoon. It is really wonderful to be back with all of you in the great Sunflower State and to have the opportunity to hear from all of our distinguished witnesses today. I appreciate very much Kansas State University hosting us, and I thank President Myers for his welcome, and Secretary Jackie McClaskey. I have to say that— Mr. Chairman, I have to clarify one thing, because Kansas State is the first land-grant university only because your State legislature beat us. We are actually the oldest—Michigan State University, Michigan Agricultural College was the oldest land-grant university, but after the law passed, you beat us to the punch. So we will share that. We are the oldest; you are the first official.

[Laughter.]

Senator STABENOW. I just have to get that straight in case any of my Spartans are watching here.

Chairman ROBERTS. I am just happy to be anywhere where I am not the oldest.

[Laughter.]

Senator STABENOW. So needless to say, we have a terrific tradition together of land-grant universities as well as agriculture production. I also want to thank Congressman Roger Marshall.

In the coming weeks, I really look forward to hosting you as well, Mr. Chairman, at the oldest land-grant university, Michigan State University, for our second field hearing. We did this before when we wrote the last farm bill together, and I am very proud of the work that was done in a bipartisan way, and that is what we can do when we work together. We had the opportunity to be in Kansas and in Michigan, and so I am looking forward to having that happen again.

Now, I do have to say, because we both like our sports teams, that I saw that the Wildcats had an impressive finish in the football season this year, winning your Bowl Game against Texas A&M. Unfortunately, Michigan State did not do so well in football this year. I was hoping we would be in a better spot going into March Madness, but I think both the Wildcats and Spartans are just hoping maybe to get in there, right? It has been a tough year for both of us. But hope springs eternal, and I am looking forward to betting you in the future when our two teams face each other.

I really do want to start the hearing, though, by thanking Chairman Roberts for his years of leadership on issues important to American agriculture. We do have a great working relationship. We have had some very, very difficult issues to work through together, and despite some great odds, we have gotten a lot done. He is one of the hardest-working Members of the Congress, and I think it is because he reminds me all the time that he is a Marine. Let me tell you, nothing says honor, courage, and commitment like battling more than 70 amendments together to get the bipartisan farm bill through on the Senate floor the last time around.

Kansas has a noteworthy history of Senators creating great legislative partnerships to advance and support American agriculture and food policy. Many of you may know the name Senator Arthur Capper as the author of the Capper-Volstead Act of 1922—I was not there, but Pat was telling me about it.

[Laughter.]

Senator STABENOW. Which authorized the creation of agriculture cooperatives, and we all know about the wonderful partnership of Senator Bob Dole and Senator George McGovern and their important work together to fight hunger.

So I am looking forward to continuing the legacy of partnerships with a great Senator from Kansas as we work together on the 2018 farm bill.

Looking back at the last farm bill, many people thought we would not get it done. The process was long. It was unconventional. We had to actually pass it twice in the Senate. We had a very tough budget situation and had to make hard choices. But we never lost sight of the fact that 16 million people—16 million people—have a job in our country because of agriculture and the food industry. So it has been our priority, and will continue to be, to support farmers and ranchers, to ensure consumers have access to affordable, nutritious food, and that we advocate for small towns and rural communities in our States and all across the United States.

Despite all the challenges we faced, we accomplished a lot: reforming the commodity programs and supporting new risk management tools; providing permanent funding for three livestock disaster assistance programs, which I believe were accessed first after we passed the farm bill because of the droughts and the weather; creating new opportunities for voluntary conservation; streamlining nearly 100 different programs, either cutting or consolidating them. These historic reforms saved billions and protected the integrity of critical safety net programs like crop insurance.

I am also proud of the work that Senator Roberts and I did together to create new partnerships on funding research, which I know is critical both here in Kansas and Michigan, and all across the country, including the creation of the Foundation for Food and Agriculture Research as a permanent agriculture research asset for us.

So looking ahead to the next farm bill, we know that the farm economy, as the Chairman has said, is not where we want it to be. Low prices have pinched margins, made it tough for many producers to make ends meet. It is a tough time. We have heard from many producers that we need particularly to take a look at dairy issues and cotton issues, and we look forward to other issues that you raise with us today.

I think our Senate Agriculture Committee members agree that we need to focus on the needs of farmers and rural communities in the next farm bill and not arbitrary cuts. We, in fact, created savings in the last farm bill. We were the only ones that offered up savings, $23 billion in cuts, in our own areas on the Committee. Now I think it is important that we address the needs that farmers and ranchers and others have.

Furthermore, the Congressional Budget Office recently estimated that the current farm bill that we wrote is projected to save about $80 billion more than initially expected, largely driven by reduced spending in nutrition as people have found jobs and no longer need help, which is the way it is supposed to work. The safety net for families is working. Now we need to make sure the safety net for farmers is working as well as it needs to work.

But savings from the current farm bill unfortunately are not allowed under budget rules to be used to address the other needs that we have, and so we will have challenges. We have a budgetary challenge facing funding 37 different key programs that do not have what we call ''budget baseline'' going forward, including beginning farmers and ranchers and veterans programs, food access, rural development, and the emerging bio-based economy.

The good news is that just last week more than 500 groups from every part of the farm and food sector came together to reject calls for additional cuts to farm bill programs, including crop insurance, nutrition, and conservation. We know the farm bill is doing more than its fair share to reduce the deficit, and further cuts would be made at the detriment of farmers and families.

In this new Congress, we face a political climate unlike any other, and if there is anyone who can come together and pass a comprehensive bipartisan bill, I believe it is our Senate Agriculture Committee. I like to think our Committee is unique, and we certainly are going to work hard to get this done.

Our interests are rooted in bipartisanship because we share the goals of supporting our Nation's farmers and ranchers who produce the safest, most abundant, and most affordable food supply in the world.

Writing a farm bill is no simple task. We certainly cannot do it alone, and that is why we are here. This is the first of many hearings we will conduct to get input, and I cannot stress enough how important your input is to all of us.

So today I look forward to learning about your priorities, what is working, what we should focus on to improve, and what is the best way to make those improvements. I am looking forward to your thoughts and ideas that we can take back as we get to work on the farm bill.

Thank you, Mr. Chairman.

Chairman ROBERTS. I thank my colleague, and thanks so much for coming to Kansas State and helping us kick off the first farm bill hearing.

The folks on this panel are leaders in the Kansas agriculture sector. These individuals have devoted tremendous time and dedication to their industries over the years. We are interested to hear your perspectives as we embark on the development of the 2018 farm bill. First let us start with brief introductions of each of the witnesses.

Mr. David Clawson of the Kansas Livestock Association, owner/operator, the Clawson Ranch Partnership, Plains, Kansas. Mr. Clawson joins us today from Plains. He is the president of the Kansas Livestock Association. He is the owner of several agriculture businesses, including a cow-calf operation, a dairy operation, a row crop farm, and he is a partner in the Plains State Bank. Mr. Clawson is a graduate of Kansas State University. David, thank you for joining us today.

Second, Mrs. Lynda Foster is here today on behalf of the Dairy Farmers of America. She and her husband own and operate Foster Dairy in Fort Scott. After earning her degree in dairy production right here at Kansas State University, she and her husband became third-generation dairy farmers, and they currently milk 170 cows, raise corn, soybeans, alfalfa, and grass hay. Her son and daughter-in-law have also joined the operation. Welcome, Mrs. Foster.

Mrs. Amy France is here today from Marienthal and is representing the Kansas Farm Bureau. Amy was raised off the farm by parents who were public educators and found her passion for agriculture later in life. She began the first 10 years of her career in a small-town lending institution at the First National Bank of Scott City. Amy now works alongside her husband, Clint, on their crop and livestock operation in western Kansas. Thank you, Mrs. France.

Mr. Lucas Heinen joins us today from Everest. He is the district 1 director and president of the Kansas Soybean Association Board of Directors. He and his wife, Kendra, farm in Brown County and work with his parents, Harold and Ruby Heinen. They have a soybean, corn, wheat, and cattle farm. Lucas has been a full-time farmer for 15 years. He graduated from Kansas State in 2000 with a degree in agronomy and worked as a crop consultant. Welcome to the panel.

Mr. Tom Lahey is here with us today on behalf of the Kansas Cotton Association. Yes, we grow cotton in Kansas. I keep reminding my colleagues from the South, when Stephen Foster wrote that old song, "those old cotton fields at home," he was writing about Kansas. He is a fourth-generation farmer and rancher from Moscow. Tom served in the army during the Vietnam War. Thank you, sir, for your service. Tom has spent more than 40 years farming and ranching in southwest Kansas. He raises cotton, wheat, corn, milo, and has a cow-calf operation. Welcome to the panel.

Kent Moore with the Kansas Corn Growers is from Iuka. He is a fifth-generation family farmer in northwest Pratt County. Mr. Moore raises irrigated and dryland corn, irrigated soybeans, and dryland wheat. He received his bachelor's degree from Kansas State University in agriculture economics. Thank you for joining us today, Mr. Moore.

Mr. Cameron Peirce from Peirce Farms in Hutchinson, Kansas, is a sunflower, wheat, canola, and soybean grower from a fifth-generation family farm in Hutchinson and Reno County. He currently serves as the vice-chairman of the Kansas Sunflower Commission. Thank you for being here today.

Mr. Michael Springer is a third-generation pork producer from Independence. He is the past chairman of the Kansas Pork Association. He, along with his wife, Christie, their two young sons, and other members of the Springer family run a family business that includes a farrow-to-finish swine operation, in addition to growing wheat and corn and soybeans. The Springer family employs 32 individuals, and they market 85,000 pigs annually. Mr. Springer is also a graduate of Kansas State University. Thank you for your testimony today, sir. Mr. Kent Winter, of Kent Winter Farms, Mt. Hope, Kansas, with the Kansas Sorghum Producers, fifth-generation farmer from Andale. Kent's family farm operation is primarily dryland and produces sorghum, wheat, soybeans, corn, and alfalfa. Kent holds a bachelor's and master's degree in agronomy from Kansas State University. Thank you for being here, Mr. Winter.

Mr. Kenneth Wood, Riverside Stock Farm, Incorporated, Manhattan, Kansas. Ken, of Dickinson County, joins us on behalf of the Kansas Association of Wheat Growers. He is the owner/operator of Riverside Stock Farm, Incorporated, near Chapman, a cash grain farm on which he grows wheat, corn, soybeans, and milo. He is a graduate also of Kansas State University. Welcome to the panel, Kenneth Wood.

We will now begin the testimonies. I ask each of the witnesses to try to keep their statements to 3 minutes. I know that is tough, especially after you have listened to us speak and the distinguished panel before us. But we are going to try to keep statements to 3 minutes. Your full written statements will be printed in the official record and are publicly available online.

Mr. Clawson, you may begin.

STATEMENT OF DAVID CLAWSON, THE CLAWSON RANCH PARTNERSHIP, ENGLEWOOD, KANSAS, AND PRESIDENT, KANSAS LIVESTOCK ASSOCIATION

Mr. CLAWSON. Thank you. Mr. Chairman, Senator Stabenow, thank you for having me. Thank you for the nice introduction. I am president of the Kansas Livestock Association, and it is a true honor and privilege to be here to speak with you today.

Development of the next farm bill is an important process for livestock producers. Whether directly or indirectly, provisions included in the farm bill can have a dramatic impact on the livestock sector. We oppose agriculture policies that pit one industry group against another, that distort market signals, and inadvertently cause economic harm to the livestock sector.

KLA opposes a Livestock Title in the next farm bill. We think provisions with industry-wide support can easily be put into the Miscellaneous Title.

KLA members oppose the involvement of the Federal Government in determining how cattle are marketed. The beef industry continues to transition toward more value-based marketing different types of methods. These systems allow cattle producers to capture more of the value of the cattle they produce.

Many KLA members see significant benefits in value-based marketing programs. They have made it clear through KLA policy that the appropriate role of our organization is to protect each member's ability to market their cattle in the manner that best fits their businesses.

With that in mind, KLA reiterates its opposition to the Grain Inspection, Packers and Stockyards Administration's interim final rule on competitive injury. The rule has been opposed by the vast majority of cattle producers since it was first introduced in 2010. Not only did GIPSA ignore the written testimony of thousands of cattlemen, they also chose to ignore eight separate Federal appellate courts. Finally, they chose to ignore the intent of language included by Congress in the 2008 farm bill.

Our analysis of the interim final rule leads us to believe that packers will offer just one price for all cattle, regardless of quality, if the rule is implemented. Packers have indicated they will not accept additional legal risk that the change in the competitive injury standard would create.

As the 2018 farm bill is developed, KLA asks you to delete the language which led to the GIPSA interim final rule. We also ask for your assistance in convincing GIPSA to withdraw this rule immediately.

We look forward to working with you on this upcoming farm bill, and thank you.

[The prepared statement of Mr. Clawson can be found on page 58 in the appendix.]

Chairman ROBERTS. With 3 seconds to spare. David, thank you so much.

Lynda Foster, Foster Dairy, Fort Scott, Kansas. Lynda.

Statement of Lynda Foster, Owner/Operator, Foster Dairy, Fort Scott, Kansas, on Behalf of the National Milk Producers Federation and Dairy Farmers of America

Ms. FOSTER. Thank you, Mr. Chairman and Ranking Member Stabenow. My name is Lynda Foster, and I own and operate Foster Dairy in Fort Scott, Kansas with my husband and son. We milk 170 cows, and we farm approximately 750 acres of corn, soybeans, alfalfa, and grass hay. I am pleased today to be here to offer testimony on behalf of Dairy Farmers of America and also the National Milk Producers Federation.

The last farm bill established a new Title I program for dairy called the "Margin Protection Program," or MPP. The final version of the program, which was originally designed by National Milk, cut the MPP benefit by 10 percent, rendering the program ineffective. That program is not working as we know it today.

The changes that Congress made to the original MPP diluted the real cost that farmers like myself face every day and diluted the effectiveness of that program. The most important change needed in the MPP is the return of that 10-percent cut. Other MPP adjustments include, but are not limited to, the feed formula calculation as it relates to milk and feed prices. This is the right program. We do not need another program. What we need is to have the original cut put back in, and with a few tweaks, I really think dairy farmers will participate at even a greater participation.

Additionally, dairy farmers want the opportunity to use—like their commodity producers, we want the opportunity to use both the RMA, or the risk management agency, programs and Title I programs without any restrictions. Give me the same opportunity to protect my dairy as my friends have to protect their crops.

A few other of the priority issues that the dairy industry is concerned about is, of course, farm labor, and I urge Congress to act immediately to address those needs for a stable and legal workforce. On our dairy farm, we chose to use robotic milkers and transitioned last September so that our labor problems are more solved because cows milk themselves now.

The trade issue is also critical. Dairy farmers export almost 15 percent of their products, so we are really dependent upon trade.

In child nutrition, I appreciate the Committee's bipartisan work on the issue of child nutrition. The dairy industry remains eager to help work with you to pass options for school kids. Kids are used to drinking what they drink at home. Research shows that they are not drinking skim milk and 1 percent flavored. They are drinking 2 percent or whole milk.

So I thank you for this opportunity to present to you what the dairy industry feels. I love the dairy industry. I am passionate about working on the farm, and I want to be able to pass this on to my son and my grandkids. Thank you.

[The prepared statement of Ms. Foster can be found on page 63 in the appendix.]

Chairman ROBERTS. Lynda, thank you so much for your pertinent testimony. I do not like blue milk either.

[Laughter.]

Chairman ROBERTS. Mrs. Amy France, France Family Farms, of Marienthal, Kansas. Amy?

STATEMENT OF AMY FRANCE, OWNER/OPERATOR/ PARTNER, FRANCE FAMILY FARMS, MARIENTHAL, KANSAS, ON BEHALF OF THE KANSAS FARM BUREAU

Ms. FRANCE. Thank you, Chairman Roberts, Ranking Member Stabenow. I am honored to represent Farm Bureau's Young Farmers and Ranchers Committee, along with my friends and family in western Kansas. Marienthal is where my husband, Clint, and I are blessed to raise our family of five, bringing them up knowing what hard work is all about and what it can accomplish. We want them to understand that it is a privilege as well as a responsibility to work our land and to feed our Nation.

We raise wheat, grain, sorghum, corn, soybeans, along with grazing our cattle on pasturelands. Our ultimate goal is to leave our operation better than we found it and to be able to pass it on to the next generation. The EQIP program has been something that is helping us do just that. Through that program we will soon be rebuilding 35-year-old terraces to help hold in moisture and improve soil quality, as well as drilling a water well for our cattle. Without the assistance, our farm would not be able to afford making such critical improvements during these tough economic times.

In lending, we are required to carry an appropriate level of crop insurance coverage. However, with the decline in our APH, that is becoming harder to do. When drought takes its tool, claims are made, APHs are lowered, insurance revenue guarantees decrease, and rates go up. Paying premiums is inevitable. But how can we increase our underlying coverage in order to stay in the system? Although as it sits crop insurance is not perfect, it has been shown to be the most timely and effective way to get money back to the farmers, unlike ARC and PLC, which can take up to 14 months after harvest.

Right now, cash wheat is $1.05 under the board price at our local elevator. We also must have a workable Commodity Title safety net. Unfortunately, in regards to USDA programs, I have heard "complex," "confusing," "burdensome," and those are just a few words I can say in front of my children.

[Laughter.]

Ms. FRANCE. Although they are intended to help the farmer, it is obvious the individuals writing and implementing these programs have little hands-in-the-dirt experience. One might even argue that these programs have caused additional risks on our operations.

One step further is regulations. We must act on EPA regulations with Congress, and if we do not, then we will have to sell our spray rigs and depend on professional applicators to do the work for us, and they are overbooked. We need Congress and EPA to let private pesticide application continue.

Senators, we thank you for spending your time with us and coming and hearing directly from us. Although some rules and proposals may sound good sitting behind a computer screen on Independence Avenue, they have real effect on me, my husband, our operation, and ultimately whether we can put food on the table tonight and in the next years.

Thank you.

[The prepared statement of Ms. France can be found on page 70 in the appendix.]

Chairman ROBERTS. Amy, thank you so much for some very pertinent testimony. Five children, right?

Ms. FRANCE. Yes, sir. Three of my very own; two I am blessed to call mine.

Chairman ROBERTS. I see. I did not mean to get into that.

[Laughter.]

Ms. FRANCE. I was not sure how to address it. I hope that is okay.

Chairman ROBERTS. We both were sort of wondering about that.

Thought you got married at 11 or something.

[Laughter.]

Ms. FRANCE. No.

Chairman ROBERTS. Okay. I will straighten up. Sorry.

Mr. Lucas Heinen, please present us with your testimony, sir.

STATEMENT OF LUCAS HEINEN, FARMER, HEINEN FAMILY FARMS, EVEREST, KANSAS, AND PRESIDENT, KANSAS SOYBEAN ASSOCIATION

Mr. HEINEN. Good afternoon, Chairman Roberts, Ranking Member Stabenow, and member of the panel and members of the audience. I am Lucas Heinen, a soybean farmer from Everest, Kansas, and I am president of the Kansas Soybean Association. We appreciate the opportunity to appear at this first hearing of your Committee on the 2018 farm bill.

I understand that the conventional view in Washington is that the cost of farm programs and other parts of the farm bill will need to be reduced again, just as they were in 2014. But this is not acceptable to producers in Kansas. Farm prices are down over 40 percent since 2013, and U.S. farm income is expected to fall for the fourth straight year, by 8.7 percent, in 2017.

Five hundred and two organizations that depend on the farm bill, including the Kansas Soybean Association and the American Soybean Association, have just sent a letter to the Congressional Budget and Appropriations Committees opposing further spending cuts in the 2018 farm bill. The letter points out that agriculture voluntarily accepted the $23 billion in cuts in 2014 which you mentioned, and that other sectors have made no contribution to deficit reduction whatsoever.

As Congress looks forward to writing the 2018 farm bill, we believe the sharp and continuing fall of farm prices and income since 2013 justifies an increase in funding to strengthen the farm safety net and to make other worthwhile investments. Soybean producers have identified the following priorities:

First, the crop insurance program needs to be protected. For many soybean producers, crop insurance is their most important risk management tool.

Second, most Kansas producers signed up for the county ARC program and want to see it continued in the next farm bill. We do need to change the yields used under the program from NASS data to RMA data, when available, to minimize county-to-county discrepancies.

Third, we support full funding of current conservation programs, including EQIP and the Conservation Stewardship Program, increasing funding for agricultural research under the AFRI, and authorization and funding for programs that promote biodiesel and bio-based products.

Finally, we strongly support doubling mandatory funding for the Foreign Market Development Program and the Market Access Program to promote U.S. agricultural exports.

In closing, Mr. Chairman, I would note the importance of keeping programs that support farmers and programs that support consumers together in the next farm bill. There is a relationship between the need to provide assistance to those who produce food and those who consume it, when either needs assistance, which explains how Congress has been able to enact farm bills for over 40 years.

Thank you again, Mr. Chairman, for the opportunity to appear today.

[The prepared statement of Mr. Heinen can be found on page 92 in the appendix.]

Chairman ROBERTS. Well, thank you, Lucas.

Tom Lahey is with us today from Lahey Farms in Moscow, Kansas. Tom?

STATEMENT OF TOM LAHEY, OWNER/OPERATOR, TOM LAHEY FARM, MOSCOW, KANSAS, AND VICE PRESIDENT, KANSAS COTTON ASSOCIATION

Mr. LAHEY. Chairman Roberts and Ranking Member Stabenow, thank you for this opportunity to provide testimony on the farm bill and policy needs of the cotton industry.

I am a fourth-generation farmer and rancher from Moscow, Kansas, and raise cotton, wheat, corn, and grain sorghum, and have a cow-calf operation. Shortly after the passage of the 2014 farm bill, cotton prices began a steep decline, the result of a build-up of global cotton stocks, decreased demand, and reduced exports. Since 75 percent of our cotton is exported, international markets heavily influence the financial condition of the U.S. cotton industry.

While U.S. cotton acres are expected to recover, a major concern still exists since cotton is not eligible for the price and revenue policies like other crops. While ARC and PLC policies have generally performed well for me in responding to the market downturn that we are experiencing in crops like wheat, corn, and grain sorghum, I continue to be largely exposed to the full market impact on cotton since it was excluded from these programs. The National Cotton Council has been working to get cottonseed designated as a covered commodity and eligible for the ARC and PLC programs. We strongly believe this policy is needed to provide a bridge until the new farm bill is enacted.

We urge the Committee to seek any opportunities to increase the Federal funding and farm policies that ensure consumers have the safest, most affordable and secure supply of food and fiber. Given the significant decline in farm bill spending, the dramatic downturn in farm income, and generally weak commodity prices, a greater investment in these critical policies for rural America should be in order.

Our industry is extremely concerned about the further payment limits and eligibility requirements since these policies are too burdensome and restrictive given the scale of production necessary to be competitive. EQIP and CSP conservation programs continue to be extremely popular across the Cotton Belt. These programs have become integral parts of many producers' operations to help improve and protect the environment.

Given our reliance on exports, it is essential that U.S. agriculture have a well-funded public-private partnership to expand export markets and grow demand. A central part of this effort is USDA's MAP and FMD programs. We believe it is justified for the new farm bill to invest additional funds in these programs.

In closing, over the past 3 years, cotton producers have struggled with low prices, high production costs, and the resulting financial hardships. This has demonstrated the need and it is imperative for the next farm bill to bring cotton back into the Title I commodity policy to access the full complement of risk management tools such as other crops.

Thank you.

[The prepared statement of Mr. Lahey can be found on page 94 in the appendix.]

Chairman ROBERTS. Kent, I am going to delay you just for a moment.

Sitting to my right, about three or four rows up is a gentleman that I think should be recognized, the former president of Kansas State University, who is going to have a hall dedicated—or not a hall, but it is an institution of learning, named after him.

When I came back from Russia and got access to a secret city over there during the days of the Nunn-Lugar program, I saw a facility that was producing pathogens—and, Deborah, you have heard this speech many, many times. I am sorry to repeat it. But the man responsible for me to come back and to really—we sat down, and we would talk about agriculture and things, and I said, "My gosh, I do not know what we can do. I do not know how we can get ready if, in fact, there was an attack on our food supply."

He said, "I know what we can do. Kansas State can do it." So the person behind the person behind NBAF is sitting right over here and has done so much for this University in Kansas. Jon Wefald, please stand up.

[Applause.]

Chairman ROBERTS. Jon always did a splendid job of officiating football games from his position in the stadium.

[Laughter.]

Chairman ROBERTS. I just cannot tell you—I do not know why the referees did not agree with us, but that is beside the point.

Kent Moore from Moore Farms in Iuka, Kent Moore, Kansas Corn Growers. Kent, please.

STATEMENT OF KENT MOORE, FARMER, IUKA, KANSAS, ON BEHALF OF THE KANSAS CORN GROWERS ASSOCIATION

Mr. MOORE. All right. Thank you. I really do appreciate the opportunity to be here and represent Kansas Corn. I am a fifth-generation farmer from Pratt County, Kansas, in the south-central part of the State.

Kansas Corn is very interested in improving and keeping the crop insurance program intact and bolstering the areas of weakness that need to be addressed during this farm bill process. But today I am going to focus my main comments in regard to Foreign Market Development and Market Access Program.

The growth potential for ag exports is greater today than any other sector, and we believe it is time to increase our efforts to provide access to these growing markets around the world. We can produce bumper crops, and we need the ability to aggressively pursue trade to sell American grains and American meat around the world. Programs like the Market Access Program and Foreign Market Development are critical in building export markets for our ag products. But these two programs have had stagnant funding levels for a number of years, and we support the efforts of the agriculture trade community to increase funding for MAP and FMD.

Over the years, the effective spending power of these programs has decreased by over 40 percent due to factors like sequestration, administrative costs, and inflation. Our farmers, through their checkoff dollars, support the U.S. Grains Council to develop export markets for corn, ethanol, and DDGS. Our checkoff dollars also support efforts to build export markets for red meat through the U.S. Meat Export Federation. The MAP and FMD programs make our farmers' investment of those checkoff dollars efficient and effective.

Many of our State's ethanol plants that provide a needed market for our corn today in the State of Kansas were started and funded by Kansas farmers who sought new markets for their corn and sorghum. Today our grain surpluses are proof that we can provide more than enough corn for feed and fuel. Our ethanol plants provide a key market for our grains, clean domestic fuel for vehicles, and a desirable feed for livestock. Ethanol plants in Kansas have been a key factor in improving the lives of many rural Kansans. Located mainly in rural communities, our 12 Kansas ethanol plants produce nearly half a billion gallons of ethanol per year.

How can the farm bill help ethanol? One way is increased funding for MAP and FMD. Exports are becoming an increasingly important segment of the ethanol industry. Ethanol and ethanol products are relative newcomers to this export world, and these programs are vital as we seek to expand international sales of both ethanol and DDGS.

While farmers continually improve and adopt new technologies in seed, inputs, and equipment that allow us to sustainably manage our fields down to the square inch, much risk remains. This is why it is imperative that Kansas farmers have a Federal farm program that provides themselves and our Nation with the security needed to navigate an increasingly complex and challenging world.

Thank you so much for the opportunity to speak.

[The prepared statement of Mr. Moore can be found on page 105 in the appendix.]

Chairman ROBERTS. Thank you, Kent.

We now have Cameron Peirce from Peirce Farms in Hutchinson.

STATEMENT OF CAMERON PEIRCE, OWNER/OPERATOR, PEIRCE FARMS, HUTCHINSON, KANSAS, AND VICE-CHAIRMAN, KANSAS SUNFLOWER COMMISSION

Mr. PEIRCE. Thank you, Chairman Roberts and Ranking Member Stabenow. Welcome to the Sunflower State. My name is Cameron Peirce. I am the vice-chairman of the Sunflower Commission, and I am pleased that you are here to listen to the farm bill programs and the impact that they have on the Midwestern producers.

Annually, Kansas plants around 90,000 acres of oil seed and confection flowers. In 2016, USDA estimated 1.6 million acres of sunflowers were planted nationwide.

Similar to other commodities, the market price for the sunflower has declined over the past 3 years while international production has increased, making it increasingly difficult for farms to be profitable. In these challenging times, farm bill programs, and particularly the risk management programs, are vital food security mechanisms that keeps

American food safe and affordable. Farm bill dollars are infused back into rural America through purchases of farm goods and services, ag inputs, and everyday household needs. These programs keep American agriculture successful and give producers a vital safety net. The volatility of weather and markets are unpredictable for the Kansas farmer; having a safety net in place ensures safe and affordable food can continue to be produced in Kansas and across the Nation.

As you look at priorities in this new farm bill, please consider that producers still need a safety net for crop failure and disaster. Crop insurance has been and still is the best tool for these situations. Full funding for the crop insurance program is the highest priority for sunflower growers, as it is for all commodities. Both production and revenue protection insurance products are important options for producers. The flexibility these options offer is important as producers weigh input costs, planting decisions, and premiums. I encourage the Committee to continue the flexibility currently found in Federal crop insurance.

Conservation programs in the farm bill are also an important part of crop production, and sunflowers benefit from having those programs in place. Sunflowers are generally part of a robust no-till rotation, a practice that has gained wider acceptance and implementation through EQIP funding. NRCS' soil health initiative has been a big success in the last few years. Producers, agribusiness, and commodity investors now understand how important soil health practices are to increasing productivity on the land and protecting our natural resources at the same time. Programs like EQIP need to be maintained at the current funding levels.

Some of the newer programs contained in the last farm bill have been important to producers, especially over the last 2 years, specifically ARC–County and PLC. These are vital tools for producers to maintain their businesses.

Both of these programs were well intentioned when authorized, but could use some improvements in the next version of the farm bill to even things out. I hope the Committee will examine some of the flaws in these programs as the discussion about reauthorization takes place.

I understand there will be many more public interests lobbying your Committee for other programs and overall debt reduction actions, so I will take this opportunity to remind you that American agriculture is the original industry that got this country started. We still produce the safest and most abundant food worldwide.

In Midwest States like Kansas, ag is still a major contributor to the State and local economies. We need your support and leadership in Congress to continue our tradition and our way of life. With the utmost respect to you and the difficult decisions you have ahead, I would ask you remember those of us out in the country that put food on your tables as you make these decisions.

Thank you.

[The prepared statement of Mr. Peirce can be found on page 136 in the appendix.]

Chairman ROBERTS. Cameron, thank you very much for that reminder. Thank you for your strong testimony on behalf of crop insurance.

Mr. Michael Springer of Springer Family Foods, Independence, Kansas.

STATEMENT OF MICHAEL SPRINGER, SPRINGER FAMILY FOODS, LLC, INDEPENDENCE, KANSAS, ON BEHALF OF THE NATIONAL PORK PRODUCERS COUNCIL

Mr. SPRINGER. Good afternoon, Chairman Roberts, Ranking Member Stabenow, and members of the Committee. I am Michael Springer, a third-generation crop and hog farmer from southeastern Kansas, and I am proud to represent the Kansas and U.S. pork industry today.

Like all pork producers, in the next farm bill I would like to see provisions that help strengthen my industry's competitiveness. I would hope it does not contain provisions that would restrict our ability to raise and sell animals or compete in the global marketplace.

The U.S. pork industry's top priority for the next farm bill is establishing a foot-and-mouth disease vaccine bank. If this country ever had an FMD outbreak, it not only would devastate my farm and the whole livestock industry, but the entire U.S. economy. An Iowa State University study estimates that an outbreak of FMD would immediately shut off our meat exports, would cost the U.S. pork, beef, corn, and soybean sectors alone $200 billion over 10 years. We need the capacity to produce enough vaccine to quickly control and eradicate the disease. We need the funds to make that happen.

Specifically, we want the farm bill to direct USDA to contract for: an offshore, vendor-maintained vaccine antigen bank that would have antigen concentrate to protect against the 23 most common foot-and-mouth disease strains currently circulating in the world; a vendor-managed inventory of 10 million doses, which is the estimated need for the first 2 weeks of an outbreak; and an international vaccine manufacturer with the capacity to produce 40 million doses of vaccine. That is a mouthful, 40 million doses.

While an FMD vaccine bank would protect the U.S. pork industry from likely inevitable crisis, a more here-and-now issue is efforts to regulate the buying, selling, and raising of animals. Chief among these efforts pushed by the last administration is the Farmer Fair Practices Rules, specifically an interim final rule that is set to take effect in a couple of months. That regulation will make it easier to sue and win Packers and Stockyard Act cases, which carry triple damages. Livestock industry experts have said this will lead to an increase in lawsuits and an increase in legal risks for the meat industry, which no doubt will take steps to reduce that risk. That likely would mean consolidation of the livestock industry, which would reduce, not increase, competition in the marketplace.

We do not need Government intervention in the market because it is working. We are seeing it work now in the U.S. pork industry. Five new producer-owned packing plants will be coming online in the next 2 years, and there is no doubt these plants will be chasing hogs, meaning producers will be good, which should mean getting some good prices for animals.

The bottom line on the farm bill, Congress should craft legislation to help farmers remain competitive and provisions that would help us compete. We ask that the Congress consider in the farm bill helping us protect our markets and help us protect ourselves from disasters like FMD so that our family can help feed your family and the rest of the world bacon.

Thank you for the opportunity, Mr. Chairman.

[The prepared statement of Mr. Springer can be found on page 152 in the appendix.]

Chairman ROBERTS. Michael, several years back, we had an exercise on what would happen with an FMD outbreak, with an attack from a foreign entity. I was asked to serve as President of the United States during that time. I think Secretary Ann Veneman came, along with all the Cabinet. During that exercise, it played out that it started in Texas, and by the time Texas closed its border, obviously it was in Oklahoma, and by the time—and you can see what happened all the way up to North Dakota. We were trying to isolate. By the time we really found out what was going on with certain strains of cattle to preserve them, that did not work either. We ended up having to terminate a lot of cattle, all sorts of problems with that, and I will not go into it.

All of our export stock—not just meat. When something like this happens, it affects all of our exports. Then we lost a lot of products from grocery stores—not only 1 year—2 years, 3 years down the road. It was just devastating. That was one of the exercises that Jon Wefald and I talked about that made us really work so hard for NBAF. So we need a vaccine, and that is a possible thing. I mean, this is not some impossible dream. We can do this. So I thank you for your comments on that, and thank you for coming.

Mr. Kent Winter, Kent Winter Farms, Mt. Hope, Kansas.

Statement of Kent Winter, Owner/Operator, Kent Winter Farm, Mt. Hope, Kansas, and President, Kansas Grain Sorghum Producers Association

Mr. WINTER. Chairman Roberts, Ranking Member Stabenow, and members of the Committee, I want to thank you on behalf of the Kansas grain sorghum farmers for this opportunity to share our views on the discussions surrounding the upcoming farm bill.

I farm near Andale in south-central Kansas, just outside Wichita, mostly dryland, producing grain sorghum, wheat, corn, soybeans, and alfalfa, and I currently serve as president of the Grain Sorghum Producers Association here in Kansas.

Kansas again last year was the Nation's leading producer of grain sorghum, coming in with 55 percent of the U.S. crop. Sorghum is used as a feedstock for ethanol, for livestock feed, and is also exported to other countries. Prices for most commodities this last year have collapsed, and lenders and farmers are very worried about producers being able to stay in business. When producers apply for a farm operating loan, the banker has two questions for them: A, what are your crop insurance guarantee levels? B, what do you anticipate in other farm program safety net payments? The ability to secure annual operating loans directly depends upon the stability of farm programs. That operating capital is what bolsters local rural economies.

The current Price Loss Coverage program is working for sorghum. As prices dropped significantly in the past year, needed support has kicked in for sorghum farmers. We appreciate a PLC program that today helps fill the void that low grain prices have caused.

Mr. Chairman, in regards to the conservation of our natural resources, sorghum is not only the Nation's premier water-saving grain crop, but it also offers many valuable conservation characteristics. Additionally, sorghum is drought tolerant and well suited for the arid conditions and is especially important in areas that draw water from the Ogallala Aquifer. Sorghum is a proven water-sipping crop and will be a solution, I think, to which many irrigation farmers will turn.

Finally, trade by way of exports remains vital for our industry. We support increased funding for the Market Access Program and the Foreign Market Development program in this farm bill.

One last item I would like to address is research. Unfortunately, our industry is being plagued by a new insect called the ''sugarcane aphid,'' which has caused significant financial and management challenges for our farmers. Research remains the answer for a long-term solution to this growing challenge, and we need help to deal with it and the damage that it is causing.

In closing, sorghum is a crop that is planted to make the most of difficult growing conditions, and it is also uniquely exposed to risk. Well-thought-out farm programs that address these risks will benefit our growers as well as our local, State, and national economies.

Thank you.

[The prepared statement of Mr. Winter can be found on page 168 in the appendix.]

Chairman ROBERTS. Kent, thank you very much, more especially your pointing out the need for forbearance in regards to our situation with credit. We are aware of that particular little fellow that is infesting our products, Kansas State is on top of it, and we hope we can get some answers for that just as quickly as we can.

Kenneth Wood—Kenneth, I do not know why on Earth you are sitting next to last and then we are reversing this. Obviously very poor staff work.

[Laughter.]

Chairman ROBERTS. The first speech I ever made when I worked for Frank Carlson was for the Kansas Wheat Growers in Dodge City. So I guess, Mr. Winter, you will not mind me saying that we saved Ken, the best, for the last and for our wheat growers. Please proceed.

Statement of Ken Wood, Owner/Operator, Riverside Stock Farm, Inc., Manhattan, Kansas, and President, Kansas Association of Wheat Growers

Mr. WOOD. Thank you, Mr. Chairman. You may want to reserve judgment on that until after I have given my testimony.

[Laughter.]

Mr. WOOD. Mr. Chairman, Ranking Member Stabenow, and members of the Committee, thank you for the opportunity to address you today. My name is Ken Wood, and I farm in central Kansas. I am president of the Kansas Association of Wheat Growers and am honored to submit the following comments:

Wheat is an important crop for Kansas. With record yields during the 2016 harvest came record stockpiles of wheat in Kansas and around the world, resulting in historically low prices. Many feel that these low prices and a struggling farm economy are what caused Kansas wheat farmers to plant nearly 1 million fewer acres last fall, the second lowest planted wheat acres in Kansas in over a century.

Low prices and rising costs are placing even more stress on the Kansas wheat farmer, forcing them to cut budgets and find efficiencies. This situation highlights the need for Federal programs like crop insurance in Title I and illustrates the vital importance of a farm safety net.

Crop insurance, for me, is the most important segment of that farm safety net. When a natural disaster looms on the horizon, whether it is a drought, flood, or in my case, a tornado, we know that crop insurance will help keep us in business.

On May 25, 2016, my farm, home, vehicles, most of my machinery, and approximately 300 acres of my crops were destroyed by an EF4 tornado. The availability of crop insurance was not the deciding factor, but certainly a contributing factor in my decision to re-build my business. I honestly do not think that I would have had the courage to start over without having the protection that crop insurance offers. I insure my buildings and machinery investment. Likewise, I want to insure my crop investment. For most of us, crop insurance will not guarantee a "good year," but it offers the promise of "another year."

Despite passage of a 5-year farm bill, some in Congress continue to come after Title 1 farm programs and the Federal crop insurance program. Efforts to cut crop insurance have come after the Federal share of premium support, either through hard caps or through establishing AGI limitations on eligibility. Such caps would limit participation and make crop insurance more expensive for all of us.

Increasing demand for wheat products is one way to help turn the agricultural economic situation around through increasing food aid and by supporting international trade. Increasing trade is one of the easiest and most effective way to increase commodity prices and improve the rural economy. Kansas ranks as the 8th largest State in terms of exports of agricultural products. Because of this, our association has been a major supporter of international trade deals such as NAFTA and TPP. On average, half of the wheat grown in Kansas is exported. Without trade, the Kansas farmer will continue to struggle.

Finally, once we do have trade deals, we need to make sure that we are taking action to enforce them. U.S. farmers are not on a level playing field in the international marketplace due to subsidies employed by other countries.

I would like to thank you for holding this farm bill hearing in Kansas, and I look forward to answering any questions that you might have.

[The prepared statement of Mr. Wood can be found on page 171 in the appendix.]

Chairman ROBERTS. Thank you again to all of you for taking the time to join us today.

Senator STABENOW. I have a few questions here, and I am going to turn to you. Then if there are any other questions that you feel that we have not covered—I am talking to the panel—please let us know.

Everybody up here has talked about crop insurance, thank goodness. Over the last couple of years, Kansas producers faced a range of natural disasters—floods, drought, wildfires, freezes—wildfire, man, that was something else in south-central Kansas—yes, even tornadoes. For years, Kansas producers have said the crop insurance program is not simply beneficial, but it is critical to managing risk. We just heard that testimony from the Kansas wheat growers.

From your standpoint and the commodities you represent, is crop insurance working to provide adequate coverage for these types of natural disasters? Ken, I am going to start with you, and just go right down the line. Where are you, Ken? Right there. Down the line and back again, if you want to.

I am sorry. Are you talking about Kent Winter? Staff. Start at that end and work back.

Chairman ROBERTS. Okay. Since there was this terribly egregious mistake that staff made, we are going to start at the end of the table and go that way. All right?

Mr. WINTER. Mr. Chairman, would you please repeat the question again?

Chairman ROBERTS. Crop insurance, how valuable—— [Laughter.]

Chairman ROBERTS. We are back to crop insurance. I am sorry. Basically, I am asking from your standpoint and the commodities you represent, is crop insurance working to provide adequate coverage for these types of natural disasters?

Mr. WINTER. Mr. Chairman, I believe that crop insurance has been working very well for our situation, and I also want to mention that the amount of assistance that we have on our premiums is what helps make this program work. I am fearful that if that was not out there, we would not have the participation level that we now have.

Chairman ROBERTS. I want to thank the distinguished Senator from Michigan for joining me and several others on the floor of the Senate where there was proposed yet another—after $6 billion and another $6 billion, they proposed another $3 billion cut with the last continuing resolution. I sort of had a conniption fit, and we took the floor. We had a colloquy, we had bipartisan support, and that cut was eliminated.

I can just tell you, in terms of crop insurance, we have to have adequate funding. If that is not going to happen, well, it is not going to happen. So I appreciate that.

Does anybody else want to contribute to that?

Mr. WOOD. I would have to agree with Kent about how important crop insurance is. It is vitally important for us as producers to know what the worst-case scenario is so we can plan from there, and along that same line, it is very important that our lenders and our bankers and people who finance us also know what our worst-case scenario is. So like I said before, it is not going to make a good year for you, but it actually gives you some stability and a little bit of confidence that you will be able to go into the next year.

Chairman ROBERTS. I appreciate that. Thank you very much.

Mr. Clawson, your testimony mentions that decisions regarding marketing of cattle and beef are best left to the industry rather than Congress. Can you describe an example where beef producers as an industry banded together to address marketing concerns?

Mr. CLAWSON. Yes. For more than a year, the National Cattle-men's Beef Association has had a working group that has been discussing issues like price discovery, market volatility and futures contract specifications. The Fed Cattle Exchange, which is an online fed cattle market, is the result of this working group that got together, and it has come to fruition. The Fed Cattle Exchange gives pricing information back into the markets, so that is one area.

Another one is our KLA working group that we are trying to come up with different ideas, and we think we have come up with more robust pricing information being available in the mandatory price reporting data. Now, this is data that is already being reported, and we have asked for access to that so we can do our analysis, and we have been denied. So we would ask this Committee's help in getting access to that data so we can do our analysis.

[Pause.]

Chairman ROBERTS. We are going to work with you on that.

Mr. CLAWSON. Thank you.

Chairman ROBERTS. I had asked simply if we have made that request, and we will be working with you to get that done.

Amy, you mentioned in your testimony some of the regulatory burdens impacting your farming operation. During these tough times, I am sure these costs can be very crippling. Can you elaborate or share other regulatory challenges impacting your farm's profitability? My next question tied into that is: Do you feel resources at the USDA, for example, conservation program dollars, are being directed to address regulatory requirements? Or would anybody else on the panel wish to add anything along these lines? Please.

Ms. FRANCE. Yes, thank you. I got a little distracted by my time limit, and you said the gavel would go down at 3 minutes. I actually wanted to address regulatory burdens. Again, with EPA restricting more and more chemicals, in turn that increases our tillage, burning more fuel and adding wear and tear on our already aging equipment. So that is another thing. For instance, atrazine is one that we use, and although there are alternatives out there, it has been forecasted that if we lost atrazine, it could cost the farmers between $30 to $59 per acre, which would be extremely devastating to our bottom line.

Another way is, unless Congress acts on the Worker Protection Standard (WPS), we will be forced to sell our spray rig and hire it done. In that case, we are the ones that know our fields better than anyone else and when things need to be done, and we cannot wait on overbooked professional applicators. So that is something as far as regulatory burden that we feel needs to be addressed.

Chairman ROBERTS. Thank you for that. Anybody else?

Mr. WINTER. Mr. Chairman? Chairman ROBERTS. Yes, sir.

Mr. WINTER. I would also like to comment on atrazine. If we lose that, that will be devastating to our industry. It is frustrating—and I will try to be respectful here, but it is very frustrating to see that the EPA is ignoring decades and decades of sound science, over 7,000 studies that have proved the safety of the chemical, the herbicide called "atrazine." A lot of what appears to be going on from my side of the fence is they are changing the rules, they are moving the goalpost to where the sound science is being discarded, and they are using models that really are not applicable to modern-day agriculture to make these decisions with.

The other thing I would like to point out is regarding the Waters of the US. I want to give you just a little bit of a sense of how that would have impacted me. A year and a half ago, in August of 2015, we learned that it was time to spray sugarcane aphids. They had come up out of Oklahoma very, very rapidly. So while we were lining up the artillery, so to speak, to take care of this situation, we did not have much time. We just had a couple of days. We did not know it at the time, but we were protecting 150-bushel-an-acre dryland grain sorghum. Had WOTUS been fully implemented, we would have been mired and mired and mired in the process for getting permit applications in order to do this spraying. So that would have been devastating to us in that particular situation.

Chairman ROBERTS. What water would WOTUS have been protecting on that ground or on that crop?

Mr. WINTER. As I understand it, the WOTUS regulations, if fully implemented, would impact and take into account every little low spot in the field, every little gully in the field that drains toward a creek or a river. We are talking about small gullies that may only have water in them a couple of days out of the year.

Chairman ROBERTS. So, in other words, WOTUS was being made applicable to dry creek beds and farm ponds where no self-respecting duck would ever land, right?

Mr. WINTER. That is correct, Mr. Chairman.

Chairman ROBERTS. Yes, that is now before the courts, and as a CRA—the Congressional Review Act—subject, we are going to have a lot of talks about that.

Senator Stabenow, I have taken way too much time here for questions. Please.

Senator STABENOW. Well, thank you, Mr. Chairman, and thank you to each of you for your input. It is very important.

I wanted to ask a little bit about our voluntary conservation practices. Many of you have mentioned EQIP and the Conservation Stewardship Program in particular. But, Mr. Lahey, I wondered if you might speak a little bit. You stated that both the EQIP and CSP programs are highly accessed by cotton farmers, and I wondered if you might share in more detail what the biggest conservation issues are for your farmers and why these working lands programs are so important to helping address those.

Mr. LAHEY. I am not in the middle of cotton country, but when I developed my testimony, I used information from the National Cotton Council. In my area we have crop rotation, so our erosion control is not much impacted. EQIP, just yesterday a neighbor talked that he was accepted into the EQIP program to idle irrigation system that will save water and he can dryland farm that. So that was one benefit of the EQIP.

The CSP programs are active and help in my area where there is water and fencing and stuff like that in my area. But I am not in the middle of cotton country, being located in southwest Kansas.

Senator STABENOW. I got you. Okay.

Mr. Heinen, you had talked about that both EQIP and CSP should be fully funded in the next farm bill. I am just wondering, as we go forward and locate all these programs in conservation, I wonder how each of you might respond to that. I know that EQIP and the Conservation Stewardship Program are used a lot in Kansas, but I wondered Mr. Clawson, if you have any thoughts on that? I wonder if you could just answer yes or no, do you think that these are two things that ought to be fully funded?

Mr. CLAWSON. Yes, the EQIP program has been very beneficial for the livestock industry. I think 60 percent of the program goes toward the livestock, and that helps——

Senator STABENOW. It does, yes.

Mr. CLAWSON. That helps us with the ponds, the lagoons, and everything, and makes sure those are getting put in correctly and right, and we get cost-share to get those done. We put in water systems in pastures and fencing systems to be able to better rotate through those pastures. I mean, there are a number of benefits to the environment because of the EQIP program.

Senator STABENOW. All right. Thank you.

Mrs. Foster, EQIP and Conservation Stewardship Program, are those priorities?

Ms. FOSTER. Well, we have not personally used the EQIP program, but we have relied on, when we wanted to do some conservation things, our extension specialist out at K–State for some of those things. We did have some ground in CRP, which just recently came out, and we are still waiting on some rules and regs to decide whether to put those back in or not.

But I do know other farmers use EQIP quite a bit, and so I would say it is very important to them.

Senator STABENOW. Right. Mrs. France?

Ms. FRANCE. I would just reiterate what I said earlier, without the EQIP program, we would not be able to rebuild terraces and install the water wells for our cattle. At this time, with the markets the way they are, we are utilizing those programs very heavily, and we are thankful they are there to assist when we cannot do it on our own with these tough economic times.

Senator STABENOW. Great. Mr. Heinen, you had mentioned before both EQIP and CSP, and in looking at the numbers, it looks like the Conservation Stewardship Program is very highly used in Kansas. Are both of those programs, do you think, important?

Mr. HEINEN. Very important. In Brown County, we have pretty deep fertile topsoil, but we need to keep it where it belongs, and EQIP money helps us with conservation practices. The CSP program, I have family across the border in Missouri—but they are farmers and they still count.

[Laughter.]

Senator STABENOW. We will let them know you said that.

Mr. HEINEN. They really rely on the CSP program for nutrient levels. They do a lot of soil testing. They do a lot of precise fertilizer application and use that money to improve soil quality and water quality. Both important programs.

Senator STABENOW. Great. Mr. Moore? We will just kind of go down the——

Mr. MOORE. I would echo what everyone here said. EQIP and CSP is something that is utilized and very beneficial to producers in Pratt County, Kansas, and all the other 104 counties in Kansas. It is critical that we have the funding in place to support the conservation efforts of that, and I would throw CRP into that mix also. I mean, I do not know that the acre cap needs to go up, but CRP has played a huge role in the State of Kansas, and it has been a benefit. Our farmers have been participants in the Conservation

Reserve Program, and we have been able to retire some land that Grandpa just should not have plowed.

Senator STABENOW. Thank you. Mr. Peirce?

Mr. PEIRCE. I have had firsthand experience with the CSP program from 2004. We were a Tier 4 qualifier, and we used that to grid-sample all of our fields and variable rate apply all of our fertilizer and stuff. So we have been able to cut back and be more efficient with what we do with that, and also that helped us kind of do our full transition into no-till as well, which has aided in water quality and soil quality. The EQIP program has kind of gone hand in hand with that.

I just had someone out just the other day to look at some terraces that were put in around the early 1980s, and the tile terrace part of it—the system was only designed to last for 20 years, and it has been almost 40, and he said it was time to redo it. But it has worked good for this long. Yes, we are big believers in the programs.

Senator STABENOW. Thank you. Mr. Springer?

Mr. SPRINGER. Fully funding CSP and EQIP is very important to the pork industry. Firsthand, I am currently working on our farm with NRCS on a pipeline and pumping project for moving livestock waste, and all livestock production, we are stewards of the environment. We have some increased uncertainty from environmental regulations. Having EQIP and programs like EQIP and CSP help us bear the financial burden that comes as some of these regulations come down the line, because whether we agree or disagree with the regulation, taking care of the waters of Kansas and the United States is very important for our family and people in our business.

Senator STABENOW. Thanks very much. Mr. Wood?

Mr. WOOD. I cannot really speak very intelligently about the CSP. It has not been used very widely in my part of the State— that I know of, anyway. EQIP is used quite a bit. I think it is kind of a carrot out there to help maybe get people to do some things that they want to do, want to be able to do conservation-wise, and it maybe just gets them a little bit over the hump to where they are able to afford to do that. So I think it is a pretty important program to maintain.

Senator STABENOW. Thanks. Mr. Winter?

Mr. WINTER. Yes, I think both programs are very important. I myself have not participated in them, but my understanding is that, as you go west in the State, more and more sorghum farmers are using them. I would like to see the CSP adjusted in a way that would encourage more grain sorghum in rotation with other dryland crops.

Senator STABENOW. Thank you.

Mr. Chairman, I will turn it back to you. I think we have a second round, do we?

Chairman ROBERTS. Yes, we do.

Senator STABENOW. I will turn it back to you. I have got a couple more questions, yes. Thank you.

Chairman ROBERTS. Just a couple more, if I might.

Lucas, you and several others mentioned the importance of the Market Access Program and the Foreign Market Development Program. That is called MAP and FMD. Do not get it confused with the other FMD. There is no question in my mind that many of the challenges you face in the current farm economy can be eased by a strong trade policy. We both have talked about that at length.

Can you provide examples as to how your industries are using the MAP or the FMD funds to develop and expand markets around the world?

Mr. HEINEN. I will do my best. I had the privilege of serving on the WISHH Committee of the American Soybean Association, and I might add I saw him in the hallway and I think he is still here, but Professor Flinchbaugh told me that Washington has its own language and the town runs on acronyms, and he is right.

Chairman ROBERTS. Let me just intervene at this particular time.

[Laughter.]

Chairman ROBERTS. The MAP program is called ''Market Access Program,'' more access for our markets. It used to be called the ''Market Promotion Program,'' and I could never get enough votes for it when I was in the House, when I had the privilege of being Chairman of the Ag Committee in the House. So I, Pat Roberts, changed an acronym.

[Laughter.]

Chairman ROBERTS. I consider that one of my top achievements. I do not know if I will ever do any better. Instead of Market Promotion Program, which nobody wanted to pay for, the Market Access Program worked. So there you go. Fire away.

Mr. HEINEN. Okay. Nice work on the acronym change.

Chairman ROBERTS. Thank you. Appreciate it.

[Laughter.]

Mr. HEINEN. We had a program in partnership actually with K–State involved with WISHH in Pakistan. It starts with FMD and MAP money, and it built the ground level, and it got funding from other sources. But it was to use soybean meal in fish farming, in aquaculture in Pakistan. It took an industry that used no soybeans at all, no Kansas soybeans especially, to a significant consumer of soybean products in a fairly short period of time. It was a win-win for us, for the university, for the Pakistani aquaculture industry.

Chairman ROBERTS. Is that still ongoing?

Mr. HEINEN. The funding—the WISHH side of that is not ongoing, no, but it laid the groundwork. The program is still in effect.

The guys in Pakistan are still using the beans.

Chairman ROBERTS. I appreciate that very much.

Mr. Moore, corn growers would like to see the ARC-County program continued and improved. Any county-based program is going to have some level of differences between counties. Can you walk us through what you see are causing the most concerns with the program in its current form?

Mr. MOORE. I think it is just the yield data discrepancies that we face, and I think a lot of that is due to the reluctance probably that we see—we were told that there were data gaps because of the farmers' reluctance to fully participate in National Ag Statistics Service surveys. I think, like it has been stated up here earlier, that—I mean, I do not see why we cannot use RMA data for those yields, because it is provided. I mean, anybody that participates in the crop insurance program is providing that yield. RMA has it. So why can't we use it? That would go a long way in leveling the playing field from county to county on getting the data that is needed to implement the programs like they are designed to run.

Chairman ROBERTS. I appreciate that. That is a very good suggestion.

Mr. Springer, the pork industry, growing in Kansas, growing in Michigan. The Ranking Member has emphasized that expansion in her State. I understand one of the three new pork packing plants will be operational in Michigan by the end of the year. Given the positive growth that industry is experiencing, what impediments to growth have you encountered as a family business and as an industry more generally?

Mr. SPRINGER. Okay. Thank you, Chairman Roberts. Uncertainty is a killer in any business project. But in agriculture, we are really good at overcoming uncertainty and the unexpected. So I would like you to think this way: When we build a hog facility or a livestock feeding facility or buy a piece of land, we are making a longterm investment. In our business, those could be anywhere from a few thousand dollars to a few million dollars. Those are 30-year investments, and they are extremely expensive to repurpose, and they basically have one function.

So we need to know the regulatory environment that we are working in when we make the investment. So anything—I would not say that there are specific things that have said, hey, that is going to stop the Springer family from growing, but when the combination of uncertainty from feed ingredient requirements, environmental regulation, if export and marketing agreements do not happen—and then the big one is animal housing. If we get an animal housing law that would prevent us from putting the number of pigs in our facility that we designed it for, then we have an issue, and it requires an investment. If we get enough of those issues at the same time, there will come a time that we say it is not worth doing anymore. So the management of the uncertainty.

Chairman ROBERTS. Thank you for that.

Lynda, you laid out quite the case for adjustments to the Market Protection Program, MPP—we have to have the acronym—in order to better serve dairy farmers. My question: For the first time in the history of mankind, can the dairy industry be able to stick together and agree to changes you would all like in the farm bill?

[Laughter.]

Ms. FOSTER. Your guess is as good as mine.

I really think in the last couple of years the dairy industry has come together far more, or we probably would not have the MPP in the first place. The way it was designed, the first year a lot of dairy farmers signed up. Personally, we signed up I think at the $6 level. But when we had low prices, because of the distorted formula through that 10-percent cut, months when it should have kicked in, it did not because the wrong margin was there. So farmers could see from what was projected it was not going to pay.

So the next year, very few signed up at $100, the basic catastrophic level, because you had to sign up, you were already in that program. Well, this last year, things did not look any better, so everybody practically signed up just at the $100 level. They were not signing up at the higher percentages because they are not kicking in.

One of the reasons is we have—the way it was designed, it said for 2 months, January-February, March-April, had to be low in each of those 2-month segments. But if you were low in February and March, it did not kick in. Where they come up with one month is better than another month and you have to have a 2-month average I have not figured out. Cows do not milk month by month. You know, you got to milk them every day. So that is one thing we would like to see changed, is some of those tweaks. But if we get some of those tweaks made, I really feel dairy farmers will come on board, because right now they are very—they are disgusted, they are disgruntled, because it is not working and we have had low prices and low margins.

Chairman ROBERTS. I really appreciate that. Thank you very much.

Senator Stabenow, do you have any further questions?

Senator STABENOW. Thank you. Just a couple. One to follow up, Mrs. Foster, on that, we grow a lot of different things, and have a lot of different producers in Michigan, but dairy is really important for us, and I have heard from my dairy producers, milk producers as well, real concerns about the new program. Everything is complicated as we have put together pieces in the farm bill, but it seems like dairy is always particularly complicated just because of the different sizes and different regions in the country and so on.

But you talked in your testimony about how other commodities have overlapping protection from the Farm Service Agency programs and Federal crop insurance, and that is not available for dairy farmers. So in addition to what we know in terms of the program that was put together that we need to fix, could you talk a little bit more about that?

Ms. FOSTER. Well, when I have my crops, I can take out crop insurance, and I can do the ARP and the—decide on those other programs. But with dairy, I had to choose either the MPP or one of those risk marketing agencies, management ones, the LGM I believe it is, Livestock Gross Marketing, which I am not personally familiar with, but I know a lot of farmers used it. But we could not use both. We had to choose one or the other; whereas, other commodity groups have several choices and can use more than one.

Senator STABENOW. That is something we need to take a look at.

Ms. FOSTER. Just by the way, I saw a few of your dairy producers from Michigan just yesterday at the meetings. They are great people.

Senator STABENOW. They are. They are.

[Laughter.]

Senator STABENOW. They are the best. Well, we cannot close out this panel, Mr. Chairman, without my asking about something that we worked so hard on together related to livestock last time, which was a huge, important, new funding piece that we included. I think the three livestock disaster assistance programs received all together, in permanent funding, something like $3 billion. It was one of the big things that we did in the farm bill. I am wondering, Mr. Clawson, how is that working from your perspective? How important are those programs to livestock industry and how much are the Kansas producers using these programs?

Mr. CLAWSON. When the drought came about, it was used very heavily, the livestock disaster—the drought protection that we got, and a number of producers were able to utilize that, and thank you for adding that.

Another provision is the Emergency Conservation Program, I think is what you call it. We had a huge wildfire last year, over 400,000 acres rangeland burnt in the southern part of the State, with fences and just totally devastated. There was a lot of people that donated hay that was needed right away, as well as fencing supplies and monetary funds. KLA and the Kansas Livestock Foundation helped disburse that. But on a longer-term fix, that Emergency Conservation Program has kicked in as a cost-share to put back these permanent fences. That has been just a godsend to those people because they are able to get that land back into production almost immediately. Where for a lot of them it might have been 3 to 10 years to get those fences back in to be able to finance them and get them put back, with this program it has been able to get the land back into production.

As you well know, grass needs to be grazed, or else we start losing production on it. So we are able to put fences back in to have a structured grazing program to be able to take care of the grass.

Senator STABENOW. Well, thank you.

Thank you, Mr. Chairman. I appreciate the excellent input from this panel.

Chairman ROBERTS. Thank you so much. Thank you so much. I think you deserve a round of applause, ladies and gentlemen.

[Applause.]

Chairman ROBERTS. We will now convene the final panel for today's hearing on the 2018 farm bill. This panel is composed of representatives who work in industries that support production agriculture and our rural communities. After all, you cannot grow food and fiber without credit or power or water and many other important functions performed by the industries on this panel. While the first panel is departing, I will introduce the second panel.

Our first witness on this panel is Shan Hanes. Shan, if you will come back. Okay. We have got the monikers, and we have the people coming aboard.

[Pause.]

Chairman ROBERTS. Our first witness on this panel is Shan Hanes. Sshhh. It is amazing how that works.

After growing up on his family farm in the Oklahoma Panhandle and graduating college, Mr. Hanes accepted the position as an ag loan officer for the First National Bank of Elkhart and Rolla in 1993, where he served as both an ag loan officer and IT officer for 13 years. In 2008, he became president and CEO of the First National Bank, a position he holds today. Shan, thank you for joining us today. You have come back, Shan.

[Laughter.]

Chairman ROBERTS. Now, that dates me an awful lot, if nobody in the audience can remember that was a movie by Alan Ladd, and he left, and little Brandon De Wilde came out and said, ''Come back, Shane.'' He is back. Now, come on.

[Laughter.]

Chairman ROBERTS. Next I would like to welcome Mrs. Catherine Moyer. Catherine, I believe our last meeting was just this past October in Allen for the Rural Broadband Roundtable that we hosted with FCC Chairman and fellow Kansan, Ajit Pai. It is good to see you again. Catherine is the general manager and CEO of Pioneer Communications, a telephone and communications company that serves residents and businesses across southwestern Kansas. She holds a bachelor's degree from Middlebury College and a law degree from Washburn University. She resides in Ulysses with her husband, Kevin. Welcome, Ms. Moyer.

Ms. Kathleen ''Kathy'' O'Brien is representing our Kansas electric cooperatives today. Ms. O'Brien is the general manager of the Nemaha-Marshall Electric Cooperative in Axtell, where she has worked in a number of capacities for the past 26 years. She currently chairs the Kansas Electric Cooperative Association Board of Directors and is the first woman to hold that position. Thank you for joining us today, Ms. O'Brien.

Our next witness is Mrs. Gena Ott. She joins us from Emporia and is representing the Frontier Farm Credit folks. Growing up on a third-generation farm in east-central Kansas, Gena developed a deep appreciation for agriculture and rural communities. She graduated from Kansas State University with a degree in agribusiness. In addition to Gena's three-decade career with Farm Credit, she and her husband have a small cattle operation. Gena, thank you so much.

Mr. Derek Peine, chairman of the board of Renew Kansas, in Oakley, our next witness, is here on behalf of the Kansas Grain and Feed Association. Mr. Peine is the CEO of Western Plains Energy located in Oakley. He is a 1997 graduate of Kansas State University. He was recently elected chairman of the board of Directors of Renew Kansas, a State trade association that represents the independent ethanol plants in Kansas as well as farmers and those who provide services to the ethanol industry in our State.

We also want to welcome here today on behalf of the Kansas Cooperative Council Mr. Greg Ruehle. Mr. Ruehle is president and CEO of Servi-Tech. That is the Nation's largest independent agronomic firm headquartered in Dodge City, Kansas, America. Mr. Ruehle manages a diverse staff of nearly 200 agronomists and laboratory technicians, information technology sales, and communications staff members across the Commission's eight-State footprint. His family lives in Dodge City and maintains a diversified family owned livestock operation in eastern Ford County. Welcome, sir.

Mr. Clay Scott, the Kansas Water Congress of Ulysses. He hails from Ulysses where he farms corn, wheat, and raises cattle. Mr. Scott currently serves on the board of directors for the National Water Resources Association, as a delegate to the Kansas Water Congress, and a board member of the Southwest Kansas Groundwater Management District. Thank you, sir, for joining us.

Cherise Tieben, city manager for the city of Dodge City, has been with the city for 26 years. Graduating from St. Mary of the Plains College, Dodge City, in 1989—God bless St. Mary of the Plains— she went immediately into full-time employment with the city and has worked in a variety of capacities leading to her current post as city manager. We sure look forward to hearing from you.

We will now begin the testimonies of the final panel. I ask each witness to try to keep their statements to 3 minutes, as we have asked the previous panel. Ms. Ott, you may proceed. Where did we go with Ms. Ott? Right there. We decided to start in the middle on this one.

STATEMENT OF GENA OTT, FINANCIAL OFFICER, FRONTIER FARM CREDIT, EMPORIA, KANSAS

Ms. OTT. Okay. Chairman Roberts and Ranking Member Stabenow, thank you for the opportunity to testify today on behalf of Frontier Farm Credit. My name is Gena Ott, and I am a financial officer and a 32-year employee of the Farm Credit System, and I have worked both in lending and in crop insurance roles. I respectfully request my testimony be entered for the record.

Frontier Farm Credit has a lending portfolio consisting primarily of corn, soybeans, wheat, and cattle. Many of our customers also depend on off-farm income and farm program payments, including ARC, PLC, CRP, and CSP, to enhance their loan repayment capacity.

To give you a high-level view of credit conditions in the Midwest generally, the upper 50 to 60 percent of our grain producers are holding their own, with many showing some minor profitability. The bottom 15 to 20 percent of grain producers are experiencing stress as a result of a combination of higher debt load, high cost of production, and overall lack of profitability.

In the cattle sector, increases in cow numbers will cause fed cattle prices and margins to be under significant pressure, while cattle feeders will get some relief from cheaper calf prices.

With our expertise and commitment to their success, adjustments are being made to sustain these operations through the present cycle. In all cases, these conversations are individual to the customer and to the operation, and we will work with them every step of the way. We were intentionally conservative in the good times so that we can be courageous during these more difficult times.

From producers, we hear daily accounts of the importance of developing strong markets and reducing regulations to improve viability of their farms and ranches.

The financial commitment required to grow an operation is especially challenging for less established producers. Frontier Farm Credit makes extraordinary efforts to support young, beginning, and small farmers. Our specialized lending programs use modified credit standards, and we underline the need for protecting against production and price risk with this segment.

Mr. Chairman and Ranking Member Stabenow, I want to thank you, both of you, for your commitment to crop insurance. It is an important public and private partnership and a critical risk management tool for farmers. The strength of the current crop insurance partnership rests in the ability for a farmer or rancher to select products that meet their needs for individualized risk protection. As you know, the program is a top priority among all ag stakeholders.

Producers who purchased crop insurance in 2012 mitigated the direct financial impact their operations would have experienced due to the drought that year. The crop insurance program performed as intended, averting the need for ad hoc disaster assistance.

Similarly, the LRP, livestock risk protection, and the pasture, range and forage program have been effective for offering some risk protection to those in the cattle and grass sectors.

Switching gears for a bit, I would like to direct your attention to my written testimony which highlights our grant programs, advancing agriculture education, young and beginning producers, hunger and nutrition, and essential services and disaster relief needs in rural communities.

Our outreach helps support the organizations such as 4H, FFA, and the Kansas Farmer Veteran Coalition and a program that I am particularly proud to be involved with, Women Managing the Farm.

Chairman Roberts, it is always great to have you back home, and we are proud of the work you do on behalf of us every day. Thank you, Ranking Member Stabenow, for coming to Kansas to listen. We know that you understand the challenges facing world communities in agriculture and ask you to share your knowledge and experience with your colleagues to help them understand, too, as you work through the farm bill.

Thank you.

[The prepared statement of Ms. Ott can be found on page 126 in the appendix.]

Chairman ROBERTS. Gena, thank you for your excellent testimony, and we are going to get straightened out here and start here with Mr. Hanes and go right down there, and if you really want to repeat that testimony, you can do that.

[Laughter.]

Chairman ROBERTS. We will jump right on down the line. Mr. Hanes, please.

STATEMENT OF SHAN HANES, PRESIDENT AND CHIEF EXECUTIVE OFFICER, FIRST NATIONAL BANK OF ELKHART, ELKHART, KANSAS, ON BEHALF OF THE AMERICAN BANKERS ASSOCIATION

Mr. HANES. Chairman Roberts and Ranking Member Stabenow, I am Shan Hanes, president and CEO of First National Bank in Elkhart, Kansas. I am proud to be an ag banker in a rural community for 20-plus years.

Just so you know, First National Bank is a $78 million bank located in Elkhart, the county seat, with a branch serving Rolla. I appreciate the western representatives that you have on our panel. We consider Ulysses central Kansas.

[Laughter.]

Mr. HANES. Dodge is eastern Kansas, since where Elkhart is at.

We have 21 employees. We are a typical ag bank in Kansas. We are the largest lender in the county.

In addition to my CEO duties, I am a member of the American Bankers Association and the Kansas Bankers Association. I appreciate the opportunity to present the views of ABA, KBA, and especially rural lenders and the impact of the Agricultural Act of 2014, better known as the "2014 farm bill."

One of the biggest successes of the 2014 farm bill, as already stated, was the continued support of crop insurance. By providing support based on each producer's proven crop yields, crop insurance continues to provide a guarantee that helps lenders secure financing for operating credit. It is important that crop insurance works for all producers, especially as commodity prices have declined.

Low commodity prices have hurt crop insurance's ability to provide a solid safety net, and this is concerning for everyone.

Another success of the 2014 farm bill is the continued support of the Conservation Reserve Program. CRP is vital to my area. It provides another avenue for farmers to find productive use for their land. In addition, the Committee should be commended for its commitment to the Farm Service Agency's guaranteed lending programs. However, I believe there is a need to consider reforms to the programs, specifically to raise the lending limit cap on guaranteed ownership and guaranteed operating loans due to the risking cost of agriculture. The guaranteed loan programs have allowed our customers to continue to access credit from banks like mine as they grow, ensuring credit access for bank customers across the country.

From a lending perspective, there needs to be consideration of changes to the ARC and the PLC programs. As you are well aware, commodity prices were much higher in 2014. With price changes significantly, producers need to have the ability to make elections on their farm programs on a yearly basis. Lastly, and most importantly, farmers currently do not receive their payments in the same marketing year. This has caused an issue for lenders as well as producers, as we cannot properly account for their payments as a part of their loan repayment strategy.

I would like to point out that in 2016 farm banks like mine increased ag lending 8 percent and now provide over $100 billion in total farm loans. It is also important to touch on the regulatory environment for lenders. Our main competitor, the Farm Credit System, has a regulator that focuses on them and only them. Banks have multiple regulators and often have to teach a regulator some of the intricacies of ag lending. This can be very frustrating when regulators go through the review of the bank both for the officer and for the borrower. Regulators often question the structure of ag loans, and every regulator seems to have a differing opinion on what is a safe ag loan. Despite these difficulties, I believe the banking industry is well positioned to meet the needs of rural America.

Thank you, and I would be happy to answer any questions you might have.

[The prepared statement of Mr. Hanes can be found on page 80 in the appendix.]

Chairman ROBERTS. Thank you, sir.

Catherine Moyer, general manager of Pioneer Communications, Ulysses, Kansas—way back east.

Ms. MOYER. Central Kansas.

STATEMENT OF CATHERINE MOYER, GENERAL MANAGER, PIONEER COMMUNICATIONS, ULYSSES, KANSAS, ON BEHALF OF THE NTCA–THE RURAL BROADBAND ASSOCIATION

Ms. MOYER. Chairman Roberts and Ranking member Stabenow, thank you very much for the invitation to speak about rural telecommunications and the 2018 farm bill. I am Catherine Moyer from Ulysses. I am speaking today on behalf of Pioneer, as well as NTCA–The Rural Broadband Association. Pioneer is headquartered in Ulysses, Kansas. We have about 113 employees, and we serve 5,000 square miles. For those comparing, it is about the size of Connecticut, with about 3 million fewer people. We provide about 21,000 total connections—that is to wireline phone, to broadband, and to video services—over a network that utilizes a mix of fiber as well as copper and co-ax. On average, we have about two customers per square mile.

To better understand our service territory as well as the subjects covered in-depth in my written testimony that I will highlight, it is really important to understand what our service territory looks like. Of our 5,000 square miles, only 15 square miles can be considered populated areas, which really leads to about 81 percent of our customers living in those 15 square miles. The remaining 19 percent of our customers live in the other 4,985 square miles, and they utilize roughly 86 percent of our network. So we are rural, and we have to serve everybody because, by legal obligation, we are a provider of last resort. So the challenges of distance and density hit very close to home.

Our broadband networks are critical for the communities that we serve to overcome these distance and density concerns. Our networks allow ag producers and other rural businesses to communicate with suppliers and sell to new markets. They enable education of our children on par with opportunities in urban America, and they make our communities places in which people want to place business and they want to relocate there and remain there. In rural America, that translates to economic development that produces jobs and a vibrant rural economy.

While the link between what rural telecom providers like Pioneer do and the witnesses you have already heard from, what might not be so obvious is why I am here talking about the 2018 farm bill. Access to capital for rural broadband projects is limited. Companies like Pioneer have few options to finance network construction. It takes a mix of private capital as well as financing from a few committed, mission-driven lenders like RUS, CoBank, and RTFC to enable us to build networks that we use to serve our communities. Pioneer is a company that has borrowed from both our U.S. and CoBank, and I currently sit on the CoBank board of directors. I can vouch for the small committed universe of capital that is essential to our industry.

It is imperative to continue to provide RUS with the resources that it needs to lend in support of rural broadband deployment. As Congress continues to grapple with where to best direct scarce resources, it is important to note that the RUS broadband loan programs make loans that must be paid back with interest—creating a win-win situation for rural broadband consumers and the American taxpayers.

We urge the Committee to continue to support the RUS broadband loan programs at or above current funding levels as you work through the farm bill reauthorization process. These programs are so vital to the ongoing deployment and maintenance of advanced communications infrastructure throughout rural America.

Working hand in hand with these programs is the Federal Universal Service Fund. USF ensures that reasonably comparable services are available in rural America at a comparable rate to those in urban America. USF promotes both availability and affordability. We continue to work with the Federal Communications Commission and urge the FCC to address the lack of sufficient USF funding for the goal of ubiquitous broadband availability.

As part of a company that is deploying broadband to a very rural, hard-to-serve part of the U.S., I know these things to be true: The sustainability of our part of southwest Kansas is dependent on a broadband network that can move more and more data.

Farms, the energy sector, and small businesses rely on our networks to make themselves more efficient and successful. Access to capital and a predictable USF program are paramount to deploying these vital networks.

I believe Congress and the FCC share my aspiration of contributing to rural America's success, and I look forward to working together to achieve that success.

Thank you very much, and I look forward to any questions that you may have for me.

[The prepared statement of Ms. Moyer can be found on page 109 in the appendix.]

Chairman ROBERTS. Thank you.

Kathleen O'Brien, representing Kansas Electric Cooperatives, please.

STATEMENT OF KATHLEEN O'BRIEN, GENERAL MANAGER, NEMAHA–MARSHALL ELECTRIC COOPERATIVE, AXTELL, KANSAS

Ms. O'BRIEN. Thank you—do you want to say something else? Chairman ROBERTS. No. [Laughter.]

Ms. O'Brien. All right. Thank you, Chairman Roberts and Ranking Member Stabenow, for inviting me to testify. My name is Kathy O'Brien. I am the general manager of Nemaha-Marshall Electric Cooperative in Axtell, Kansas. While the first business priority of electric co-ops is to deliver reliable, affordable electricity to our members, our purpose is much greater than that. We are the engines that drive economic opportunity across much of rural America and improve the lives of our members. That is why the farm bill is essential for co-ops, for Kansas, and for the country. It contains important rural development tools that support our efforts to strengthen our communities.

Since 1936, loans from the REA, now called the "Rural Utilities Service," have helped build, expand, and improve the infrastructure necessary to provide power, deliver clean water, and other necessities across rural America. It has been the most successful public-private infrastructure investment program in the history of the country. RUS loans help electric co-ops reduce costs and improve reliability for our members by financing basic maintenance like replacing poles and wires. But it also helps us fund projects to make our systems more modern, efficient, and secure.

In just the last decade, RUS loans have helped my own co-op move from a system where co-ops read their own meters and paid their own bills based on a rate chart to a more technologically advanced, cost-effective system that allows us to read meters remotely and allows members to monitor their own electric usage.

We have historically enjoyed strong support for robust funding for RUS, in large part because we are such a good investment for the Federal Government. We ask that you help maintain that support.

We have also appreciated working with the Committee over the years to help make the RUS more streamlined and efficient, and we look forward to exploring new ways to continue to improve the program.

In addition to investing in the electric cooperative network, the fees paid on RUS loans are used to fund rural economic development loans and grants. Five years ago when I was here, I gave an example of how these zero interest loans helped finance an expansion of Koch and Company—pronounced "cook" in northeast Kansas, "coke" in Wichita—a cabinet maker in my home town of Seneca, Kansas. I am pleased to say that original $450,000 investment continues to yield a great return. They have more than doubled their payroll since 2011 and now employ around 650 people in several States. Electric cooperatives continue to enjoy a productive partnership with the Federal Government and with the communities we serve to promote the health of rural America.

We look forward to continuing to work with you toward that important goal, and I am happy to answer any of your questions.

[The prepared statement of Ms. O'Brien can be found on page 122 in the appendix.]

Chairman ROBERTS. Thank you, ma'am.

Derek Peine, chairman of the board, Renew Kansas, Oakley, Kansas.

STATEMENT OF DEREK PEINE, CHAIRMAN, RENEW KANSAS, AND CHIEF EXECUTIVE OFFICER, WESTERN PLAINS ENERGY, LLC, OAKLEY, KANSAS

Mr. PEINE. Thank you, Chairman Roberts, Ranking Member Stabenow, for providing me the opportunity to be with you here today. My name is Derek Peine, and I am here today representing Renew Kansas, our State trade association that represents the 12 independent ethanol production facilities in Kansas and those who provide services to our industry. I currently serve as the chairman of the Renew Kansas board, and I am also the CEO of Western Plains Energy, a mid-sized ethanol plant located in northwest Kansas.

Let me start by sharing a key point about the ethanol industry. Western Plains Energy, like most ethanol plants today, was founded with two simple goals in mind. First, ethanol was a chance to provide additional demand for local crops to increase grain values. Second, it was an opportunity to provide much-needed jobs and economic value to our rural communities. Today, the 12 plants in Kansas do just that. We produce over half a billion gallons of ethanol annually, and we create a local stable market for approximately 200 million bushels of Kansas-grown corn and sorghum. Each of these plants is located in a rural area, and we provide more than 380 direct jobs spread across the State.

Over the last 10 to 12 years, the ethanol industry has been the predominant outlet to absorb the ever-increasing corn and sorghum production volumes. Today more than a third of those grains grown across the U.S. is converted into biofuel. However, we are now reaching the point again where crop yield improvements are outpacing demand, and the farm economy is struggling due to oversupply and depressed pricing.

The good news is that the ethanol industry can help to absorb those increased volumes. We are working hard to increase the demand for our products and simultaneously invest in innovation and improvements to increase our own production capacity.

As an industry, we are starting to grow domestic demand by developing markets for E15, a mixture of 15 percent ethanol and 85 percent gasoline. We have worked successfully with the privately funded Prime the Pump Program and USDA's Biofuel Infrastructure Program to provide consumers with a choice to purchase E15 fuel.

We have also focused on increasing product demand internationally, and the USDA Foreign Ag Service trade promotion has been a key component to ensuring we can expand those export markets.

The ethanol industry can provide additional support to the farm sector by providing an outlet for the increased grain supplies, but we need your help. As Committee members and policymakers, we need your leadership and advocacy for policies supportive of renewable fuels, including those not related to the farm bill.

My written testimony provides more specific details, but in short, we need your support to help us open free market access for consumers to purchase cleaner, cheaper, and better E15 fuel. We need to continue to advocate for fair trade with our international partners with countries such as China. Finally, we need support to not change the Renewable Fuel Standard. While this policy is not related to the farm bill, it is the integral component to the success of farmers here in Kansas and America.

I want to close by thanking you for allowing me the opportunity to testify here today. We are proud of the work that America's ethanol industry does to help the American farmers and ranchers succeed. Thank you.

[The prepared statement of Mr. Peine can be found on page 130 in the appendix.]

Chairman ROBERTS. Thank you, Derek.

We have now Mr. Greg Ruehle, president and CEO, Servi-Tech, Inc., in Dodge City, Kansas.

Statement of Greg Ruehle, President and Chief Executive Officer, Servi–Tech Laboratories, Dodge City, Kansas, on Behalf of the Kansas Cooperative Council

Mr. RUEHLE. Mr. Chairman and Senator Stabenow, thank you for the opportunity. Let me join the chorus of folks who have recognized your commitment to kick off the field hearings on the 2018 farm bill here in Kansas.

I am here today representing the Kansas Cooperative Council, of which we are a member, and I will talk about that a little bit before I get into the statement. Servi-Tech is a federated cooperative, and, Senator Stabenow, I really appreciate your reference to the Capper-Volstead Act. Obviously, those of us who represent the cooperative community know well and appreciate the value of that act and the opportunity for us to do business.

As a federated co-op, we are owned by 63 other cooperatives, so we may be kind of the unicorn up here at the table, and we really appreciate and value that cooperative model, and we are always happy to speak to that.

The Kansas Cooperative Council, though, has a broad base of membership. Lots of them are represented up here at the table, and I want to be careful not to repeat testimony that has come from them, whether it is in electricity or telecommunications, lending, et cetera, but focus in on really two areas that the Co-Op Council has a tremendous interest in.

The first is the Working Lands Programs, and I appreciated that dialogue in the first panel around how to make those programs better. There were some good references both around EQIP and around CSP and the CREP program.

One of the things I think we are undervaluing, though, is the level of technology that has evolved around conservation tillage, so no-till, limited tillage, vertical tillage, all of those practices are increasing in their application on acres today. Their ability to help hold that soil in place is valuable to us, and I think it allows us then to look at those working programs with maybe a different perspective in the 2018 farm bill, and that is to really focus the dollars on the acres where the impact can be the greatest.

Those other acres, we are going to need to feed a growing global population. We are going to need those acres in production growing row crops. Whether that is a crop of corn under irrigation or a crop of sorghum in a dryland situation, those are important crops to us from a domestic and international standpoint. So the council would strongly encourage the Committee to give a hard look at those programs to make sure that they are relevant to the level of technology that is available in agriculture today. The role that farmers and ranchers play in conservation is significant, and we do not need a Federal farm policy that ties one of their hands behind their backs. So in that vein, we would be happy to work with the Committee as the debate goes forward.

The other area is the area of credit, and you heard a lot about that in the first panel as well, the role and then the need for credit that we have today in a growing global agricultural environment. At Servi-Tech, we utilize both Farm Credit Service lending and private lending. It is important for us to have those opportunities and to be able to tap into both of those markets. So we will just continue to make sure that we encourage those programs being in place. Strong support for crop insurance as we go through the debate in the 2018 farm bill.

With that, I would wrap it up, and I would let the folks in the audience know that the screens up here start at 3 minutes and they go to zero, and then it turns red, and I am waiting to see if lasers or something shoot out of that if you go too long. So I do not want to make the lasers come out, so with that, Mr. Chairman, I will wrap up my remarks, and I would be happy to answer questions.

[The prepared statement of Mr. Ruehle can be found on page 139 in the appendix.]

Chairman ROBERTS. Well, whether or not there are lasers is highly classified.

[Laughter.]

Chairman ROBERTS. But I think the worst you could expect is [tapping] from me, and also from the distinguished Ranking Member. I have not done that because every one of you has tried to stay within the 3 minutes, plus the fact every one of you has given us very valuable information. So when that turns red, well, take a chance and keep going.

[Laughter.]

Chairman ROBERTS. Mr. Clay Scott of the Kansas Water Congress, from Ulysses, Kansas.

STATEMENT OF CLAY SCOTT, KANSAS WATER CONGRESS, ULYSSES, KANSAS

Mr. SCOTT. Ranking Member Stabenow, welcome to Kansas. Chairman Roberts, welcome home. Thank you for holding this hearing today and for your attention to the many issues facing rural America and our Nation. The farm bill is one of the most important pieces of legislation the Congress will consider over the next few years, and this legislation—and its effects on water infrastructure—helps ensure our Nation has a diverse, safe, reliable, and affordable supply of food.

My name is Clay Scott, and in addition to farming and ranching, I am actively involved in water, presently serving as a delegate to the Kansas Water Congress, a member of the National Water Resources Association, and a current board member of our local Southwest Kansas Groundwater Management District, as well as other local and regional groups working on water conservation.

The NWRA and Kansas Water Congress members provide water to millions of individuals, families, and agricultural producers through local, State, and national water projects that support our communities, the economy, and the environment. The connection between agriculture and water is clear and of great importance. As a reliable supply of clean water is key to providing healthy, high quality, and inexpensive foods that our families enjoy, the extent of this was greatly challenged during the recent drought in Kansas, and much of the Nation was put under real challenges, especially in our industry, which spurred further review and focus to conserve and extend our resources and implement new technologies and practices for greater efficiency and higher-value uses. It also revealed the irreplaceable value of water infrastructure and the need to maintain and improve its management. Properly done, we are able to provide water for our cities, farms, and livestock and affordably transport our grains and fertilizers while capturing flood flows and resupplying depleted reserves.

As this new farm bill is written and implemented, our Nation's water infrastructure systems, which carry the fuel, fertilizer, and grains throughout the heartland and supply water for drinking and irrigation across the West, are aging past their projected life spans. The adequate care and updating of our water management systems remains key, not just for food production but for power generation, manufacturing, health, and safety.

As ranches and farms and cities look to the future, a secure supply of water is critical to further development and adoption of new technology. Water conservation and generating real opportunities for our next generation fall right in line with this.

As many individuals, groups, and organizations here are working hard to improve the livelihood of agriculture in Kansas and the United States, and from my local water board and the Kansas Water Congress, who represent many of my neighbors and much of Kansas, to State and national organizations such as the National Water Resources Association, we appreciate your time and consideration of our testimony and hope you will utilize their expertise when needed. The new farm bill must change from the era of the past and focus on the needs and vision of the future of agriculture, and while placing a strong commitment on water infrastructure.

Thank you for your time.

[The prepared statement of Mr. Scott can be found on page 144 in the appendix.]

Chairman ROBERTS. Thank you.

Cherise, thank you so much for coming, and thank you for putting up with Ken Strobel all those years. Thank you for taking over, and it is good to see you here.

STATEMENT OF CHERISE TIEBEN, CITY MANAGER, DODGE CITY, KANSAS

Ms. TIEBEN. I am pretty confident I can be shorter than Ken. [Laughter.]

Ms. TIEBEN. Mr. Chairman and Ranking Member Stabenow, welcome to Kansas. I am Cherise Tieben, city manager of Dodge City, Kansas, the proud home community of Senator Pat Roberts that is now recognized as rural. Thank you for allowing my testimony about a rural housing challenge with a positive outcome as a result of your successes in the last farm bill.

In 2008, community leaders recognized a significant housing shortage, and a housing study was commissioned to find out why the lack of quality affordable housing did not exist in Dodge City— or existed in Dodge City, why people were living in unlivable conditions and paying dearly to do so, why the housing limitations were posing barriers to recruiting, retaining, and expanding the local workforce, and why employers were housing new recruits in hotels and the individuals would leave the community after 6 months because they could not find affordable housing.

The housing study indicated that we needed to build 568 single family homes and 379 multi-family homes varying in price ranges in a period of 5 years. We had built 64 units in the previous 5 years. So the task did seem rather monumental.

The housing assessment highlighted the serious lack of inventory for starter homes for first-time home buyers. We had 44 homes on the market and should have had 140. We needed owners to graduate up in the market to make homes available for those desiring to enter the ownership world. We addressed that locally with new developments. However, the increasingly conservative nature of banks and the lack of available stock were obviously problematic, especially for our young families looking to purchase their first homes.

The study revealed that USDA rural development programs were available in Ford County but not in Dodge City, forcing individuals needing assistance to buy or build outside of the city limits, which were stretching our abilities to provide service.

We brought this to the attention of Senator Roberts, who successfully went to work on our behalf to increase the population limits. Since May of 2014, the effective date of the population expansion, Dodge City alone has had 94 USDA-guaranteed loans issued totaling $9.9 million in investment.

There are four southwest—wait, it is eastern Kansas, right?— four southwest Kansas communities of like size, and we have all had similar successes utilizing USDA rural development. Businesses are now being retained and recruited to our communities and regions due to the population changes in the last farm bill. For that, we thank you, Senator Roberts, for being our champion, and to you, Senator Stabenow, for the hard work. The rewards can easily be seen in southwest Kansas.

Thank you for the opportunity to testify, and I am pleased to answer any questions.

[The prepared statement of Ms. Tieben can be found on page 167 in the appendix.]

Chairman ROBERTS. Thank you, Cherise.

Senator Stabenow, I have two or three here, and then I will recognize you. Then we are going to wrap it up.

Thank you all for coming and taking time out of your valuable schedule to share your testimony with us. Clay, your testimony touches on an issue that is terribly important to Kansas farmers, particularly those out in the western part of our State where the Ogallala has been. There used to be as much water in the Ogallala as one of the Great Lakes, and now that is just not the case. Water is the lifeline for agriculture. What policy changes should Congress consider as it reviews USDA conservation programs—I do not want Federal water management. We can do that ourselves, thank you very much. But what policy changes should Congress consider as it reviews USDA conservation programs to further incentivize the efficient use of water while also supporting agricultural production?

Mr. SCOTT. Thank you. I think one of the most beneficial programs we have seen at times has been the EQIP program, especially in times of drought when conservation is needed the worst. It enables farmers who are already suffering from the effects of a drought to utilize programs that, even though it is probably pretty dire financial times, they are able to go ahead and make those adjustments and changes.

Another aspect of that is there is a lot of conservation being done over the aquifer right now, regardless of whether or not it is through a Federal program or not. I think in the great majority of southwest Kansas over the aquifer, that new production was shut down in the early 1990s for new appropriations and at the direction of local farmers and water users.

We are making steps forward to continue to reserve that while improving the economy. Around Ulysses, we are in the heart of the dairy boom, and with the new plant in Garden City of Dairy Farmers of America, several hundred million dollars' worth of investment there, we continue to see that expansion. I see a lot of it done without the Federal assistance side, just from real hard work.

The EQIP program, though, has its values, and especially just in this last year, I participated in a Conservation Innovation Grant with the Dragon-Line, as it is called by commercial standards, the vertical drip lines for sprinklers. That is an outstanding product. It saves water, it maintains the yields, and it preserves and extends the aquifer.

Chairman ROBERTS. Thank you for that. In visiting the Nation of Israel, which used to be a water importer and food importer, they are a food exporter and a water exporter now. They have wave energy. They have evapotranspiration. They have conservation on the water that they use constantly and then run it through a process. It is not potable water, but it certainly can be used on crops. They discovered wells. It is just an amazing thing.

But one of the things they really use is drip irrigation, and not with pipes but with a plastic that is a new kind of plastic that is just rather amazing. I am very hopeful that K–State and the person that I met that really was the godfather of this effort, who I said he ought to come and visit K–State, and I am still trying to get that worked out. But I was a little stunned by the progress that they made, and a lot of it was like southwest Kansas when they started out. I think they are about 5 to 10 years ahead of us. I know that we have a lot of investment with regards to circle irrigation, a very expensive thing to do, but also if you do not do that, why, you are not in irrigated farming. I would hope we could encourage people to take a look at that drip irrigation, which I think is what you have been talking about. Thank you for that. I think this is one of the biggest problems that we face out in our country.

Greg, in your testimony you highlight support for the Rural Economic Development and Loan Grant program. It is important to link cooperatives with their local communities to spur economic development. Could you provide an example of how these programs impact not only businesses like yours but the rural communities they serve as well?

Mr. RUEHLE. Certainly. I am going to go back and play off of Cherise's point a minute ago. With our headquarters in Dodge City and the growth that we see in our company from a staffing standpoint, a great challenge was to be able to entice people to move to southwest Kansas when there was not affordability housing available to them. I am one of those. Our family just moved to southwest Kansas about 2–1/2 years ago—or a year and a half ago, and we are one of the folks who benefits from the fact that there were rural housing funds available to develop an area of the city. Builders have come in. They build homes there now. They are priced in all different price ranges, which fits the population of Dodge City very well. So that is one of the areas.

I think the other is—and this is partially federally funded. I do not know that it falls under as directly as maybe your question requested, Senator, but it plays back in Mr. Scott's reference to some technology on pivots that allows us to more efficiently utilize limited water resources in an irrigated agricultural environment. Now, whether that is a line that drags on the ground and emits close to the ground, you lose that evapotranspiration loss, whether it is the drip tape that you mentioned a minute ago, the ability to fund those through either Federal funds or through the groundwater management districts, which there is a lot of that work being done in the groundwater management districts in western Kansas, need the kind of support that I think you are speaking of here, and it is going to take a partnership of Federal funds and local funds and private funds, frankly, to be able to make that happen.

Drip tape installation can cost several thousand dollars an acre, and with commodity prices at the point that they are, it is tough to make that work without a concerted Federal, local, and State partnership.

Chairman ROBERTS. I appreciate that.

Catherine, 2 years ago, we held a high-tech precision agriculture event in Gypsum with K–State's Polytechnic campus, a number of our Kansas equipment manufacturers and producers. They even got me to fly a UAV capable of producing high-resolution images, measuring a number of variables such as plant health, the presence of pests, weeds, and so on. Can you talk about the role our rural providers play in supporting these advancements in precision agriculture? It was not that hard. I just took control, it went this way, it went that way, this way, that way. We can do that.

[Laughter.]

Chairman ROBERTS. I do not know what the hell we are going to do with it in Washington, but at any rate, what got me was — I mentioned to somebody there, I said, "What about the farmer who goes in his pickup with his dog every day just to check the low point in his ground?" I do not want those days—I mean, what are you going to do if you cannot do that? But at any rate, please answer the question if you can sort of discern what I have been trying to say.

[Laughter.]

Ms. MOYER. Well, first I would suggest you do not fly a drone in Washington. That probably leads to trouble. But I think UAVs or drones allow our farmers to have a really unique look at their farmland and their cattle operations. The data that they are going to gather, they are going to be held on board or be transmitted to a viewing device via radio transmission. So I think the question is really what you do with that data once you have gathered it, and that really is bringing it back to your office, your desktop, your computer, downloading it, and then combining it with other forms of precision ag.

I talk to the farmers in our service territory, and they use it for looking at water application and seed application, fertilizer application and soil, and take all of those things together, and it is the big data analytic piece of it, I think, that is the most important.

Now, the question, I think, that really goes to my wheelhouse is: How do you move that data? Because they are going to move it from farm to farm or within the farm, but they are also going to move it to seed companies and fertilizer companies to ask for help to discern what this data looks like.

So we are in a very unique position to supply those pieces, the broadband, the high-speed broadband data connections, the transit to those seed and fertilizer companies, as well as the cloud storage that you need to aggregate it all to read it. I think that is where we work hand in hand with agriculture. You know, I think that's the piece that really makes our farmers much more efficient, and in today's world, especially with input prices going up and the low commodity prices, that efficiency piece, and then how to best make your farm efficient and then productive is the key piece, and that is really where I think we step in to form that partnership and look forward to continuing that.

Chairman ROBERTS. I appreciate that very much, and I enjoyed that experience very much.

Kathy, in your testimony you highlight some regulatory decisions made during the last administration, specifically the Waters of the US. Staff is going to really get upset with this, but we had Gina McCarthy and we had 11 Senators. The bill was two pages, Deborah, and in that, it said normal farming operations are exempt. Do you remember that?

Senator STABENOW. I do.

Chairman ROBERTS. Yeah. Then there was 88 pages of regulations in about 10 point font. I mean, you really had to get a magnifying glass to figure out what was going on. No lawyer of any farm organization or commodity group or anybody could figure out where we were with regards to WOTUS. Now, of course, that is in the courts. We do not have a CRA on it, which is what I said before, but that is not accurate because it has to work through the courts.

Then we have the lesser prairie chicken. Everybody knows about the lesser prairie chicken. Did you know that when Mother Nature came to our rescue and it rained, the habitat for the lesser prairie chicken increases? Then the lesser prairie chicken comes back.

Then he or she becomes the greater lesser prairie chicken.

[Laughter.]

Chairman ROBERTS. I tried to convince the EPA of that, or the Department of Interior, and I could not get to first base. Now, that is just crazy. Then I want to know who is really counting the lesser prairie chickens. We even had a situation where you could not have an oil rig on your land because the—I cannot remember which falcon it was, but it was a very mean falcon because it would go after the prairie chicken. So you could not have an oil rig on your land if it is working. They did not know that that particular falcon was slower than the lesser prairie chicken, who is a pretty fast lesser prairie chicken. I mean, that is why they call it the lesser prairie chicken.

So I understand that our Nation's electric co-ops have concerns regarding the Clean Power Plan. Have you or any other co-ops been able to produce any real-world numbers, whether that could be an economic impact or the reliability impacts in rural America? Give me some hope here.

Ms. O'BRIEN. Well, I am not quite an expert on the Waters of the US, but for the Clean Power Plan and addressing the lesser prairie chicken, I do not have specific numbers because primarily the local impacts in Kansas may differ from what may impact the Nation. But whatever the impact, even a small increase would impact the farmers. Just as the farmers in the previous panel strive to be good stewards of the land, electric cooperatives understand the importance of being good stewards of the environment. Even so, co-ops across the country want to be part of a solution to the Clean Power Plan.

Initial measures taken to meet the mandates, because we thought it was going to progress, have already increased our wholesale power costs and in turn have increased the electric bills on the farmers you just heard from on the previous panel. While we cannot predict the negative economic or reliability impact of the Clean Power Plan, we in Kansas have already seen the lack of economic development because of the lesser prairie chicken and the increased costs associated with protecting the species. Electric co-ops have even had to recommend to people who run electric power that they might have to bury lines, and the cost is just so prohibitive.

We are happy that these rules are on hold, and we think we have a lot to offer in the conversation going forward on the Clean Power Plan. The lesser prairie chicken, too, we in northeast Kansas do not have the lesser prairie chicken, but we are sympathetic to the issues that our friends in southwest Kansas—or eastern Kansas, whichever—are having because we do not know what the next species might be. So we certainly have an interest in that.

Chairman ROBERTS. I appreciate that. Senator Stabenow.

Senator STABENOW. Well, thank you, Mr. Chairman, and thank you to each of you. You really reflect the breadth of issues involved in what we call the farm bill, which is really the economic development plan for small towns in rural America, as well as food policy for everybody. I very much appreciate all of the things that you are involved in.

When we look at rural development, as an example, this is really about quality of life. When I think about growing up in a small town in northern Michigan, one of the real concerns has always been when we go off to college, who will come home, and start the business and go back to the farm and be in the community? Will there be a rural hospital? Will there be doctors? Will there be the ability to have a business? Will there be broadband? All of those things that allow people to live and stay in small towns.

So because I think broadband is so important, I wondered, Ms. Moyer, if you might just expand a little bit on some of the challenges around broadband infrastructure. I have an ongoing small business tour in Michigan and I stop in small towns. Inevitably I hear about the fact that somebody has started or wants to start a small business, and they want to sell, they want to export, they want to stay in their small town but still have access to the world. Broadband is incredibly important to making that happen.

Telemedicine is also a very big deal. We have a lot of rural hospitals in Michigan and across the country. The ability of the University of Michigan Hospital or Michigan State or the other major hospitals to connect and partner with each other, as well as to connect with people in their home through telemedicine is so important.

So when you look at the challenges, to me this is an incredibly important piece that touches so much in terms of creating quality of life and economic development and so on. Is it technical assistance? Is still just an issue of capital? Is it both? I mean, what really needs to be done so that we are providing those opportunities in small towns?

Ms. MOYER. I think you have highlighted exactly why we need it, whether it is telemedicine or attracting and retaining businesses and encouraging people to come back once they have graduated from high school, gone to college, and let us bring them back.

I think personally speaking, from the Kansas provider perspective, it really still comes down to capital. It is access to capital, but then also a way to pay back the capital that you borrowed. It is not an easy business plan to make, especially when you talk about extremely sparse population in our service territories. When you talk about, as I said having 19 percent of our customers living across over 4,900 miles, you cannot make that business plan with an expectation that only they pay for the entire transport network. That is where we go hand in hand with universal service, and it really falls under the purview of the Federal Communications Commission as well as Congress. But those two pieces go hand in hand. It is the ability to actually access capital and have a predictable and sufficient universal service program that will put some of that money back into those areas.

I do want to highlight here that the universal service program is not—they do not hand out money to people; rather, we borrow the money, we spend it, and a couple of years later, we start to get some money back from the universal service program but also from our end-user customer. So those are the pieces, I think, that are so important to building a robust broadband network throughout rural America.

Senator STABENOW. Well, I hope that we are going to be able to help with that, not just through the farm bill but through other mechanisms as well, because I think it is absolutely critical and touches the complete quality of life in rural America.

Mr. Peine, I cannot let you go without talking about the importance of the Renewable Fuel Standard, and it certainly is something that impacts us in Michigan as well as Kansas and across the country. I have to say, as somebody who is a big NASCAR supporter, we do two big races in Michigan every year. Mr. Chairman, you are welcome to come. We would love to have you. They drive E15.

Mr. PEINE. Correct.

Senator STABENOW. Right? That is all they drive is E15. So, if you want a faster car, that is what you want to drive.

I wonder if you might speak a little bit more about the Biofuels Infrastructure Program. There are a lot of opportunities in the biobased economy, and one of the things that was important to me was to have a funded Energy Title in the farm bill. We have had Energy Titles before, but they have not had any money in them, or just authorizations, and we actually put dollars in there for not just biofuels infrastructure and energy efficiency, which is really important, but the bio-based economy. Before you answer, let me just say I will do a commercial for Michigan. We are doing a lot of work around bio-based economy, as you know, in materials, with corn-based or wheat-based, soy-based materials and so on as materials and products—clothing and soaps. One of the things that we do now is seats of cars, and this is not made with corn, but with soy. I am sure it is in a lot of vehicles, but I know right now if you buy a Ford vehicle, for instance, you get a new F–150 truck, you are sitting on soy-based foam in the seats. There is soybean in the seats, so if you get hungry, you have got something you can chomp on while you are driving along.

But I raise that only because—and I know I can go on about corn-based products the same way—corn in the automobile, is used in the plastic cup holders and the dashboard, and you can do all kinds of things with it. But when we look at jobs and bringing together agriculture and manufacturing, I think there is a lot of opportunity in what we call the bio-based economy that is really exciting, and I wonder if you might just speak about what you see in that area.

Mr. PEINE. Sure. Thank you for the question. Your first comment was about the Renewable Fuel Standard, and the RFS is really the bedrock that has helped launch the ethanol industry that is based on corn and sorghum today. But the broader industry is really about bio-based technology. As the ethanol industry has expanded, one of the things I see happening today is that bio-based economy is starting to peak out a little bit. We are starting to see ethanol companies that have learned how to run a biotechnology refinery start to look at new technologies, whether that is converting their existing plant to a new biotechnology end product or putting on Bolt On technologies that could supplement with their ethanol plant.

Once you take the starch from the grain into sugar, your opportunity to turn that into lots of new materials beyond just ethanol becomes wide open. But the challenge is always around economics and the incentives to have people invest their money with surety that the Government will stand behind them. The Renewable Fuel Standard is a great example. It has helped blossom the industry, but as time has gone on, there has been pushback regarding repealing and reforming the Renewable Fuel Standard.

The challenge to our company and to investors around the country is if there is no confidence or if the confidence is shaken that the Renewable Fuel Standard could change or be eliminated, you are more resistant to put in that capital. You are more resistant to go down the road of a new biotechnology product.

Senator STABENOW. Mr. Chairman, I have a lot more questions, but I know we are coming to the end of the afternoon, so thank you to all of you. I did want to just say, Mr. Scott, I appreciate your work in bringing agriculture's voice to the Kansas Water Congress. Coming from a State surrounded by water—we have 20 percent of the world's fresh water all around Michigan—we like to say we are the ocean without the salt or the sharks. So we welcome everyone to come and have a chance to see that beauty. But I did appreciate the fact that you talked about a Conservation Innovation Grant, which was something that we had added to the conservation portfolio in the last farm bill, and so I was very interested in your using that as well.

Thank you very much, Mr. Chairman.

Chairman ROBERTS. Thank you, Senator.

Shan, come back once again. I am worried about and I know the Senator from Michigan is worried about and everybody on the Ag Committee is worried about forbearance, and Banking Committees as well in the Congress, and Farm Credit for struggling farmers with the tough times, with the tough patch that we are in.

I certainly do not want to ever again see the days where regulators would pull up black vehicles in front of the community bank and come in and want to look at your loan portfolio, which was performing. It was performing, but it did not meet some conscription or some yardstick that somebody had come up with and said you had to have X here or X there or Y here. Those were tough days. We lost a lot of folks. That was tragic.

So can you tell me some of the ways that our Kansas bankers are working with customers and young and beginning farmers to ensure producers in our rural communities are able to weather the current economic storm? Where do you see forbearance coming? Or will there be forbearance from the regulators? Or have you seen the regulators yet? Well, I know you always see the regulators.

[Laughter.]

Mr. HANES. I really do not want to see the black cars pull up either, frankly.

Chairman ROBERTS. Yes.

Mr. HANES. Obviously, that is mission critical right now. We are in the middle of our renewal season. We are trying to get operating funds secured for everyone. Typically, as you would know, when prices go through the low cycles, we can typically use real estate to restructure lower payments, ease up the cash flow, that sort of thing. The challenge, I am afraid this time, is we are also looking at a time where rates are going to start moving up instead of down, and so that is actually going to make that much more of a challenge moving forward. But we can still use that because there is good equity in the land. When prices were good, a lot of banks increased loan margins, had a quicker repayment because the cash was there, and so we have got good equity in equipment and in real estate.

When you get to the young and beginning farmers, however, typically they either do not have real estate to fall back on to restructure, or what they do have they have not had very long, and so there is not a lot of equity there to put cash, inject capital/cash back in the operation. So it becomes vitally important to educate the borrowers. They have to know their breakeven, their real breakeven of operating inputs, debt repayment, a real breakeven.

I see a time now kind of going back to the mid-1990s where we may be marketing the entire year where the price of that particular commodity barely meets the breakeven, barely gets over it; and if it does, it is only going to be there for a very short period of time. So we have been very proactive in educating our borrowers so that they know what that breakeven is, and so they are in a position to act and respond and take advantage of that price when it does get there. So that is really what we are trying to do for our borrowers because that is the long-term projection.

To that end, the last thing for the young and beginning farmer is Farm Service Agency and those guaranteed loans. That is a great source of comfort both to the bank and to the borrower. If they meet certain numbers and certain returns, we can get a 5-year guaranteed line of credit, and so that gives that borrower some assurance that, hey, as long as I meet this standard, I will be able to have my note renewed.

The challenge is that what 20 years ago was a small young, beginning farmer and a $100,000 line of credit and $200,000 of equipment, that is not a beginning farmer. That is a hobby farmer now. So those loan limits we bump up in that 1.4 or 1.399 guaranteed limit rather quickly, even with a beginning farmer. So that is the challenge I see even for those guys.

Chairman ROBERTS. Gena, we started with you. I think we are going to end with you. I had a question on crop insurance, but I would like you to maybe respond to the same question that I asked Shan. What is your take on this in terms of forbearance, where we are headed, ample farm credit, et cetera, et cetera?

Ms. OTT. In my written testimony, we talked a little bit about different adjustments that producers could make. We encourage then to look at their fixed costs and those four R's: to reamortize, if they have short real estate loans, to try to stretch them out to lower those payments through this lower cycle; refinance if they have got equipment debt and such, they may be able to restructure that and, again, lower the debt service on that, stretch it out some.

We have talked about—I am going to forget my R's as I go along here. We are going to reassess family living needs, our costs of doing that. We got perhaps comfortable at some level when profitability was in the industry, and sometimes we need to look at that and make sure that we are careful about that while the cycle is at the bottom.

Forgive me on the spot here. The other thing we have done is added staff that is dedicated entirely to working with people that are in a tough situation. So they have more tools to rework some of the financing, help them understand their costs. We have talked a lot, too, about making sure they are marketing when they can, when the profit is there. Shan alluded to that. If they use their crop insurance guarantee, they are able to price at a time where they do not have the product on hand, but they can forward-price knowing that that guarantee—that the crop insurance is there so they can market a great percent of their production knowing that that is there to protect them when they have an opportunity to do so.

Chairman ROBERTS. I put you on the spot. Well done.

Thank you to all of our witnesses for joining us here in Manhattan, Kansas, America, the Little Apple. We appreciate you sharing your experiences and thoughts today, and thanks to those in the audience, those still remaining and those who have listened from around the country for your interest.

A special thanks to my colleague and friend, Senator Stabenow. Welcome to Kansas. I look forward to going to Michigan. I think I look forward to going to Michigan. It is green and white, folks. It ain't purple.

Senator STABENOW. That is right.

Chairman ROBERTS. As I said when I took the gavel 2 years ago, this Committee is the voice of the producer. This Committee will not only provide folks a platform to spread the word about the value of production agriculture, but also be the forum for our farmers and ranchers and rural communities to participate in the shaping of our next farm bill.

Today we started that process. We have heard about agriculture research, crop insurance, some of the other policies that are working well, and we have heard about the burdens of Government regulation and programs, and we need to raise more questions and craft solutions, including the ARC program.

We will continue to listen to farmers and ranchers and other stakeholders at additional hearings in the countryside and in Washington. We will keep asking tough questions and reexamining programs to determine their effectiveness.

We have less than 2 years to pass the next farm bill, and, yes, there will be another farm bill. But we have our work cut out for us. We need bold thinking, new ideas to address today's challenges during these tough economic times. We must face the realities head-on. Our producers in their fields are being asked to do more with less, and we also have to be willing to find solutions that stay within our budget caps and trade rules. Yes, those trade rules. I hope we have trade rules. I hope we have trade opportunities.

We will be crafting a bill that meets the needs of producers across the countryside, and if we embrace the attitude of our producers' optimism and ingenuity, we can certainly get that done.

To my fellow Committee members, I ask that any additional questions you may have for the record be submitted to the Committee clerk 5 business days from today or by 5:00 p.m. next Thursday, March 2nd.

That concludes our hearing. The Committee is adjourned. Thank you all so much.

[Whereupon, at 5:03 p.m., the Committee was adjourned.]

APPENDIX

Testimony for Hearing from the Heartland: Perspectives on the 2018 Farm Bill from Kansas, Submitted to the United States Senate Committee on Agriculture, Nutrition and Forestry, Senator Pat Roberts, Chair, Submitted by David Clawson, Englewood, Kansas, February 23, 2017, Manhattan, Kansas

Mister Chairman and members of the committee, my name is David Clawson. My wife Jeanne and I reside near Englewood, Kansas, and are part of a family partnership that includes a commercial cow-calf operation and both dryland and irrigated farming. We also are partners in a dairy and my family's bank. I am President of the Kansas Livestock Association (KLA) and serve on the Board of Directors of the National Cattlemen's Beef Association (NCBA), of which KLA is an affiliate. I am very pleased to be with you today.

KLA, formed in 1894, is a trade association representing nearly 5,200 members on legislative and regulatory issues. KLA members are involved in many aspects of the livestock industry, including seedstock; cow-calf and stocker cattle production; cattle feeding; dairy production; swine production; grazing land management; and diversified farming operations.

The beef industry is a key segment of the Kansas economy and the Kansas beef industry is a major piece of the U.S. beef industry. Kansas ranks third nationally with 6.4 million cattle on ranches and in feedyards. Those cattle generated $8.8 billion in cash receipts in 2015. Kansas is a national leader in cattle feeding and beef processing. The Kansas beef cow herd is the sixth largest in the country at 1.57 million head. Kansas is home to a growing dairy industry, both in production and processing. In 2016, Kansas dairy farmers produced more than 3.3 billion pounds of milk. Also, the presence of Kansas State University, the Animal Health Corridor and the proposed National Bio and Agro-Defense Facility makes Kansas a world leader in animal health research.

Development of the next farm bill is an important process for livestock producers. Whether directly or indirectly, the provisions included in the farm bill can have a dramatic impact on livestock producers' businesses. We oppose agriculture policies that pit one industry group against another, distort market signals and inadvertently cause economic harm to the livestock sector.

The vast majority of my fellow livestock producers believe the livestock industry is best served by the process of free enterprise and free trade. Even with its imperfections, free trade is relatively more equitable than regulated and subsidized markets which retard innovation and distort production and market signals. We oppose attempts to narrow the business options or limit the individual freedom of livestock producers to innovate in the management and marketing of their production.

We oppose inclusion of a "Livestock Title" in the next farm bill. Items with industry-wide support can be included in the "Miscellaneous Title." I ask for the support of members of this committee in opposing a Livestock Title in the next farm bill.

Marketing Issues

KLA members, and the vast majority of cattle producers, oppose the involvement of the federal government in determining how cattle are marketed. The beef industry continues to transition toward more value-based marketing methods. These systems allow cattle producers to capture more of the value of the cattle they produce.

These value-based marketing methods also facilitate the transfer of market signals from consumers back to producers. We believe these signals have helped drive a significant improvement in Quality Grade, a predictor of a satisfactory eating experience, in the cattle being produced today.

While many KLA members see significant benefits in value-based marketing programs, they have made clear in KLA policy the appropriate role of the organization is to protect each producer's ability to market their cattle in the manner that best fits their business.

With that in mind, KLA reiterates its opposition to the Grain Inspection, Packers and Stockyards Administration (GIPSA) interim final rule on competitive injury. The rule has been opposed by the vast majority of cattle producers since it was first introduced in 2010. In issuing the interim rule, GIPSA ignored the comments submitted by thousands of cattle producers in opposition to the rule, the decisions of eight separate federal appellate courts and the intent of language included by Congress in the 2008 Farm Bill.

Our analysis of the interim final rule leads us to believe packers will offer one price for all cattle, regardless of quality, if the rule is implemented. Packers have indicated they will not accept the additional legal risk the change in the competitive injury standard would create. GIPSA claims the rule is needed to protect producers. However, since it would eliminate value-based marketing programs, it would negatively impact producers and make it more difficult to provide the types of beef products desired by consumers.

As the 2018 Farm Bill is developed, KLA asks you to delete the language which led to the GIPSA interim final rule. To that end, we support language striking SEC. 11006, Part 1 of the Food, Conservation and Energy Act of 2008. In the interim, we ask for your assistance in convincing GIPSA to withdraw the rule.

KLA also opposes any attempts to restrict the ownership of livestock. During development of previous farm bills, some members of Congress have proposed language placing restrictions on packer ownership of livestock. These types of restrictions would limit the marketing options available to KLA members and would represent unwelcome interference by the federal government in the marketplace.

With regard to country-of-origin labeling (COOL), KLA reiterates its opposition to mandatory COOL programs. Repeal of the previous mandatory program was appropriate and necessary since it provided no market benefit to beef producers and violated trade agreements with two of our largest trading partners. We ask the committee to resist any attempt to reinstate this failed program.

Conservation Title

Several conservation programs authorized in previous farm bills have played an important role in assisting farmers and ranchers enhance our nation's natural resources for food production, wildlife habitat, and water quality. In Kansas, the Environmental Quality Incentive Program (EQIP) is improving habitat for grassland-nesting birds under consideration for listing as threatened or endangered species, enhancing the health of grazing lands, improving water quality near lakes used for public drinking water, improving soil quality, conserving groundwater and reducing soil erosion. One important feature of EQIP has been its focus on livestock operations. We recommend a continued focus of 60% of EQIP funds toward livestock projects.

We appreciate the addition of the Anderson Creek Wildfire Initiative to the EQIP program. As landowners work to recover from the effects of the fire, cost-share assistance through the program will be very valuable in restoring and enhancing the quality of the rangeland.

The Agricultural Conservation Easement Program (ACEP) is in strong demand by our state's agricultural landowners who desire to sell their development rights to protect their lands for future generations of farmers and ranchers. In many instances, selling a conservation easement has been a helpful tool for estate and succession planning as today's landowners prepare for the next generation of farmers and ranchers.

I encourage members of this committee to remind your colleagues that federal funds spent on conservation are a good investment in our country's natural resources and the ultimate beneficiary is the general public. In addition, conservation program spending is not an entitlement as participants are required to use these funds on the land and, in many instances, are required to invest their own time and personal funds as a match or cost-share contribution.

Foreign Animal Disease Response

KLA supports enhancements to our foreign animal disease (FAD) response capabilities. Key to this effort is the development of a more adequate foot-and-mouth disease (FMD) vaccine bank. While we recognize and agree with the preference for vaccination over culling for controlling the spread of FMD, the current availability of vaccine is completely inadequate for an outbreak of any significance.

KLA participated in an FAD exercise last December. The exercise scenario included confirmation of FMD at one feed yard and two dairy farms in the state. Kansas animal health officials determined in such a scenario, an immediate request for 1.5 million doses of FMD vaccine would be necessary. That represents the entire supply of vaccine expected to be available to the U.S. in the first week of an FMD outbreak.

KLA supports additional funds dedicated for the development of a more adequate FMD vaccine bank. In addition, KLA supports additional work around FAD response plans that recognizes the limitations of vaccination in an FMD outbreak.

Other Issues

KLA supports increased funding for research on production practices, genetics, animal diseases, economics, nutrition, food safety, environmental impacts, and the impact of environmentally sensitive lands and species on agricultural operations is a critical component in advancing animal agriculture. Increased investment in this type of research is vital to the security and viability of our agricultural industry and food supply.

KLA members strongly support the beef checkoff program. This industry-funded self-help program has been essential to efforts to increase demand for beef. While maintaining the current program is important, we seek opportunities to enhance the program to better meet the needs of the current marketing environment.

Conclusion

As you can see, the vast majority of cattle producers believe markets free from government interference best serve the beef industry. We prefer a farm bill that does not restrict our marketing options nor distort market signals. We look forward to working with you as the next farm bill is developed.

Testimony of Mrs. Lynda Foster, Foster Dairy, Ft. Scott, Kansas, Field Hearing in Manhattan, Kansas, on Behalf of the, National Milk Producers Federation and Dairy Farmers of America, February 23, 2017

Mr. Chairman, Ranking Member Stabenow, members of the Committee, my name is Lynda Foster. Along with my husband and son, I own and operate Foster Dairy, located in Ft. Scott, Kansas.

Foster Dairy has been in operation since the late 1940's. We milk 170 cows and farm approximately 750 acres of corn, soybeans, alfalfa and grass hay.

I am a third generation dairy farmer and have been dairying all my life. I majored in dairy production at Kansas State University, met my future husband there, and we returned to the farm in 1978 to farm in partnership with my parents, Conrad and Beverly Davis. We took over the farm on our own in 1999, and our son and his wife joined us in the operation approximately ten years ago. I am proud to be able to continue the tradition of producing safe, nutritious food and working with the next generation.

I am also proud to be a spokesperson for good nutrition and about modern agriculture. Throughout my career I have served in several leadership roles in the Kansas Farm Bureau, Kansas Dairy Association, local and regional dairy promotion entities, and I am serving my last year of six on the National Dairy Research and Promotion Board.

I am pleased to be delivering testimony, not just on my behalf, but also for my cooperative, Dairy Farmers of America, and that of the National Milk Producers Federation (NMPF). Only by working together – farmer, milk marketing cooperative and national trade advocacy organization – can we move forward to make real changes in dairy policy in the next Farm Bill.

Introduction and Margin Protection Program

Over the past few years, dairy farmers across the country have faced a number of financial challenges. In 2014, Congress passed legislation establishing a new safety net under Title I for dairy farmers. During the legislative process, changes were made to the original dairy program designed by NMPF and other dairy leaders around the country. Unfortunately, the safety net, known as the Margin Protection Program for Dairy Producers (MPP), has failed to provide the level of protection envisioned in the original program.

Like many farmers, I was supportive of the MPP and thought it would finally give our farm a tool to manage the extreme volatility we had experienced in the market. In the first year, I, like many others, signed up for the program and purchased supplemental coverage at the $6.00 level.

Also like others, since that first year I have only enrolled at the minimal $4 margin level, which to be perfectly honest, Senator, is meaningless. MPP remains the right model for the future of our industry, but changes are needed if Congress wants to provide relevant tools to our sector.

Unfortunately, many dairy farmers participating in the MPP have become disenchanted with the program. In calendar year 2015, dairy farmers paid $70 million into the MPP program and received $730 thousand. In 2016, those figures were $20 million and $13 million, this was particular hard in a year where more program support was needed. Let me be clear, I understand that MPP has two components: a true, free safety net and then a risk management tool. We are not asking for a program that provides a profit to producers, neither do we want a program that will enhance or incentivize production. However, the changes that were made to the original MPP by Congress diluted the real costs that farmers face every day and diluted the effectiveness of the program. If MPP was more reflective of the true costs I saw on my farm, I believe active participation would rise dramatically.

In fact, since its inception, MPP has actually made the government a profit, equal to $66 million in fiscal year 2015 and $37 million in fiscal year 2016, according to the Congressional Budget Office. All we are seeking is a program that provides a safety net for dairy farmers when they need it most – something that delivers on the risk management promises dairy leaders and Congress committed to. In order to do that, we must make adjustments to the program.

Given the concerns that producers have expressed since the program's inception, the NMPF has embarked on a review of the program Congress enacted. As the voice of America's dairy farmers in Washington, DC, NMPF represents the vast majority of producers across the country. The NMPF process began in early 2016 and has included the voice of dairy farmers and the dairy cooperatives they own, as well as industry experts, academia and others to ensure proposed changes to MPP will provide the protection to farmers that is expected from a Farm Bill.

As we consider ways to improve MPP, one issue in particular continues to rise to the surface. When USDA determines the margin for dairy farmers under MPP, there are two factors - the "All Milk Price" and feed costs. The former is a definite number, reflecting a long-reported price for all milk sold by farmers in the United States for processing into different dairy products. We need to work with USDA to better understand how this reported price reflects, on average, what dairy farmers received in their check. The latter, though, is more concerning. During the lead-up to the 2014 Farm Bill, NMPF worked closely with economists, veterinarians, nutritionists and farmers to develop a model for average feed costs for dairy cows. This process took nearly a year and included industry experts who understand the real cost of feeding cows. When NMPF presented this information to Congress, the formula, while respected as being accurate, was cut by 10 percent. This cut resulted in a skewed margin program, a flawed calculation for MPP and a much less useful program. For example, in the period of May through June 2016, the MPP margin was reported to be $5.76 per cwt. Had the original, more accurate, feed cost formula been in the law, the margin would have been $4.77 per cwt, enabling a much larger group of financially-stressed producers to benefit from MPP. As a result of this change, a number of farmers who purchased higher coverage levels in 2015 did not opt to do so in 2016 because of the likelihood of no payment during times of need.

There are other adjustments that should be considered regarding MPP. These include, but are not limited to, the feed formula calculations as it relates to corn and alfalfa hay prices. We dairy farmers also want to have access to as many tools as possible. Unlike other sectors in agriculture, Congress arbitrarily limited the ability of dairy producers to use Risk Management Agency (RMA) products as well as Title I programs. Although all other commodities can use both RMA and Title I programs without any restrictions, dairy farmers cannot used the Livestock Gross Margin for Dairy Cattle (LGM) program, which remains a popular tool for producers. Due to restrictions in MPP, a producer must decide at the beginning of the Farm Bill cycle whether to cover their milk under LGM or the MPP. This restriction leaves dairy farmers without the tools that other farmers have at their disposal regarding federal support for their operations. As stated above, I have more tools available to manage risk on my corn acres. I can participate in both Title I programs as well as crop insurance programs to protect my business. I do not have the same opportunity for my dairy. In fact, a look at an analysis of 2014 Farm Bill programs for major commodities demonstrates that dairy program costs are miniscule.

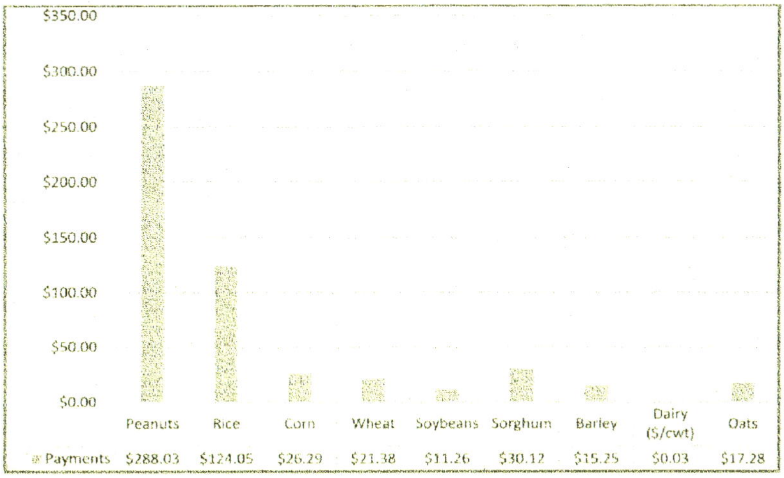

Average Farm Program Payments per Base Acre; *ARC, PLC, MMP.*

The above graphic is startling and demonstrates why improvements to dairy support programs are necessary to ensure that dairies of all sizes and in all regions have tools to weather challenging financial times.

Dairy Market Situation

For the past decade, times have been generally tough for America's dairy farms. In 2009, following several years of expanding U.S. dairy exports, world dairy markets collapsed in the worldwide recession, taking domestic milk prices with them. Farm income over feed costs, as measured by the MPP margin formula, fell to $2.25 per hundredweight of milk in June of that year, well below the $4.00 minimum margin coverage level, which is commonly referred to as "catastrophic" under the current program. The MPP margin formula averaged $3.87 per hundredweight during the first ten months of the year. Three years later, widespread drought drove feed prices to historic highs in 2012 and sent the MPP margin back into catastrophic territory.

The margin bottomed out at $2.67 per hundredweight that year and averaged $3.63 during the six months of March through August. Many dairy farms did not survive this one-two knockout punch, and the many that did are still struggling to recover. Although 2014 was a record year for milk prices and margins, world markets again collapsed in 2015 and most of 2016, which had a large effect on U.S. milk prices and gross dairy farm income. Revenue from milk sales dropped from $49.4 billion dollars in 2014 to $35.7 billion in 2015. U.S. Department of Agriculture (USDA) data indicates that it was down again in 2016 to $34.4 billion dollars.

The value of the fresh milk America's dairy farmers produced in 2016 was worth 19 percent less than it averaged over the five previous years. The difficult economic conditions and tighter operating margins over the last 10 years have resulted in the loss of more than 18,500 dairy farms in the United States. The present environment of depressed market prices could result in even more farm closures. While USDA is projecting that milk prices and margins will be better in 2017 than last year, milk production is showing signs of expansion following an extended period of almost static production. U.S. milk production grew by 1.3 percent from 2014 to 2015. This annual growth rate expanded to 1.6 percent from 2015 to 2016, but averaged 2.4 percent during the fourth quarter. USDA is currently projecting that milk production will grow again this year at an annual rate of 2.3 percent. During 2015 and 2016, total commercial use of milk, in both the domestic and export markets, increased at an annual rate of 1.8 percent. The recent and projected expansion of milk production has a real possibility of outpacing demand, which will weigh heavily on milk prices again.

Finally, dairy farmers deserve better. We need Congress to act swiftly this year and make the necessary changes in order for our industry to be able to protect ourselves from the bad year that could arrive at any time, even in years where experts are predicting higher margins. We dairy farmers are doing our job. We are producing safe, nutritious milk for the market. If that market goes sour or our costs soar because of drought, we must have the ability to protect our equity and our investment. Please do not leave us behind. Act now.

Farm Labor

I am lucky that the majority of my farm's labor needs are met with family laborers. Until very recently, we had only one full time hired hand. She made up 25 percent of my labor force. We have recently hired a part-time employee to help us through a family health-related issue. The issue of farm labor is important whether you are a dairy of my size or one like my colleagues in southwest Kansas, where farms are milking thousands of cows. No one here in Manhattan, in any corner of town, is hoping to one day secure a job milking cows. In all my years in agriculture, I have witnessed a decreasing interest, not increasing interest, in careers on the farm. These agricultural jobs pay well and come with benefits. Additionally, they are located in a great part of the country! We try in vain to find interest by American workers, but dairy farmers, like others in agriculture, have had to look to qualified foreign-born workers to meet our labor needs.

According to a University of Texas A&M report, released in August 2015 (and conducted in coordination with NMPF), 51 percent of all dairy farm workers are foreign born, and the farms that employ them account for 79 percent of the milk produced in the United States. How are dairies like mine, or any others, supposed to operate if we do not have access to a reliable workforce? In dairy, we cannot turn the cows off when there are not enough employees to do the job, we have to milk them. This is the reason that NMPF and my cooperative, Dairy Farmers of America, have urged Congress to act immediately to reform our immigration system in a manner that addresses agriculture's needs for a legal and stable workforce. I fear that if we don't, we as a country will have to face the reality that the term, "Made in America," will not apply to the milk you drink or the cheese you eat. I believe that in the future, the milk U.S. consumers enjoy will be milked by foreign-born workers. The question is, are they milking cows here in Kansas or are they doing it in their home country?

The new plant DFA is building in Garden City, Kansas will benefit all of us here – and farmers all over the country, as most of the product will be exported. To keep the plant filled, southwest Kansas dairy farmers will have to maintain milk production. How can they do that with their current labor strain?

My family decided to address part of our labor needs by purchasing robotic milkers. These milkers allow me to spend time on other parts of my operation. This was the only solution we could come up with – but it is expensive and complex. I hope the investment is worth it in future net savings. Additionally, my answer is not the answer for all dairy farmers. The larger farmers in southwest Kansas likely do not have the right infrastructure on their operation to use this technology. For once, this is a technology where smaller farmers are the target for adoption.

Trade

The dairy industry has come a long way on trade in the past several years. Our nation has gone from exporting dairy products valued at less than $1 billion in 2000 to exporting a record $7.1 billion in 2014, an increase of 625 percent. Although low prices brought that number closer to 5 billion last year, we remain the largest exporter of skim milk powder, whey products and, depending of the month, the number one exporter of cheese in the world. That reflects not just a tremendous jump on a value basis, but also a dramatic increase in the proportion of U.S. milk production that's finding a home overseas.

Fifteen years ago we were exporting roughly five percent of our milk production, now we are at three times that level, even as overall U.S. milk production has continued to grow. That means the equivalent of one day's milk production each week from the entire U.S. dairy industry ultimately ends up overseas, making exports integral to the health of my farm and our dairy industry at large. It is critical that Congress protects the progress we have made as the Administration updates trade agreements like the North American Free Trade Agreement (NAFTA).

I also urge a strong rejection by Congress of the European Union's (EU) aggressive stance on confiscating common food names. Names like Parmesan and Feta belong to everyone, not just a handful of producers in Italy and Greece. Our industry has built markets here and overseas. We need to protect those markets. We can be competitive and increase sales in markets as diverse as Latin America, the Middle East and Asia. What we need are well-negotiated agreements and the necessary tools to achieve and implement them.

The Market Access Program (MAP) and Foreign Market Development (FMD) program are some of those tools. I urge the Committee to maintain those programs, but allow for USDA to review the distribution of monies so those like dairy, that have expanded exports significantly in the last 10 years and are matching with funds and efforts, are awarded by providing enough funds to continue the work.

Environmental Sustainability

Farmers are the original environmentalists. As a dairy farmer, I care deeply about the land, air and water that I raise my herd and my family on. In recent years, however, federal and state regulators have applied significant pressure on the dairy sector to reduce nutrient output to improve water quality in dairy-producing regions across the country. We, as an industry, have invested significant resources to proactively respond to this challenge, and we continue to work to embrace the best possible environmental practices. In 2008, the dairy industry voluntarily set a goal of reducing greenhouse gas (GHG) emissions from fluid milk by 25 percent by 2020, and has since undertaken several projects intended to help meet that goal.

In a demonstration of continued leadership, the dairy industry is seeking proactive policy solutions that will help turn an environmental liability, such as manure, into a valuable asset. To that end, we are grateful to you, Chairman Roberts, for partnering with Senator Brown in the last Congress to put forward the bipartisan Agriculture Environmental Stewardship Act. This legislation creates an Investment Tax Credit to cover the upfront capital costs of nutrient recovery and biogas systems, which can play an important role in reducing the environmental impacts of dairy farming and, in turn, improve water quality in every region. We look forward to working with you again this year to introduce, gain support for and pass this legislation.

Like other sectors of the economy, dairy farmers are impacted by political, legal and regulatory uncertainty. Producers are committed stewards of a healthy ecosystem, but we need certainty regarding the application of environmental policies and regulations to their operations. In this context, we support the bipartisan Farm Regulatory Certainty Act, which is pending in the House and soon forthcoming in the Senate. This act is intended to reaffirm the intent of Congress that dairy farmers and other agricultural producers were not to be subject to solid waste laws passed more than four decades ago. As dairy farmers, we strive to comply diligently with any law we are subject to, but legal and regulatory certainty is critical to our efforts in this regard.

Child Nutrition

I want to thank you for your work in the last Congress with Senator Stabenow and others to reauthorize child nutrition programs. As you know, Child Nutrition programs in schools serve as part of the backbone of America's education policy. As a mother and grandmother, I know when my kids are well fed they are more productive, more responsive and more active. As an advocate for balanced diets and good nutrition for the nation's youth, I know that milk has been a key piece of meals served in schools, even predating the current school breakfast, lunch and dinner programs. However, recent changes made by the Obama Administration precluded schools from having access to a variety of dairy beverages based on outdated science regarding milk fat.

Mr. Chairman, when you and millions of other Americans go to the grocery store, surveys show that you are likely to purchase 2 percent or whole milk. You have a choice to make between the various products. When children go to school they do not have that same choice, despite the widely recognized benefits of all milk. They are limited to three options: skim white milk, skim flavored milk or 1 percent white milk. This is not the milk they drink at home, and they are unlikely to do so when they go to school. When you have a product like milk that provides nine essential nutrients and vitamins, and that even the folks at USDA say is under-consumed, an important question must be asked. If the point of school meal programs are to provide the nutrients and sustenance children need, why eliminate the option of nutrient rich, healthy foods like 1 percent flavored milk or 2 percent milk if children simply throw away what they are currently served? The science tells us that expanding options for schools to offer milk that will help children meet their nutrient requirements is a good nutrition policy and good public policy and it should be addressed by this Committee. In fact, even former Secretary of Agriculture Tom Vilsack testified before the House Education and Workforce Committee (June 16, 2015) on the issue of expanding milk options for schools, stating "if adding that option [1 percent flavored milk] would encourage kids to drink more milk, we should do that."

Mr. Chairman and members of the Committee, I appreciate the opportunity to share the thoughts and concerns of those in the dairy industry with you, and I look forward to your questions.

Amy France, Owner/Operator/Partner of France Family Farms in Kansas, Senate Agriculture, Nutrition, and Forestry Committee, Hearing from the Heartland: Perspectives on the 2018 Farm Bill from Kansas, February 23, 2017

Chairman Roberts, Ranking Member Stabenow, and members of the committee. It is an honor and privilege to sit before you today. My name is Amy France. I live near Marienthal, an unincorporated community in Wichita County, Kansas. While I am a first-generation agricultural producer, my husband Clint and his family have been farming in the High Plains of western Kansas for three generations. We understand the risk associated with farming and ranching in a region that averages less than 20 inches of rainfall annually. Add in the fact that only three percent of the ground the good Lord blessed us with is irrigated, I sit before you today without a doubt in my mind the necessity of the Farm Bill and the federal crop insurance program. Clint and I have five children. Our oldest son recently came back from school to help on the family farm. We pray they will continue the family farm and become the 4th generation to farm the rolling lands of western Kansas. Today our family operation consists of 6,000 acres where we grow wheat, corn, sorghum and soybeans. We also are blessed to graze our 300 head cattle operation on 4,000 acres of beautiful pasture. We treasure the land we are blessed with. We do all we can in preserving it so our children will have the opportunity to continue our passion and livelihood.

As congress begins to research, discuss and plan the next five-year Farm Bill, I encourage you to double down on what is working and to revamp or eliminate areas that need improvement or flat out just do not work. Without question, the most important USDA program is federal crop insurance; and I'm not alone in that belief. In Kansas, 84% of the soybean acreage, 88% of the grain sorghum, and 95% of both corn and wheat acreage are insured through USDA-Risk Management Agency (RMA) policies. For the 2015 crop year, that represented more than 18 million acres, specifically, high risk areas like where my family farms, to plan for next year's crop. If it were not for the federal crop insurance, the Livestock Forage Program (LFP) and similar safety net programs, many of my neighbors would no longer be in business. We're able to sign loan papers at the bank, consult with our agronomist, seed salesmen, equipment dealer or commodity broker, and even plan for increased crop diversity and rotation. Crop insurance offers risk protection to many agricultural commodities and when disaster strikes, the indemnity check is in our bank account much sooner than any other USDA program. As crop insurance continues to evolve and participation rates increase to historic levels, we need to make sure the Risk Management Agency continues to improve the program. For example, having a workable limited irrigation practice developed will help many areas of Kansas as scarce water becomes a more precious natural resource. As new seed traits and technologies continue to be developed, reviewing insured commodity planting dates and the benefits of cover crops to insured commodities will be key to ensure producers participate at the highest coverage levels possible. However, crop insurance is not without its shortcomings. Due to a prolonged drought in western Kansas, many of my neighbors' Actual Production History (APH) has declined. With commodity prices being as low as they are today, some producers have little to no revenue protection offered through crop insurance due to the APH and price calculation. Many are leaving the program to self-insure until prices rebound considerably or congress finds a solution to the eroded APH. Another contributor to reduced APH's is purely a procedural glitch in adjusting for losses. In a drought year, aflatoxins are sometimes present in corn, and spring rains occurring when wheat is pollinating can often contribute to the presence of vomitoxins in wheat. Both mycotoxins are poisonous to livestock and humans, reducing the crops value. Crop insurance adjusts for this by multiplying a Quality Adjustment Factor (QAF) by the bushels produced, resulting in "production to count" which is multiplied by the crop insurance price to obtain the revenue per acre determination. The problem is that this adjusted production to count also goes into the farmers' APH calculation for the next 10 years. A simple solution would be to multiply the QAF by the crop insurance price instead of bushels delivered.

Another concern with crop insurance is that while the Commodity Exchange Price Provisions (CEPP) that are used to set projected and harvest prices for revenue protection products truly provide a market determined price, they do not adequately account for differences in basis (cash price minus futures price) which can vary greatly across the state. For example, according to Kansas State University's AgManager website, the five-year average wheat basis in Garden City, near my home, is ($0.51), while in Salina, it is ($0.074); creating a nearly $0.44 per bushel gap in my safety net relative to central Kansas farmers. At 40 bushels per acre, that's a $17.60 gap in my crop insurance per acre safety net because I farm in a different part of the state.

Additionally, in years like 2016, when grain supplies exceed available storage capacity and Chicago Board of Trade (CBOT) Kansas City Hard Red Winter Wheat (KC HRW) futures are not converging at delivery points, an even greater gap in our wheat income safety net is created. This is because it is the July KC HRW futures contract that is used for the Revenue Protection (RP) crop insurance policies, and when July wheat futures are not accurately reflecting market fundamentals, our wheat income safety net is further adversely affected.

USDA commodity programs administered through FSA are also extremely vital to France Family Farms being able to pass the operation along to the next generation. Farming is inherently a risky business. Until we better understand (and control) Mother Nature, we are one hail storm away from going out of business. The 2014 Farm Bill injected additional, unnecessary risk to the producer by forcing producers to decide between signing up for a revenue program (Agricultural Risk Coverage), with a national price trigger and a county or individual yield trigger, or a counter-cyclical price program (Price Loss Coverage) which paid out only when prices for commodities grown in Kansas reached extreme lows. Farmers make decisions daily about their business operations but having the government force a decision between what is the greatest risk – price or yield – is a decision many wish they could change less than three years later. To make matters worse, whichever program a producer signed up for, USDA paid the producer more than a year after the financial strain of the revenue or price loss and long after the bank required payment on an operating line of credit. This is no better than the ad-hoc disaster programs congress used to pass every election year – it is too little, too late. And, in the case of ARC-County, Kansas producers farming in multiple counties received vastly different USDA payments due to the uncertainty and unpredictability surrounding which data sources (NASS vs. RMA vs. other) and the hit and miss approach of when they were used in calculating ARC-County benchmark yields and annual triggers. I understand congress has tough decisions to make, and often budget bean counters push you down a less desirable path, but there are real consequences of locking into a government-sponsored safety net program only to see that safety net offer little to no protection within a year or two of starting the five-year commitment. Unfortunately, in the case of ARC and PLC the federal government added additional risk to farmers rather than reducing it. As you begin the task of writing a new bill I urge you to look closely at these programs and find a better way to offset the risk of farming on the High Plains and elsewhere.

As a young producer USDA programs can be overwhelming and quite burdensome. While program sign up timelines seem to be relayed to us that "time is of the essence," after jumping through the hoops, you are often met with road blocks and delays out of our control. It is obvious that the individuals creating these government programs and national regulations have little "hands in the dirt" experience. Furthermore, farmers young and old, must rely on the understanding and expertise of the federal employees working in our local USDA service centers for information, a better understanding of how programs work in our part of the country, and what our legitimate chance of being selected for specific programs are.

Additionally, while USDA efforts to ensure that payments only go to eligible farmers is commendable, the complexity and required reporting that are part of the “actively engaged” rules create real hardships and unduly punish business operations in Kansas. I would hope that one of the goals of the Farm Bill is to assist farm families so they can remain a viable part of rural communities. Sometimes, to pull together the capital needed to form a viable farming operation, multiple family members from different local farm families is needed. Today’s actively engaged rules penalizes these family farms and the way they structure their businesses. We encourage the committee to reassess the actively engaged rules and reporting requirements so these family farms are treated in the same manner as all other farms.

Another major title of the Farm Bill is conservation. This title has evolved over time and Kansans rely on the multitude of programs to ensure we continue to keep, build and restore the soil, water and air required to pass the farm on to the next generation. It seems over the more recent years we have had to utilize USDA conservation programs in order to keep the U.S. Fish and Wildlife Service (USFWS) at bay with their threatened listing under the Endangered Species Act (ESA) for the lesser prairie chicken (LPC). For example, in total in Kansas we have just over two million acres enrolled in the Conservation Reserve Program (CRP), but in the 39 western Kansas counties located within the LPC range, there are 1,349,648 acres enrolled in the CRP, broken down as:

- 476,986 acres and 4,110 contracts; CP2 - Native Grass Plantings
- 252,591 acres and 2,989 contracts; CP4D - Wildlife Habitat

- 483,764 acres and 4,819 contracts; CP25 - Rare and Declining Habitat
- 7,168 acres and 382 contracts; CP33 - Upland Bird Habitat Buffers
- 129,139 acres and 2,453 contracts; CP38 - State Acres for Wildlife

This is in addition to the acres enrolled in voluntary range-enhancement programs as part of NRCS's Lesser Prairie Chicken Initiative (LPCI).

It was also extremely concerning when the EPA and the U.S. Army Corps of Engineers proposed the Waters of the United States (WOTUS) rule a few years ago at the same time USDA proposed a rule that listed several agricultural practices that were offered protection from WOTUS regulations. Unfortunately, the USDA list did not cover all of the modern-day agricultural best management practices we implement today under the proposed protections. Even more concerning to me is the ongoing use of voluntary conservation practices, which come with limited cost share, being used to cover regulatory mandates from other federal agencies. As a producer, I feel like I'm being squeezed in the vice clamp between federal regulations that make no sense, were drafted by a bureaucrat sitting behind the computer screen, in a basement with no windows 1,000 miles away and a consuming public that has less and less of an understanding where their food, fiber and energy comes from with every passing year. Farmers and ranchers were the original conservationists because without keeping our soil in the field, our waterways usable and the air breathable there is no way we would be able to pass an operation down the family line; nor would we allow our young children to work in an environment that would put them in harm's way. It becomes increasingly frustrating to explain to an urban public the importance of cost share dollars being leveraged when putting conservation practices on the ground, and the societal benefit of such actions and programs. To that extent, Farm Bureau strongly supports working lands conservation programs such as the Environmental Quality Incentives Program (EQIP) and the Conservation Stewardship Program (CSP). Looking at the most recent year data available (2015), there were 594 Environmental Quality Incentive Program (EQIP) cost-share contracts awarded in Kansas, providing for additional conservation practices to be applied on more than 125,000 acres; and there were 510 Conservation Stewardship Program (CSP) cost-share contracts awarded, covering an additional 1.03 million acres. We have been able to utilize the EQIP program several times on our farm with the rebuilding of terraces and drilling a well for our livestock. We understand how vital terraces are to our land and with the cost-share assistance available through EQIP we are now able to rebuild 35-year-old terraces. Another example of how EQIP is helping our farm is with the drilling of a water well for our cattle. Without programs like these, we would not be able to financially make these changes and updates that are key to caring for our soil, our livestock and our local economy. If anything, though, these programs could be streamlined and simplified through the regulatory process to get conservation practices started and completed in a timely manner. It would be helpful if NRCS reworked their requirements for the DUNS and SAMS numbers across all forms of business structures. Furthermore, producer friendly administration of programs and transparency of the ranking system for prioritizing conservation practices across states and regions would benefit all producers and USDA local employees, alleviate duplicative paperwork and minimize frustration from multiple trips to the local field office, and curtail administrative paperwork errors.

The Rural Development title of the farm bill receives much praise across the state and nation but is often out of sight, out of mind. In the 21st Century farmers and ranchers need access to precision agricultural tools, split second market information and technology data packages that allow for value-added sales and modern-day communication – at a competitive price point with reliable service. I sit before you today and tell you this is not the case in many areas of rural America, including the France home in Marienthal. In fact, while I was drafting this written testimony last week, I lost internet service four times in a single evening. Like it or not, the world continues to get smaller and spin faster. Unless government steps up like they did during the Rural Electrification Act in 1936, America will be split between the urban areas, connected along major transportation routes where urbanites require connection points, and truly rural or frontier regions, such as where I live, will continue to struggle with reliable and cost effective technology access. Technology connection is an absolute necessity to business survival not only on our farm but also along rural Main Street and among rural healthcare providers.

Another area where the Senate Agriculture, Nutrition, and Forestry Committee along with USDA could be a true champion of the American farmer is on the regulatory front. Due to overzealous regulators, we are being buried in compliance paperwork and restrictions and our international competitors continue to take an increasing amount of market access. While I could spend hours discussing the growing list of regulatory concerns, I am hopeful this committee will conduct at least one issue surfacing and oversight hearing on regulatory concerns within agriculture and rural America. Today I will discuss just a few of the many items that keep me and my husband up at night. First, the proposed WOTUS rule would put our operation out of business overnight should a citizen lawsuit or an EPA/Army Corps regulator determine one of the ephemeral streams on the land we farm is a Water of the United States. In an area that receives less than 20 inches of rainfall annually, the streams, creeks, and sloughs that "flow" across Wichita County and western Kansas don't contribute to any navigable flow. On those years where the good Lord blesses us with moisture, we are lucky to have flowing water in the road ditch or terrace channel once or twice a year. And when it happens, we want every drop to soak into the soil profile and recharge the underground Ogallala Aquifer. Second, EPA has been on a rampage the past few years revoking tolerances of many commonly used pesticides. These synthetic chemicals are necessary to produce the bushels we are capable of today and act to keep weeds, pests and funguses at bay. Without the ability to use EPA-restricted-label-use pesticides, our operation would return to a bygone era of increased tillage, increasing the risk of erosion and soil loss, increasing the amount of fuel needed to run the operation, and putting additional wear and tear on our equipment and employees. Again, I do not wish to put myself, my husband or our children in harm's way. If there is sound science presented that shows a need to use less or revoke a tolerance completely then I trust that science; but, constantly fighting activists who believe the smallest amount of every synthetic or natural chemical product means the end of the world does not compute with reality when farmers across the globe are required to produce more bushels of grain to meet the nutritional needs of more than seven billion people globally. Kansas farmers and ranchers desperately need the federal government to return to utilizing risk-based science, common sense and allow American ingenuity to once again flourish when it comes to producing agricultural commodities and animal protein.

Third, to start this year the EPA finalized their Worker Protection Standard (WPS). While not fully understood or implemented, this regulation will increase costs on our farm. It forces significant changes to the longstanding private pesticide applicator license the Kansas Department of Agriculture administers. Thanks to WPS, some private applicators, who have been licensed and conducted their pesticide application fully under state and national law, will choose not to reapply and instead will be forced to hire a professional pesticide applicator to apply registered pesticides. This additional cost, all due to a change EPA implemented beginning in January 2017, will increase a cost of production agriculture we could better control prior to the change.

Fourth and my final point on overregulation, the 2013 ammonium nitrate fertilizer explosion at the West Fertilizer Company in West, Texas, was a tragedy and our thoughts remain with those affected. However, anhydrous ammonia was not the cause of the explosion and has never been an explosive material. Yet, the Occupational Safety and Health Administration (OSHA) proposes to change the regulations pertaining to storing and transporting anhydrous ammonia. If this were to be fully implemented, it would limit our access to the most cost-effective source of nitrogen fertilizer available. Also, depending on how businesses who sell the fertilizer comply with the rules, the proposed rule change could force producers to travel farther, taking on additional risks, in finding a business to supply their farming operation with a necessary nutrient to grow grain commodities. Thankfully, congress continues to put language in appropriations bills to prohibit OSHA from severely limiting our access to anhydrous and I strongly encourage this committee to be a champion for the farmer on this issue.

Due to the regulations listed above along with many others, my husband and I are continuing to diversify our farming practices and operation. We know on the France Farm we are not the only ones experiencing tough economic times. Although we know conventional farming is the only way to truly feed the world, and I would add we strongly believe conventional farming is safe and effective, we have begun the process of converting 1/3 or our wheat fields to certified organic. The regulations on chemicals that truly work are becoming so burdensome that the costs involved are more than our farm can handle. In addition to diversifying our input costs, we are able to market our grain and negotiate for better prices at different delivery locations than where we take conventional grains we raise on 2/3 of our acres. Furthermore, last year, while looking for ways to supplement our income, we tried our hand at raising pumpkins. With just a 1/2 acre utilized, we were able to supply our area communities with pumpkins. Although it was hard work, it was an opportunity for us as a family to work together on something new and found we were able to make a significant profit by identifying a need and being willing to take a chance and further diversify. Will we convert our entire 6,000 tillable acres to pumpkins? No but on small acreage, when our family labor resources allow, we will continue to look for ways to add profit to our operation.

In closing, it is an honor to sit before you today and testify on behalf of Kansas Farm Bureau and our more than 30,000 farm and ranch family members across Kansas as you begin to plan for the next farm bill. In summary, crop insurance is without question the number one program we rely on to keep our business operating year to year. The commodity, conservation, and rural development titles are also extremely important. Many of the programs USDA administers have benefited our operation and we are thankful for the opportunity to utilize technical assistance and program experts when we sign up for various USDA programs. Without question, technology continues to advance, the business and structure of agriculture evolves, and risk associated with farming only increases. Some of this is due to market structures and global demands, while some of it can directly be tied to how USDA programs are executed. In more recent years, attacks have come from other federal agencies with little understanding and appreciation for what farmers and ranchers do every day to put food on the table, fuel in the tank, and clothes on the backs of Americans. I look forward to continuing the discussion, watching how agricultural policies will be altered, and seeking out how my fellow producers will be relieved of many regulatory burdens over the next two years by discussing how the next Farm Bill will be written.

Testimony of Shan Hanes, On Behalf of the American Bankers Association, before the Agriculture, Nutrition and Forestry Committee of the United States Senate, February 23, 2017

Chairman Roberts, Ranking Member Stabenow, and members of the Committee, my name is Shan Hanes, and I am the President and CEO of First National Bank in Elkhart, Kansas. First National Bank is a $78 million bank with a main location in Elkhart, Kansas and one branch serving Rolla, Kansas and the surrounding area. We have 21 employees and we predominantly lend to the agricultural sector. Despite our small size, the bank is the largest lender in the county. We represent an average sized bank in rural Kansas.

I am also a member of the American Bankers Association's Agricultural and Rural Bankers Committee. I appreciate the opportunity to present the views of rural lenders and the impact of the Agricultural Act of 2014, better known as the 2014 Farm Bill.

The American Bankers Association is the voice of the nation's $17 trillion banking industry, which is composed of small, regional and large banks that together employ more than 2 million people, safeguard $13 trillion in deposits and extend over $9 trillion in loans. ABA is uniquely qualified to comment on agricultural credit issues as banks have provided credit to agriculture since the founding of our country. Over 5,000 banks – over 82 percent of all banks – reported agricultural loans on their books at year end 2015 with a total outstanding portfolio of over $172 billion.

The topic of today's hearing is very timely. There have been many successes within the 2014 Farm Bill that have directly affected agricultural lenders. However, the agricultural landscaped has changed considerably since the passage of the last Farm Bill. Agricultural lenders have often been the first group to feel the effects of the changing agricultural landscape, and the role that public policy has played in shaping that landscape.

The agricultural economy has been slowing, with farm sector profitability expected to decline further in 2017 for the fourth consecutive decline. However, farm and ranch incomes for the past five years have been some of the best in history. With the 2014 Farm Bill in place, farmers, ranchers and their bankers achieved a level of certainty from Washington about future agricultural policy. Interest rates continue to be at or near record lows, and the banking industry has the people, capital and liquidity to help American farmers and ranchers sustain through any turbulence in the agricultural economy.

Banks continue to be one of the first places that farmers and ranchers turn when looking for agricultural loans. Our agricultural credit portfolio is very diverse – we finance large and small farms, urban farmers, beginning farmers, women farmers and minority farmers. To bankers, agricultural lending is good business and we make credit available to all who can demonstrate they have a sound business plan and the ability to repay.

In 2015, farm banks – banks with more than 15.5 percent of their loans made to farmers or ranchers – increased agricultural lending 7.9 percent to meet these rising credit needs of farmers and ranchers, and now provide over $100 billion in total farm loans. Farm banks are an essential resource for small farmers, holding $48 billion in small farm loans, with $11.5 billion in micro-small farm loans (loans with origination values less than $100,000). These farm banks are healthy and well capitalized, and stand ready to meet the credit demands of our nation's farmers large and small.

In addition to our commitment to farmers and ranchers, thousands of farm dependent businesses – food processors, retailers, transportation companies, storage facilities, manufacturers, etc. – receive financing from the banking industry as well. Agriculture is a vital industry to our country, and financing it is an essential business for many banks, mine included.

Banks work closely with the USDA's Farm Service Agency to make additional credit available by utilizing the Guaranteed Farm Loan Programs. The repeal of borrower limits on USDA's Farm Service Agency guaranteed loans has allowed farmers to continue to access credit from banks like mine as they grow, ensuring credit access for farmers across the country.

We remain concerned with certain areas of the agricultural credit market. In particular, we are worried that the Farm Credit System – a government sponsored entity – has veered away from its intended mission and now represents an unwarranted risk to taxpayers. The Farm Credit System was founded in 1916 to ensure that young, beginning, and small farmers and ranchers had access to credit. It has since grown into a $315 billion behemoth offering complex financial services. To put this in perspective, if the Farm Credit System were a bank it would be the ninth largest in the United States, and larger than 99.9 percent of the banks in the country.

This system operates as a Government Sponsored Entity and represents a risk to taxpayers in the same way that Fannie Mae and Freddie Mac do. It benefits from significant tax breaks – valued at $1.3 billion in 2015 – giving it a significant edge over private sector competitors. Moreover, the Farm Credit System enjoys a government backing, formalized by the creation of a $10 billion line of credit with the U.S. Treasury.

The Farm Credit System has veered significantly from its charter to serve young, beginning, and small farmers and ranchers, and now primarily serves large established farms, who could easily obtain credit from the private sector. In fact, the majority of Farm Credit System loans outstanding are in excess of $1 million. Any farmer able to take on over $1 million in debt does not need subsidized credit. Moreover, the volume of small borrower loans accounted for 14 percent of all new Farm Credit System loans in 2015.

Our nation's farmers and ranchers are a critical resource to our economy. Ensuring that they continue to have access to adequate credit to thrive is essential for the wellbeing of our whole nation. America's banks remain well equipped to serve the borrowing needs of farmers of all sizes. An important step in ensuring credit availability is to review entities such as the Farm Credit System and ensure that they stick to their charter of helping young, beginning and small farmers.

In my testimony today I would like to elaborate on the following points:

- Banks are a primary source of credit to farmers and ranchers in the United States.;
- The 2014 Farm Bill was successful by supporting crop insurance, the conservation reserve program and by removing term limits on USDA Guaranteed

Farm Loan Programs. However, the next Farm Bill will require some necessary changes to ARC and PLC programs, especially on the timing of payments;

- Banks work closely with the USDA to make additional credit available via the Guaranteed Farm Loan Program but there is a need to increase the loan cap within these programs;
- The Farm Credit System has become too large and unfocused, using taxpayer dollars to subsidize large borrowers and congress should consider legislation that would level the playing field with the Farm Credit System.

Banks Are a Primary Source of Credit to Farmers and Ranchers in the U.S.

For my bank and for many ABA members, agricultural lending is a significant component of their business activities. ABA has studied and reported on the performance of "farm banks" for decades and, we are pleased to report that the performance of these highly specialized agricultural lending banks continues to be strong. ABA defines a farm bank as one with more than 15.5 percent farm or ranch loans (to all loans).

At the end of 2015, there were 1,976 banks that met this definition. Farm lending posted solid growth during 2015. Total farm loans at farm banks increased by 7.9 percent to $100.3 billion in 2015 up from $94.6 billion in 2014. Approximately one in every three dollars lent by a farm bank is an agricultural loan.

Farm real estate loans grew at a faster rate than farm production loans. Outstanding farm real estate loans grew at a pace of 9.1 percent, or $4.2 billion, to a total of $50.6 billion. Farm production loans rose by 6.6 percent, or $3.1 billion, to $49.8 billion. Farm banks are a major source of credit to small farmers – holding more than $47.8 billion in small farm loans (origination value less than $500,000) with $11.5 billion in micro-small farm loans (origination value less than $100,000) at the end of 2015. The number of outstanding small farm loans at farm banks totaled 761,192 with the vast majority – over 496,200 loans – with origination values less than $100,000. Farm banks are healthy and well capitalized and stand ready to meet the credit demands of our nation's farmers large and small.

Equity capital —often thought of as the strongest form of capital—at farm banks increased 4.9 percent to $47.7 billion in 2015. Since the end of 2007, farm banks have added $19.5 billion in equity capital, building strong high-quality capital reserves. These capital reserves will enable farm banks flexibility as the agricultural sector adjusts to lower commodity prices — allowing bankers to work with and serve the needs of our nation's famers — and will also act as a buffer, proving insulation from the risks associated with any downturn in the agricultural sector.

One area of concern for farm bankers and their customers has been the rapid appreciation in farmland values in some areas of the country. The run up in farmland values has not been a credit driven event. Farm banks are actively managing the risks associated with agricultural lending and underwriting standards on farm real estate loans are very conservative. The key consideration in underwriting any loan is the ability of the customer to repay regardless of the collateral position in the loan. To further manage risk, we regularly stress test our loan portfolios to judge repayment capacity under different scenarios.

Farm Banks Exhibit Solid Farm Loan Growth

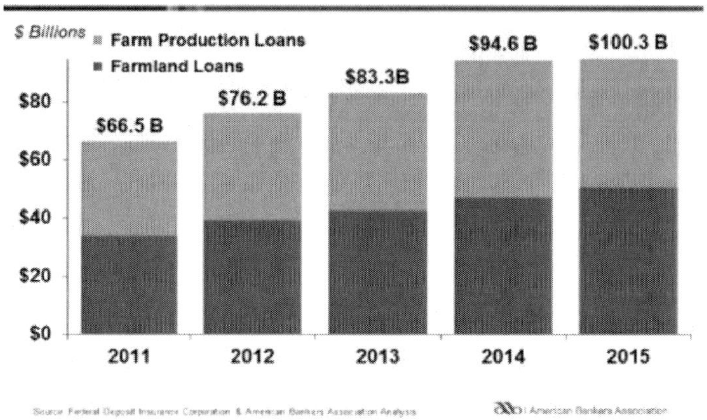

Farm Banks Increase High-Quality Capital

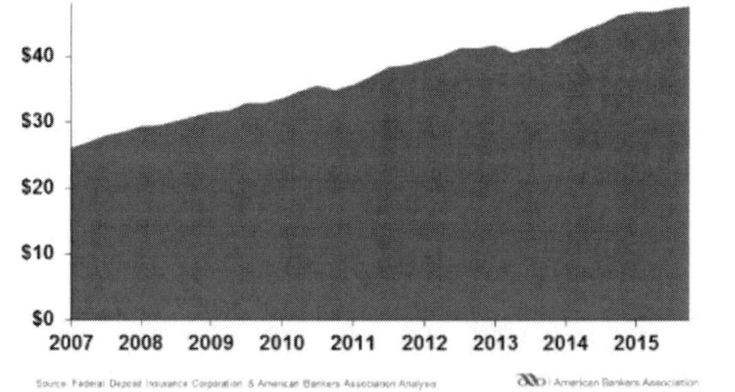

After several years of large increases in farmland values, the consensus view among bankers I know is that the increase in cropland values has slowed. USDA estimates of lower commodity prices for the third consecutive year in 2016 seem to have modestly cooled off the demand for farm real estate. We watch the farm real estate market very closely, as do my customers. In recent years, over four-fifths of the agriculture sector's asset values were held in real estate. USDA estimates a 1.2 percent decline in the value of farm real estate in 2016.

The Agricultural Act of 2014 Had Many Successful Components, but Improvements Remain Necessary

One success of the 2014 Farm Bill was the continued support of crop insurance programs. Agricultural lenders use crop insurance as a guarantee to help secure financing for operating credit. With crop insurance, a lender has the ability to provide support based on individual producers' proven crop yields. This allows lenders to tailor a loan to a producer's operation and allow for year-to-year adjustments within that operation. Without crop insurance acting as a safety net, producers would be in a much more challenging financial situation in the event of disaster. Crop insurance has allowed lenders to provide the best possible terms for operating loans because it helps to lower the risk for the lender. ABA has been a long-time supporter of crop insurance programs and would like to see the programs expanded to help as many producers as possible.

Another success of the 2014 Farm Bill was the continuation of the Conservation Reserve Program (CRP). CRP is vital in rural areas as it provides another use for land that may be otherwise unsuitable for farming. From a lender perspective, CRP is another tool in the toolbox for landowners to use when they are trying to diversify their holdings. Additionally, CRP can provide a steady stream of income for producers, especially older producers.

I would like to thank Congress, especially the Agricultural Committees, for repealing borrower term limits on USDA Farm Service Agency guaranteed loans in the 2014 Farm Bill. Term limits restricted farmer access to capital, and with the expansion of the farm economy over the past ten years, there are some farmers who are not able to obtain credit from banks like mine without a guaranty from USDA. The USDA's Farm Service Agency guaranteed loan program has been a remarkable success. Today, nearly $12 billion in farm and ranch loans are made by private sector lenders like my bank and are guaranteed by the USDA. There are nearly 43,000 loans outstanding – of course some farmers have more than one guaranteed loan, so this number is not to be confused with the number of individual farmers and ranchers, but the numbers of individuals accessing credit under this program is very significant.

This program has grown over the past five years, with less than $9 billion outstanding at the close of FY 08 to nearly $12 billion today. The loans made by banks like mine under this program are modest in size. The average outstanding guaranteed real estate loan is $439,000 and the average outstanding guaranteed non real estate secured loan is $250,000. Clearly, we are reaching customers who have modest-sized operations, who are in the process of starting their farm or ranch operation, or who are recovering from some sort of financial set-back. Despite the fact that these customers do not have either the earnings or collateral to qualify for conventional credit, losses in the program have been extremely small. Over recent fiscal years losses have ranged from a high of 0.6

percent in FY10 to a low of 0.3 percent in FY13. These are extremely low losses – especially for customers who are perceived to be a higher risk than other customers, hence the need for the USDA credit enhancement. Bankers who utilize the guaranteed farm loan programs offered by USDA know what they are doing and work very closely with their farm and ranch customers to properly service these loans. The Farm Service Agency deserves a great deal of credit for administering such a successful public/private partnership. We urge you to continue to support this very worthwhile program.

I want to reiterate that the 2014 Farm Bill was very successful from a lender's perspective. However, there are some substantial changes from the lender's perspective that need to be considered as Congress starts working on the next Farm Bill.

When the 2014 Farm Bill was written and approved, commodity prices were considerably higher than after implementation of the programs. As you are aware, the 2014 Farm Bill required that the producer make a one-time election between ARC and PLC. This become problematic because while producers were making the election in July 2013, corn futures were over $7 per bushel, with wheat futures were over $9 per bushel. Now, corn is less than $4 per bushel, and wheat $4.50 per bushel. This dramatic drop in prices could not be foreseen by any producer.

Coupled with the drop in prices, the decision to use county yields instead of state yields should have provided assistance to the individuals most in need when yields were low, but this was often not the case. Instead, due to the variability in National Agriculture Statistics Service (NASS) data, two fields on each side of a county line, may have drastically different payments, with my customers seeing the difference as high as $90 per acre. Additionally, from a lender's point of view, NASS data has not been as accurate as data from the Risk Management Agency (RMA), which led to difficulties in yield calculations.

While crop prices and a one-time program election were both issues, the timing of payments greatly impacted lenders. Payments could not be calculated until the final county yield was determined and the marketing year was complete. This means producers do not receive payments during the same year in which the crop was planted, and lenders were left to deal with the fallout of this timing issue. For example, we are currently completing renewals for our farm customers. We look at their financial progress for 2016 and set their operating lines for 2017. However, we cannot calculate 2016 payments until October of 2017. From a lender perspective, this has caused a real problem with our regulators, as we cannot use a payment that may be received a year later in the profits calculation for this year. Furthermore, lenders should not be making educated guesses on what payment might be received. Instead, there should be certainty within the programs to allow for an accurate calculation.

Banks Work Closely with the USDA's Farm Service Agency to Make Additional Credit Available by Utilizing the Guaranteed Farm Loan Programs

As I mentioned before, the removal of term limits on USDA's Farm Service Agency Guaranteed Loan Programs was a much needed reform to the Guaranteed Loan Programs. However, the current loan limit of $1.399 million on Guaranteed Operating Loans (GOL) and Guaranteed Farm Ownership Loans (GFO) is simply not keeping pace with the growing cost of agriculture. It is much more costly for a young, beginning or small farmer to get into agriculture, and the guaranteed loan programs need to reflect this reality. ABA has endorsed H.R. 831, the Beginning Agriculturist Lifetime Employment Act of 2017 (BALE Act). This legislation would increase the cap on GFOs and GOLs to $3.5 million. We believe this increase is necessary to ensure lenders are able to assist as many producers enter and grow into the future of agriculture.

With any increase to Guaranteed Loan Programs, there will need to be an increase in funding for the programs. Unfortunately, there has been a shortage of funds for the past three years, so it is vital that the necessary funds are appropriated for the programs in advance. These programs continue to create a great public-private partnership between lenders and USDA, and future funding should reflect the strength of the programs.

The Farm Credit System Has Become a Large, Unfocused Government Sponsored Entity at the Expense of American Taxpayers

I mentioned earlier in my testimony that the market for agricultural credit is very competitive. I compete with several other banks in my service area, finance companies from all of the major farm equipment manufacturers, several international banks, credit unions, life insurance companies and finance companies owned by seed and other supply companies to name a few. The most troublesome competitor I face is the taxpayer-backed and tax-advantaged federal Farm Credit System (FCS). The FCS was chartered by Congress in 1916 as a borrower-owned cooperative farm lender at a time when banks did not have the legal authority to make long-term farm real estate loans. Over the ensuing 100 years the FCS has received numerous charter enhancements, and has ventured into areas that are not appropriate for a farmer-owned farm lending business.

Today *the FCS is a large and complex financial services business with $315 billion in assets*. If it were a bank, it would be the ninth largest bank in the United States. It is tax-advantaged and enjoyed a combined local, state, and federal tax rate in 2015 of only 4.2 percent—a rate lower than what 75 percent of American taxpayers pay. The tax advantages enjoyed by the FCS in 2015 was worth $1.296 billion or 28 percent of the Farm Credit System's net income in 2015.[1]

[1] Federal Farm Credit Banks Funding Corporation; 2015 Annual Information Statement of the Farm Credit System; March 7, 2016. Page F-3.

Today's Farm Credit System is a large, unfocused Government Sponsored Entity presenting the same kind of potential threat to the American taxpayer as Fannie Mae and Freddie Mac. As a Government Sponsored Enterprise (GSE) like Fannie Mae and Freddie Mac, the American taxpayer is the ultimate back stop should the Farm Credit System develop financial problems. This reality was formalized in 2013 when the Farm Credit System Insurance Corporation arranged a $10 billion line of credit "with the Federal Financing Bank, a federal instrumentality subject to the supervision and direction of the U.S. Treasury – to which the Federal Financing Bank would advance funds to the [Farm Credit System] Insurance Corporation. Under its existing statutory authority, the [Farm Credit System] Insurance Corporation will use these funds to provide assistance to the System Banks in exigent market circumstances which threaten the Banks' ability to pay maturing debt obligations. The agreement provides for advances of up to $10 billion and terminates on September 30, 2014, unless otherwise extended."[2] The agreement has been extended each year since.

We believe the farmers who own stock of the Farm Credit System—and the American taxpayers who back it—deserve a better understanding of what transpires between the Farm Credit System and the U.S. Treasury, but very little information is available to the public. Unlike the housing GSEs which are subject to reform efforts to lessen the taxpayer's exposure, the Farm Credit System seems to be increasing its dependence upon the U.S. Treasury.

Congress created the Farm Credit System as a public option for farm finance when farmers were having trouble getting the credit they needed from non-government sources. The conditions that led to the creation of the Farm Credit System nearly 100 years ago no longer exist, and yet we continue to have a government assisted, tax advantaged farm lender providing credit to customers who would be able to easily borrow from taxpaying institutions like mine. In fact, the heavily subsidized credit that FCS lends goes to those who need it least. Despite amendments to the Farm Credit Act of 1980 requiring each FCS lender to have a program for furnishing credit to young, beginning and small farmers and ranchers (YBS), the share of new YBS loans to total new FCS loans continues to ***be dismal***—even as the assets of the system have expanded enormously. Loans to small farmers have steadily drop over the past several years with small farm loans declining from a high of 30 percent of total new loan volume in 2003[3] to just 14.1 percent in 2015. Clearly, those who would benefit the most from the taxpayer subsidized credit made available by the FCS are not receiving the benefits that Congress intended them to receive.

---

[2] Federal Farm Credit Banks Funding Corporation; 2013 Annual Information Statement of the Farm Credit System; February 28, 2014, page 23.

[3] "FCA's Annual Report on the Farm Credit System's Young, Beginning, and Small Farmer Mission Performance: 2013 Results." Office of Regulatory Policy, June 12, 2014 Board Meeting.

Conclusion

The banking industry is well positioned to meet the needs of U.S. farmers and ranchers. U.S. agriculture has begun to adjust to lower commodity prices after enjoying one of the longest periods of financial prosperity in history. USDA projected that at year-end 2016, farm and ranch solvency ratios — debt-to-asset and debt-to-equity ratios — would rise to 13.23 and 15.25 percent, respectively. Even as these measures have increased, each remains low relative to historical levels. During the past few years, while farmers experiences unprecedented high commodity prices and rising farm profits, farmers used their excess cash profits to retire debt and to acquire additional equipment and land. As a result, farmers and ranchers today have the capacity to tap their equity should there be a decline in farm profitability resulting in diminished cash flows. While no farmer or rancher wants to take on additional debt, the strength of the U.S. farm and ranch balance sheet gives producers options to do so if the need arises.

The banking industry remains cautious as it looks forward to the next Farm Bill. There is a very real concern that declining commodity prices will negatively affect the farm economy and make credit situations tighter. This is why the banking industry will continue to be involved in the Farm Bill process and will continue to offer assistance to Congress as it writes the next Farm Bill. With the changes that have been outlined earlier, the banking industry will continue to help producers remain strong into the future. Bankers still see great opportunities in agriculture and will stand with their partners in agriculture to develop the best Farm Bill for all.

Thank you for the opportunity to express the views of the American Bankers Association. I would be happy to answer any questions that you may have.

Statement of Lucas Heinen, President, Kansas Soybean Association, before the Committee on Agriculture, Nutrition, and Forestry, United States Senate, February 23, 2017

Good morning, Chairman Roberts, Ranking Member Stabenow, and Members of the Committee. I am Lucas Heinen, a soybean farmer from Everest, Kansas, and President of the Kansas Soybean Association. We appreciate the opportunity to appear at this first Congressional hearing on the 2018 farm bill.

I understand that the conventional view in Washington is that the cost of farm programs and other parts of the farm bill will need to be reduced again, just as they were in the 2014 farm bill. This is not acceptable to producers in Kansas. Farm prices are down over 40 percent since 2013. Soybean prices in Kansas are down from $14.40 to $9.12 per bushel in the last three years. Hard Red Winter wheat prices have been hit particularly hard, down from $7.56 to $3.16 per bushel. And U.S. farm income is now expected to fall for the fourth straight year, by 8.7 percent, in 2017.

The anticipated cost of the current farm bill is significantly less than the level estimated by the Congressional Budget Office when it was enacted in 2014. While commodity program costs are projected to be up by $14 billion over the next ten years due to lower prices, the cost of crop insurance is down about $10 billion for the same reason. And the cost of food stamps, or SNAP, is down by $84 billion over the same ten year period due to the improved economy.

A large number of farm organizations, including the Kansas Soybean Association and the American Soybean Association, have just sent a letter to the Congressional Budget and Appropriations Committees opposing further spending cuts in the 2018 Farm Bill. The letter points out that agriculture voluntarily accepted $23 billion in cuts in the 2014 bill, and that other sectors have made no contribution to deficit reduction whatsoever.

As Congress looks toward writing the 2018 Farm Bill, we believe the sharp and continuing fall of farm prices and income since 2013 justifies increasing funding to strengthen the farm safety net and to make other worthwhile investments. Soybean producers have begun to identify priorities and they include the following:

1) First, the crop insurance program needs to be protected. For many soybean producers, crop insurance is their most important risk management tool.
2) Second, most soybean, corn and wheat producers in Kansas signed up for the county ARC program. While support under ARC has declined with the lower prices and revenue we've had in recent years, Kansas farmers want to see this program continued in the next farm bill. We do need to change the yields used under the program from NASS to RMA data, when available, to minimize county to county discrepancies. This could incur some additional cost, but it would make this important program more accurate and defensible as an option in the next farm bill.
3) We support funding of current conservation programs, including EQIP and the Conservation Stewardship Program, at their authorized levels. We support raising annual funding for agricultural research under AFRI to the full authorized level of $700 million. And we support continued authorization and funding for Energy Title programs, including the Biobased Market Program, the Bioenergy Program for Advanced Biofuels, and the Biodiesel Education Program.
4) We strongly support doubling mandatory funding for the Foreign Market Development program and the Market Access Program to spur promotion of U.S. agricultural exports. Funding for these programs has been frozen for over ten years while our foreign competitors are massively outspending us on market promotion.

We are aware that other crops have issues that need to be addressed, and which may add to the cost of the bill. It is important for farm organizations to work together to achieve legislation that everyone can support. Soybeans will continue to lead this effort, and to oppose proposals from farm bill critics on both the left and the right to weaken or eliminate programs that are important to producers.

In closing, Mr. Chairman, I would note the importance of keeping programs that support farmers and programs that support consumers together in the next farm bill. There is a relationship between the need to provide assistance to those who produce food and those who consume it, when either needs that assistance. This bond explains how Congress has been able to come together and enact farm bills for over 40 years.

Thank you again, Mr. Chairman, for the opportunity to appear today. I'm happy to answer any questions.

Testimony of Tom Lahey, Vice President, Kansas Cotton Association, before the Committee on Agriculture, Nutrition, and Forestry, U.S. Senate, Manhattan, Kansas, February 23, 2017

Introduction

Chairman Roberts, Ranking Member Stabenow, and Members of the Committee, thank you for the opportunity to provide this testimony regarding the current farm bill and the policy needs of the U.S. cotton industry in the next farm bill.

My name is Tom Lahey, a fourth generation farmer and rancher from Moscow, Kansas. I raise cotton, wheat, corn, and grain sorghum, the majority under pivot irrigation, and have a cow-calf operation. Nearly 20 years ago, I was one of the first two farmers to grow cotton in southwest Kansas. In 2002, we built the first cotton gin in Kansas, Northwest Cotton Growers Inc. (NWCG), in the western part of the state.

I serve as vice president of the Kansas Cotton Association, and I am a producer delegate to the National Cotton Council (NCC). NCC is the central organization of the United States cotton industry. Its members include producers, ginners, merchants, cooperatives, warehouses, textile manufacturers and cottonseed processors and merchandisers.

Current Industry Conditions

As you know, the current economic situation for much of production agriculture is bleak, including for U.S. cotton farmers. The passage of the 2014 Farm Bill coincided with significant changes in the global cotton market. Shortly after the bill was approved, cotton prices began a significant decline, the result of a build-up of global cotton stocks, especially in China, decreased demand, and reduced exports. This led to the lowest U.S. cotton acreage for 2015 in over 30 years. While cotton prices and acreage have increased from the lows experienced in 2015, producers are still struggling with prices at levels not adequate to cover all production costs.

To understand the challenges facing cotton farmers, it is important to review the dynamics at work in global cotton demand. USDA estimates world mill use at 112 million bales for the current 2016 marketing year. However, even with very modest growth, world cotton demand remains almost 13 million bales below the peak demand observed in 2006. Slumping demand is largely the result of the tremendous increase in polyester use. During the 2006-2015 period when cotton mill use fell by 13 million bales, polyester's production capacity, primarily located in China, increased by 145 million bales. Excess production capacity, in many cases fueled by government support, is contributing to polyester prices in Asian markets of approximately 55 cents per pound. While consumers continue to express their preference for cotton products, the tremendous increase in low-priced polyester production has created extraordinary hurdles for increasing cotton demand.

I highlight these issues because of the critical influence of international markets in the financial conditions of U.S. cotton farmers. In recent years, approximately 75% of U.S. cotton production enters export channels. Policies that directly affect international production, consumption and trade have a direct bearing on U.S. market prices.

For 2017, NCC is estimating 11 million acres of cotton plantings, with 45,000 acres in Kansas, a 42% increase from 2016. This increase in Kansas is reflective of several factors, including the availability of seeds with a trait that provides tolerance to 2,4-D herbicide, the yield potential of cotton coupled with minimal water use requirements, and the relative returns compared to other crops.

Cotton Policy and the Farm Bill

While cotton acres across the U.S. are expected to recover, a major concern still exists since cotton is not eligible for the same price and revenue policies as other crops. As you know, these Title I policies in the farm bill are designed to help producers withstand periods of price declines and depressed market conditions. While the ARC/PLC policies have generally performed well for me and other producers in responding to the market downturn we are experiencing in crops like wheat, corn, grain sorghum, and soybeans, I continue to be largely exposed on cotton since it was excluded from these types of programs. Under the current farm bill, cotton has access to the Stacked Income Protection Plan (STAX) crop insurance policy and the marketing loan program with an adjustable loan rate based on prior year market prices. Cotton is the only traditional 'program' crop that does not have any long-term price or revenue protection policy in the 2014 Farm Bill.

Cotton policy in the 2014 Farm Bill was largely dictated by a World Trade Organization (WTO) trade challenge brought by Brazil against components of U.S. farm policy and some cotton policy specifically. This resulted in cotton having to rely largely on STAX as the core safety net for cotton. But just like any revenue based crop insurance policy, STAX is not equipped to address periods of extended low prices, which is exactly what cotton producers experienced beginning the year the farm bill was approved.

For more than a year, the NCC has been working with Congress and the previous Administration to try to get cottonseed designated as a covered commodity and be eligible for the ARC and PLC programs in the farm bill. Cottonseed remains an important co-product of cotton production, along with the cotton fiber. Our industry believes support can be provided for cottonseed without running afoul of the agreement with Brazil that settled the WTO case. We strongly believe we need to get a cottonseed policy in place to help provide support to our producers as a bridge until the new farm bill is enacted, which will hopefully be by the 2019 crop.

NCC is beginning internal discussions on cotton's policy objectives for the new farm bill. We know that a meaningful safety net for cotton must be included in Title I of the farm bill. Better protection in times of depressed markets can take on several forms, and our industry will continue to pursue the best avenue to provide growers adequate protection for the revenue generated by both cotton fiber and cottonseed.

In order for Congress to be able to address the current shortcomings in U.S. cotton policy and to shore up other areas of need in farm policy, we strongly oppose any attempts to reduce the budget for the next farm bill. Further, we urge the Committee to seek any opportunities to increase the Federal investment in farm policies that ensures the U.S. consumer continues to have the safest, most affordable and secure supply of food and fiber in the world. In the January 2017 Congressional Budget Office baseline projection, the cost of the current farm bill is expected to be more than $100 billion less than estimated when the bill was enacted in 2014. Given this significant decline in farm bill spending, coupled with the significant downturn in farm income and generally weak commodity prices, a greater investment in these critical policies for all of rural America should be in order.

In addition to a meaningful safety net, our industry relies heavily on a properly functioning marketing loan program, so maintaining that policy, with minor adjustments, is also a priority.

Maintaining a strong crop insurance program is also critical since in agriculture, one thing is for certain, crop losses will occur in some part of the U.S. each year. Annual losses incurred by farmers clearly demonstrate the need for crop insurance protection and the public-private partnership of program delivery. Farmers, ranchers, their lenders, input suppliers and other stakeholders agree that crop insurance protection should remain a viable, affordable tool for managing risk.

In 2016, 96% of cotton acres were covered by either multi-peril "buy-up" insurance or catastrophic coverage. 88% of these acres were covered by multi-peril insurance. The STAX policy was purchased on over 2.5 million acres covering 26% of total insured acres.

In 2016, crop insurance was purchased on 84% of cotton acres in Kansas and 79% of those acres are covered with multi-peril insurance. Unfortunately, STAX coverage has been used in very limited amounts on Kansas cotton acres. While there are likely several reasons for this low level of participation, it is imperative that cotton producers have access to the same complement of risk management policies and tools as other producers, including commodity policies in Title I, along with crop insurance.

Federal crop insurance provides an effective risk management tool to farmers and ranchers of all sizes when they are facing losses beyond their control, reduces taxpayer risk exposure, makes hedging possible to help mitigate market volatility, and provides lenders with greater certainty that loans made to producers will be repaid. The public-private partnership of program delivery works very well, allowing for timely and outstanding service to producers when they need it the most and providing much-needed jobs across rural America.

While the insurance program is working well and should be defended, there are a few areas that can be improved. NCC is currently working with the Risk Management Agency (RMA) to improve quality loss provisions that have proved inadequate for many producers in the Southeast region who suffered through extensive rains during the 2015 and 2016 harvest seasons. RMA has been a good partner in identifying and pursuing improvements to this feature of the product. Another area that is particularly important here in the Southwest region that was allowed in the 2014 Farm Bill is the ability to insure Enterprise Units by practice. In our view, the RMA has not implemented this provision in the way intended by Congress and should be reconsidered by USDA, and if necessary, further clarified in the next farm bill.

Our industry will work to prevent any further tightening of payment limits and eligibility requirements, as we believe these policies are already too burdensome and restrictive in light of the size and scale of production agriculture necessary to be competitive and viable in a today's global market.

In addition to the above policies discussed for upland cotton, there are important policy considerations for Extra Long Staple (ELS) or Pima cotton as well. The industry is evaluating the potential for an increase in the loan rate for the ELS loan program to better reflect the relative market value of Pima cotton. Since this is a non-recourse loan without marketing loan provisions, there should be little, if any, additional government cost or exposure. Also, the ELS Cotton Competitiveness Program is not currently functioning as intended given the recent shift in the countries that are major producers, importers and exporters of ELS cotton. For the intended objectives of this program to be met, USDA needs to take steps to update the key price data being used.

Conservation programs continue to be extremely popular across the Cotton Belt. Specifically, the Environmental Quality Incentives Program and the Conservation Stewardship Program are both heavily accessed. I commend the Committee for streamlining conservation programs in the 2014 Farm Bill. I believe this will make them easier for NRCS to administer, but more importantly easier for producers like myself to utilize. These programs have become integral parts of many producer's operations and achieve the goal of improving and protecting the environment while also improving our farming operations.

Between 1997 and 2008, the amount of cotton used by U.S. textile mills experienced a precipitous decline, falling from 11.3 million bales down to 3.5 million bales. Since 2008, the U.S. textile industry has stabilized, however there has been a slight decrease in domestic mill use for the current marketing year at 3.3 million bales.

The recent years of stability and expected future growth can be attributed to the continued benefits of the Economic Adjustment Assistance Program (EAAP), first authorized in the 2008 Farm Bill. Recipients must agree to invest the proceeds in equipment and manufacturing plants, including construction of new facilities as well as modernization and expansion of existing facilities. EAAP funds have allowed investments in new equipment and new technology, thus allowing companies to reduce costs, increase efficiency and become more competitive against imported textile products. By allowing U.S. textile mills to make the new investments necessary to remain competitive, the program supports a manufacturing base that is keeping jobs in the United States.

Given the tremendous reliance by our industry on exports of raw cotton fiber and yarn, it is essential that the U.S. agriculture industry have a strong, well-funded public-private partnership to help leverage private resources to expand export markets and grow demand for U.S. agriculture products. A central part of this effort is USDA's Market Access Program (MAP) and Foreign Market Development (FMD) program. Even though the U.S. continues to be heavily outspent by other major agricultural producing and exporting countries, MAP and FMD investments have not increased in more than a decade. For this reason, we believe it is justified for the new farm bill to invest additional funds in these programs.

Conclusion

In closing, for the past three years, U.S. cotton producers have struggled with low cotton prices, high production costs and the resulting financial hardships. While current cotton futures markets have increased from year-ago levels, many producers continue to face economic challenges. The projected increase in cotton acreage is largely the result of weaker prices of competing crops and improved expectations for water in some regions that were experiencing severe drought conditions. As such, it is imperative that the next farm bill bring cotton back into the Title I commodity policy so that cotton is able to access the full complement of risk management tools as other crops.

NCC looks forward to working with the Committee, the other groups and commodities represented here today, and all commodity and farm organizations to develop and pass a new farm bill that effectively addresses the needs of all commodities and producers in all regions of the country.

Thank you for this opportunity to present testimony, and I would be pleased to respond to any questions.

Chairman Roberts and Ranking Member Stabenow:

Let me be among the first to welcome you to the Big First Congressional District of Kansas, our nation's largest agricultural-producing district.

You are now in the leading state for wheat and sorghum production, the largest district for beef sales and home of the fastest growing dairy industry- a fitting place to launch a review of our current farm programs and discuss solutions for the upcoming 2018 bill.

You are also at ground zero for the challenges facing America's farmers and ranchers. The hurt in farm country is real. I'm confident that today you will hear from folks in the trenches of this current economic downturn. I'm looking forward to hearing their ideas and solutions to take back to Washington.

For me, the downturn in the ag economy we all hear about becomes very real when I see the Kansas Farm Management Association reporting that net farm income in Kansas was less than $6,000 in 2015. I can't imagine trying to live and raise a family on that income level. We know those levels will fall when they are reported for 2016, and unless something changes, they will be even lower for 2017.

I know today's hearing is focused on the 2018 Farm Bill, but I want to instill this: we can't make farm policy in a vacuum. Monetary, trade, regulatory and economic policy all impact our producer's bottom lines just as much as the programs we'll be discussing today; perhaps, none more so than trade. A robust agricultural trade agenda would work hand-in-hand with our safety net programs to provide revenue from the marketplace, and opportunity for our producers to succeed.

While I don't have all the answers or any silver bullets for our current crisis, I am committed to working with my colleagues across the aisle and across the Capitol as we begin to write the 2018 Farm Bill. It is my hope that we can identify the areas where the 2014 bill fell short, correct them, and ensure we have farm, food and nutrition policy that works for our farmers, ranchers and consumers.

Written Statement for the Hearing from the Heartland: Perspectives on the 2018 Farm Bill from Kansas, by Jackie McClaskey, Kansas Secretary of Agriculture, February 23, 2017

On behalf of the state of Kansas, I’m pleased to welcome you today and I’m glad to see so many people in attendance for this very important event. It is particularly meaningful to host this first Farm Bill hearing right here at Kansas State University, the first land-grant university, which still prides itself on leading the way in preparing the next generation of agriculture leaders. I am especially happy to welcome Senator Pat Roberts, a K-State graduate, a loyal Kansan and a respected advocate for the agriculture industry. Kansas is fortunate to be represented by a leader of this caliber who understands and respects the importance of agriculture. Senator Roberts has spent more than 30 years serving the needs of Kansas, first in the U.S. House of Representatives and then in the U.S. Senate since 1996. Senator Roberts was the first member of Congress in history to have chaired both the House Agriculture Committee and now the Senate committee. His position as Chairman of the Senate Agriculture Committee gives him a unique opportunity to be a voice for American agriculture.

Today provides an opportunity to look at the future of agriculture as it is addressed through the Farm Bill, and I appreciate that opportunity. As I do so, however, I want to go well beyond the subject of the Farm Bill itself, and share with you an update on the significant efforts being made here in Kansas as we work to grow agriculture. Our focus is on strategic growth, and while much of that requires work at the local level, it also highlights the critical need for federal partnerships on many levels and on many issues. I want to address some of those places where federal partnerships can make a significant difference to the farmers, ranchers and agribusinesses of Kansas.

Agriculture is Kansas' largest industry, employer and economic driver. Sixty-six agriculture, food and food processing sectors combine to provide nearly $65 billion in total economic contribution to the state, approximately 43 percent of the total economy. The industry employs over 234,000 people, nearly 13 percent of the Kansas workforce. If food retail is included, the economic contribution rises to over $74 billion, about 50 percent of the state economy, and employs nearly 20 percent of the workforce.

In Kansas, there are 46,137,295 acres of land. Farmland accounts for 88.9 percent of all Kansas land. More than 21 million acres in Kansas are harvested for crops and over 16 million acres serve as pastureland for grazing animals. In addition to growing crops and raising livestock, the Kansas agricultural sector includes renewable energy production, food processing, research and education, agribusiness, technology entrepreneurship, and many value-added enterprises. Between Columbia, Missouri, and Manhattan, Kansas, sits the single largest concentration of animal health interests in the world. Kansas farmers and ranchers make a global impact. In 2015, Kansas exported more than $4.1 billion in agricultural products. The top five exports include wheat, beef and veal, soybeans, feed and forage, and corn.

Kansans embody the pioneer spirit that brought their forefathers to an uninhabited prairie to seek their fortunes in a new land. The values of hard work and achievement have stood the test of time in Kansas. The same pioneer spirit that converted Kansas from a vast sea of grassland into a major producer of our nation's food supply lives on today as we seek new opportunities and relationships to improve the largest industry in our state.

Kansans are known for their work ethic, valuing education and exhibiting a willingness to persevere through challenges.

In the light of depressed commodity prices, Kansas farmers, ranchers and agribusinesses face an abundance of challenges, but industry leaders clearly expressed the need to continue to look forward and plan for short- and long-term expansion of the state's agriculture industry. As the nation's agriculture industry positions itself for growth in order to meet the needs of a growing population with changing demands, Kansas is well-suited to be a home for that growth. Kansas has the right leaders and priorities and the right tools and resources to be a nationwide leader in agricultural growth.

The success of the Kansas economy is directly linked to the success of the agriculture industry. We know that to grow the Kansas economy, the agriculture industry must grow. Strategic industry growth requires communication, coordination and collaboration, so Kansas agricultural leaders have begun the process of developing a strategic growth plan for all sectors of agriculture, based on the opportunities in and the barriers to economic growth. In August 2016, the Governor's Summit on Agricultural Growth was held in Manhattan, Kansas, bringing together nearly 400 leaders from across industry sectors under one roof to talk about barriers, challenges, opportunities, growth goals and next steps. Feedback from that Summit, along with input from one-on-one meetings with industry leaders, has been compiled and utilized to develop desired objectives and action plans for each agricultural sector in Kansas. While some of these outcomes simply require government to let industry work and function, there are some that have a role for state government and some that will require cooperation with our partners in Congress and within federal agencies. Progress reports and continued focus on the future will take place at the next Summit, which will take place in August 2017.

As we look toward future growth opportunities for Kansas agriculture, we are fortunate to have a strong foundation on which to stand. Kansas was built on a values system of family, hard work, faith and entrepreneurship. Those values continue to be integrated into a pro-growth, pro-business, pro-agriculture culture. This small-town, family environment, combined with an innovative, proactive nature, is evident across the state. Maintaining that approach will require partners on a federal level, both in Congress and in the administration, who share the desire for pro-growth, pro-business policy.

Kansas is naturally suited for effective and efficient agricultural production. The semi-arid climate offers abundant sunshine, available moisture and irrigation and reasonable humidity, making for good growing seasons and harvesting conditions. Kansas takes pride in providing some of the best roads and rail systems in the nation. These transportation systems provide easy access to markets and make moving people and goods in the state simple and inexpensive.

The foresight of agriculture leaders has resulted in state-level regulatory standards and legislation that make Kansas a great place to farm, ranch and run a business. Environmental standards allow production agriculture and environmental preservation to work hand-in-hand. Kansas legislation protects animal agriculture against threats from activist groups focused on dismantling the industry because Kansas is not a ballot initiative state. Business-friendly tax exemptions, longstanding property tax policy, being a Right to Work state, and a business-friendly regulatory culture make Kansas "open for business."

Kansas is the home to Kansas State University — the first land-grant university in the U.S. — and Fort Hays State University. These institutions, along with the other Regents universities, community colleges and technical schools, are all key partners in growing the workforce needed to serve Kansas agriculture. In addition, career and technical education at the high school level, especially agricultural education programs, are growing and prospering.

The long-term availability of water in Kansas is dependent on local leadership, responsible use, management and policy development. In 2013, Kansas Governor Sam Brownback issued a call to action to develop a long-term plan for water in Kansas, which was followed by a comprehensive statewide effort to seek input throughout the state and to craft a plan. The resulting *Vision for the Future of Water Supply in Kansas* and the development of innovative water policies focused on individual management and local control are helping extend the life of the Ogallala aquifer and the reservoir system to allow for long-term sustainable growth.

As the Kansas agriculture industry works toward economic expansion, we know that growth has barriers as well. Farmers, ranchers and agribusinesses must balance a lengthy list of challenges and variables, many of which they cannot control, as they work to grow and raise food for families across the globe. The variability of agriculture is inevitable. Weather extremes, volatile markets, diverse consumers, and lawmakers and regulators with less understanding about agriculture are factors the agricultural industry confronts and manages through on a daily basis. The role of the Kansas Department of Agriculture is to serve as a partner to the industry, eliminating unnecessary, overly burdensome, or outdated barriers to growth, and fostering an environment that encourages and welcomes expansion of the industry. Some of those challenges and opportunities can be addressed in the 2018 Farm Bill.

Kansas is poised to work collaboratively to help craft quality legislation aimed at serving our farmers and ranchers. Several specific items related to the Farm Bill and other federal issues and barriers were identified during the process of developing sector-specific desired outcomes for the state's strategic growth project, and those are listed in the attached document. They were based on direct input from stakeholders in the industry in one-on-one meetings and at the Summit.

Continuing to maintain a regulatory environment at the state level designed to help agriculture rather than hinder it, while looking for ways to improve and streamline state systems, is a must to further growth. More importantly, state government and industry must work together with the state's congressional leadership to push back against and, when possible, dismantle over-reaching, excessive, burdensome federal regulations targeted against agriculture. We are encouraged with initial actions taken by the Trump administration to reduce regulatory challenges and we will seek opportunities to work with the administration to eliminate barriers to growth that are due to overly burdensome and unnecessarily costly regulations or those that impede businesses or innovation in agriculture.

As spring planting approaches and as wheat begins to exit its stage of winter dormancy, Kansas farmers, much like farmers across the country, are entering into the fourth consecutive year of the current downturn in the agricultural economy. Average net farm incomes have plummeted from record levels of nearly $160,000 to less than $5,000 in 2015, with negative incomes predicted for 2016 and 2017. These levels have not been seen since the early 1980s. It is in times like these that risk management tools, including Title I commodity programs and federal crop insurance, need to kick in to provide the safety net they were designed to deliver.

Animal agriculture represents the largest segment of the Kansas agricultural industry, so a threat to animal health would be devastating to the Kansas economy. Foreign animal disease preparedness is a priority for the state. KDA has the lead responsibility within Kansas for an agricultural emergency response, and we intend to be the best prepared state in the country. In the last seven years, Kansas has held five major animal disease exercises, each involving more than 250 participants and including players from the county, state and federal levels, as well as from university and industry organizations. It is clear from these exercises that an effective animal disease response requires a realistic, executable plan that involves federal coordination of state responses and federal resources based on state needs and state implementation.

We are aware of the efforts being made to enhance availability of vaccines to address disease outbreaks, but vaccination funding should not be seen as a silver bullet. Throwing money at vaccine development does not address the practical challenges related to dissemination, or the response time lost while vaccines are being prepared. Additionally, the fact that the proposed amount of vaccines is clearly not enough if it is to be used in all species, and the potential problems with reopening international market access have not been fully considered. Serious discussion needs to occur among state and federal leaders, in addition to animal health officials, to develop a more realistic plan and approach. Vaccine is currently being sold as "the solution" and circumstances dictate that in a real situation it will be only one tool. We know the best way to stop the spread of the disease is to stop movement, so our approach in Kansas is very different from other states and from what is recommended by USDA: As soon as there is a presumptive positive FMD case, we're stopping movement. We have seen the importance of stopping movement as well as traceability, and believe these elements are key to disease control, but they will only work if all affected states are working in concert. These are challenges we are continuously working to address both internally and with partners in industry, other states, and the federal government.

As the National Bio and Agro-Defense Facility (NBAF) continues construction in Manhattan, it reinforces the animal health sector in this region and confirms the state's prominence in the animal health and bioscience sector. This facility will strengthen our nation's ability to respond to animal disease events, and we support all efforts on a federal level to prioritize animal health, including conducting research, developing vaccines, diagnosing emerging diseases, training veterinarians, and developing countermeasures against large animal foreign animal diseases and zoonotic diseases.

Consumers across the state, nation and globe want to know more about where their food comes from and the story of the people who raised it. The agriculture industry must work together to provide an increasingly open and transparent food system that meets the needs of consumers and creates value-added benefits for farmers and ranchers. While these demands for a transparent food system can present a challenge to the status quo, this demand is also an opportunity to work with our partners in the industry to develop a voluntary traceability system that not only serves to enhance consumer confidence and trust but also to manage a disease outbreak, protect food safety, and potentially, provide opportunities to access export markets. We are prepared to move forward with federal partners to progressively address the feasibility of a national traceability system.

Robust support for agricultural research and extension is critical to the vitality of agriculture, both in Kansas and across the United States. As previously mentioned, Kansas State University is the nation's first land-grant university and it is an important partner in our state's agricultural industry. The research that is done at K-State leads to advancements in precision agricultural production practices, food safety, animal care, efficiency, and more. We know that research and development in agriculture are key to growing the industry, and we support expanded research in areas important to agriculture in Kansas, and continue to look for public/private partnerships which will advance this research.

Kansas is blessed with abundant natural resources, and it is necessary to continue to build private-public partnerships to protect and conserve the state's water supply and be good stewards of the land. We have seen success with voluntary conservation programs that are locally driven and provide flexibility to water users, and we support increased investment in those programs. Kansas has a track record of progressive and innovative protection of the important waters of the state, whether under federal jurisdiction or not, noting that not all waters are equally important. We are among the nation's top states in terms of sediment reduction and phosphorus reductions through best management and conservation practices. We have promoted federal policies which encourage conservation without penalizing qualification for crop insurance. We commend USDA Risk Management Agency for developing limited irrigation crop insurance coverage options for corn and soybean in counties over the Ogallala aquifer in Kansas. Allowing for states' administrative discretion without ubiquitous, counter-productive federal oversight, ensures the critical waters of the state, as well as the nation, will be protected.

We know that growing agriculture in Kansas means we need access to more markets around the globe. Access to international markets and expanded global market share is critical to nearly all agriculture sectors in Kansas. Public-private partnerships focused on gaining additional market access, along with national leadership in trade negotiations and partnership, are necessary for sustainable agricultural growth. During the past 12 months, while domestic commodity prices were low, exports of agricultural products were a high point in the industry. Expanding market access and increasing food and agricultural exports not only boosts farm receipts but create jobs here at home. We support efforts to open new doors for trade through bi-lateral and multi-lateral trade agreements that seek to level the playing field by eliminating tariff and non-tariff barriers to trade, and will continue working to build international relationships through focused trade missions.

The prosperity of agriculture is closely linked to the prosperity of rural communities. Continuously improving infrastructure in rural areas, whether that means rail access, rural housing, or broadband and mobile networks, is critical to rural development. Grants and other programs which support rural business development have been instrumental in providing opportunities for individuals, businesses and the state to prosper.

A challenge facing all of us in agriculture is ensuring we have an adequate workforce to meet our industry needs. In addition to leaders and innovators, it is essential to have a workforce that includes people willing to work in production and processing facilities, and the federal government must be a viable partner to meet that need in the workforce. Another potential source of workers we are interested in utilizing is our nation's heroes. More than two million veterans are transitioning out of active duty and looking to identify opportunities to make a living, and many of them have shown an interest in agriculture. This is an opportunity in Kansas and around the nation to address workforce challenges in the agriculture industry. Meeting workforce and talent demands in agriculture means we have to think creatively to identify willing, interested and capable employees for our farms, ranches and agribusinesses.

Though it's been just a few years since the 2014 Farm Bill was enacted, it has been anything but a quiet three years for the industry. Since 2014, farmers and ranchers across the nation have experienced droughts, floods and fires. They have seen markets at their highest point, and they have experienced fast declines in commodity and livestock prices. This diverse, rapidly changing, incredibly important industry is vital to the nation's economy and security. Agriculture is critical to the nation's food supply, natural resources, and public health and safety, and the decisions made today carry great weight as we preserve the future of American agriculture.

Despite the complex challenges facing the Kansas agriculture industry, the strength and commitment of the farmers, ranchers and agribusinesses of Kansas will continue to carry agriculture into the future to grow and thrive. As the state agency that supports this complex industry, the Kansas Department of Agriculture is committed to our Vision, *Kansas will provide an ideal environment for long-term, sustainable agricultural prosperity and statewide economic growth.* Through our collaborative efforts with industry organizations, academic institutions, and state and federal lawmakers, we know this Vision can become a reality.

The Kansas agricultural community has appreciated the many relationships that have been developed with our federal partners. We look forward to continuing those relationships and creating opportunities for new partnerships as we work together for a strong and prosperous future for agriculture.

Testimony of Kent Moore, Iuka, KS, On Behalf of the Kansas Corn Growers Association, before the U.S. Senate Committee on Agriculture, Nutrition & Forestry, February 23, 2017, Manhattan, KS

Thank you for the opportunity to speak at this hearing. My name is Kent Moore. I farm in Pratt County. I serve on the board of the Kansas Corn Growers Association and I am also Chairman of the Kansas Corn Commission, the state's corn checkoff. While the checkoff works to increase the profitability of corn through market development, research, promotion and education, the association is involved in policy and regulatory issues. Today, I am honored to appear on behalf of the Kansas Corn Growers Association.

I am the fifth generation of my family to farm in northwest Pratt County. We typically grow over 3,000 acres of irrigated corn and 750 acres of dryland corn. We also normally grow 500 acres of irrigated soybeans and 850 acres of dryland wheat. Our farm is located in the area covered by Big Bend Groundwater Management District #5. GMD 5 was an early adopter of safe yield criteria to manage the long-term sustainability of the region's water resources. And I believe that strategy of water resource management has been successful in my farm's capacity to produce crops to feed and fuel our state and nation in a responsible manner.

Kansas is a unique state because most of our farms are diversified. There are few Kansas farmers who grow only one or two crops. Kansas farmers grow corn, wheat, soybeans, sorghum and other crops. Many of our grain farms also have livestock. Because of this, our association continually advocates for cooperation among our commodity groups, especially in the formulation of the farm bill. Our national organizations have indicated an unprecedented level of cooperation among farm groups in initial discussions, and we hope that cooperation continues. In a time when a large part of the agricultural sector is in an economic decline, it will be necessary and beneficial to have a united effort.

The last farm bill was written in a time of high prices. This one will be written in a time of low prices. We've been blessed with bumper crops. More than ever, our farmers need a strong safety net to protect production and revenue, and we need robust federal support for programs that expand and develop export markets for our grains, meats, fibers and fuels.

As the 2018 farm bill begins to take shape, you'll hear from a lot of farmers. But you'll also hear from many well-funded groups including budget hawks, environmental groups and anti-agriculture groups that will villainize the needed safety net the farm bill provides. Members of the Senate Ag Committee know this, but it bears repeating that the farm bill represents a miniscule part of our nation's budget, and commodity programs represent a miniscule part of the Farm Bill. The bulk of the funding in the Farm Bill is found in the nutrition title, and we strongly support keeping nutrition in the farm bill. It is key to the bill's passage. But we all know, our nation's budget woes can't be fixed with agriculture's small part of the overall farm bill.

The crop insurance program will be attacked by special interest groups during the farm bill process. I wonder if anyone understands the need for a solid crop insurance program more than the Kansas farmer. Drought, hail, wind and floods can ravage farms and sometimes Kansas farmers can experience all of these disasters in the same year. Unlike car insurance, crop insurance protects us against systemic risk. Every year, we hope we don't collect a crop insurance payment, but when we do have a loss, crop insurance provides critical support to farmers and the rural communities that serve agriculture.

Kansas farmers benefit from the revenue protection programs, ARC and PLC, in the current farm bill. In times of high crop prices, we saved the government billions of dollars in farm program payments. We won't get credit for that. When prices are low, critics are quick to point out the cost of these safety nets. While our groups work to build domestic and export markets to increase the value of our crops, commodity pricing remains virtually out of our control. The ARC program in particular has been an excellent tool for Kansas farmers, and we'd like to see it continued and improved. Some Kansas farmers who chose the ARC program have been hurt financially due to data gaps. We believe these inequities could be fixed in the current farm bill, without reopening it, by allowing the state FSA more flexibility in yield data. As we look to the 2018 farm bill, we support continuation of revenue-based programs and improved implementation of those programs.

When I speak of the need to provide a safety net for agriculture, I'm not only speaking for the corn growers, I am speaking for our state's economy. Agriculture is our state's top economic driver. Our industry is volatile, and without a strong safety net, it's impossible to predict what would happen to our state's economy.

Farms aren't just rows of crops. Our farms are what makes the Kansas economy tick. Our corn fuels livestock feeders, dairies, ethanol plants, grain elevators, trucking and rail companies, implement dealers and many other ag-related industries that directly employ many thousands of people in our state. Our corn, and other ag products also create an economy and tax base that funds our local schools, hospitals and highways. Farmers and others with careers in agriculture eat at our local restaurants, shop at the local grocery store, buy cars, pickups and farm machinery. We serve on the school board, the church committee and volunteer in our communities.

The growth potential for ag exports is greater than any other demand sector today. We believe it is time to increase our efforts to provide access to these growing markets around the world. We've produced bumper crops, and we need the ability to aggressively pursue trade to sell American grains and American meat to other countries. Programs like MAP and FMD are critical in building export markets for our ag products, but these two programs have had stagnant funding levels for a number of years. We support the efforts of the agriculture trade community to increase funding for MAP and FMD. Over the years, the effective spending power of these programs has decreased by over 40% due to factors like sequestration, administrative costs and inflation. Our farmers, through their checkoff, support the US Grains Council to develop exports of corn, ethanol and DDGS. Our checkoff dollars also support efforts to build export markets for red meat through the US Meat Export Federation. The MAP and FMD programs make our farmers' investment of checkoff funds for foreign market development efficient and effective.

Many of our state's ethanol plants that provide a needed market for corn today were started and funded by Kansas farmers who sought new markets for their corn and sorghum. Today, our grain surpluses are proof that we can provide more than enough corn for feed and fuel. Our ethanol plants provide a key market for our grains, clean domestic fuel for vehicles, and a desirable feed for livestock. Ethanol plants in Kansas have been a key factor in improving the lives of many rural Kansans. Located mainly in rural communities, our twelve Kansas ethanol plants produce nearly half a billion gallons of fuel per year. How can the farm bill help ethanol? One way is through increased funding of MAP and FMD programs. Exports are becoming increasingly important to the ethanol industry. Ethanol and ethanol products are relative newcomers to the export world, and these programs are vital as we seek to expand international sales of both ethanol and DDGS.

If you spend any time in our state, you will see a great deal of positive economic activity, and much of it is due to agriculture. Like any business, many farmers go to banks for operating loans and other financial tools. The programs in the farm bill give our farmers a degree of financial stability. Without strong farm bill programs, availability of agricultural credit will be endangered as banks won't be able to justify working with many family farmers. There may be simply too much risk for the lenders to assume in their increasingly highly regulated banking industry.

Our farms are businesses like no other. We put our investments into dirt and leave them exposed to storms, scorching heat and hopefully some rain. Then we leave the product of our investments to the will of a commodity market. This may sound careless, but it is the way we produce needed crops. In this time of crop surpluses, people may question the need for our productivity, yet less than five years ago, many were decrying a corn shortage that would lead to a food crisis. This is the nature of our business. Unpredictable, uncontrollable weather and markets are part of our job. Strong farm programs allow us to ride through these ups and downs.

While farmers work to continually improve and adopt new technologies in seed, inputs and equipment that allow us to sustainably manage our fields down to the square inch, much risk remains. This is why it is imperative that Kansas farmers have a federal farm program that provides themselves and our nation with the security needed to navigate an increasingly complex and challenging world. Thank you for the opportunity to speak here today.

Statement by Catherine Moyer, Chief Executive Officer and General Manager, Pioneer Communications, Ulysses, Kansas, on Behalf of NTCA–The Rural Broadband Association, before the United States Senate, Committee on Agriculture, Nutrition, & Forestry, Hearing from the Heartland: Perspectives on the 2018 Farm Bill Manhattan, KS, February 23, 2017

Introduction

Chairman Roberts, Ranking member Stabenow, and members of the committee, thank you for this opportunity to testify before you about rural telecommunications and the 2018 Farm Bill. I am Catherine Moyer, CEO/General Manager at Pioneer Communications. My remarks today are on behalf of Pioneer, as well as NTCA–The Rural Broadband Association, which represents approximately 850 member-owned cooperatives and commercially-owned carriers in 45 states that are largely based in the communities they serve and offer a variety of communications services throughout the rural far reaches of the nation.

Small, rural telecom providers like Pioneer connect rural Americans with the world, and these companies make every effort to deploy advanced networks that respond to consumer and business demands for cutting-edge, innovative services. Fixed and mobile broadband, video and voice are among the numerous services that rural Americans can access thanks to our industry's commitment to serving sparsely populated areas. Small rural telecom providers have always been at the forefront of resourceful entrepreneurship and technological innovation, being" first movers" in the telecom industry by converting to digital switched systems, providing wireless options to their hardest to reach customers, enabling distance learning and tele-health applications, and deploying as the chance permits future-proof all-fiber systems.

I have been part of the industry for more than 15 years, spending most of those years at Pioneer Communications. Pioneer is a local telecommunications provider with 113 employees serving a 5,000- square mile area – an area roughly the size of Connecticut, but with three million-plus fewer people than that state. We provide 21,000 total connections to wireline voice, high-speed broadband and video services over a network that utilizes a mix of fiber, copper and coax facilities. On average, we have just over two subscribers per square mile. However, when considering that 81 percent of our customers live in our small population centers, the "density" of our rural subscribers per square mile drops to just under 0.5. Put another way, 81 percent of our customers reside in approximately 15 square miles, while the remaining 19 percent reside in the other 4,985 square miles. In actual network terms, we have deployed 375 route miles (14 percent of our route miles) to serve that 81 percent of our customers, while it takes 2,325 route miles (86 percent of our route miles) to serve the remaining 19 percent of our customers. While one might ask why we serve these areas, we are the provider of last resort – in addition to its legal obligations to serve these consumers and businesses who were left behind long ago when larger companies picked first where to serve, if Pioneer does not provide them now with service, there is no one else available to do so. And atop all of that, our largest population centers are still tiny compared to even Tier 3 or Tier 4 "cities" – and our serving area is roughly 400 miles away from major cities like Denver or Kansas City. So at Pioneer, like many other NTCA members that serve agricultural communities and other rural areas, the challenges of distance and density hit very close to home.

Our broadband-capable networks are critical for the communities we serve to overcome these challenges; if anything, cutting-edge networks and advanced services are more important for rural consumers than in urban areas where distance is of little to no concern and densities are high. Our networks allow agricultural producers and other rural businesses to communicate with suppliers and sell to new markets, they enable education of our children on par with opportunities in urban areas, and they make our communities places to which people and businesses want to relocate and/or remain. In rural America, that translates into economic development that produces jobs, not only in agriculture, energy and other industries with a strong rural presence, but in the healthcare sector, and just about any other retail industry that requires broadband to operate.

As this committee deliberates the upcoming Farm Bill reauthorization, it should be mindful that access to capital for rural broadband projects is limited. Although there are a few options for the smaller broadband providers like Pioneer and other NTCA members to finance network construction, the fact is that there are truly just a few. Small rural broadband providers cannot walk into large commercial banks to obtain loans for networks where the addressable market of consumers is so small, the costs are so high, and the payback is therefore often measured in decades rather than years. There is no

"Wall Street" financing for rural broadband. Cost-effective Rural Utilities Service (RUS) loans offered through the U.S. Department of Agriculture (USDA) are therefore an essential resource for small businesses looking to deploy broadband in rural America. In the end, it takes a mix of private capital and financing from a few committed, mission-driven lenders like RUS, CoBank, or the Rural Telecommunications Finance Cooperative (RTFC) to enable small rural providers to build networks in their communities, with the complementary cornerstone of universal service funding then helping to justify the business case for such construction. Universal service funding ensures that consumers can afford to adopt services on the constructed networks and make continuing use of those networks over time.

The State of Rural Broadband Deployment Progress

In the face of the challenges just described, Pioneer Communications and other NTCA members have made remarkable and substantial progress in deploying advanced networks in their communities. In the spring of 2016, NTCA surveyed its members on their activities in providing broadband services and Internet availability to their customers. Responses from 131 member companies indicated that they use a variety of technologies, even within individual serving areas, to find ways to offer the best possible broadband to their customers: 49 percent of respondents' customers are served via fiber-to-the-home (FTTH), 29 percent via copper loops, 15 percent cable modem, 6 percent fiber-to-the-node (FTTN), 0.5 percent fixed wireless, and 0.1 percent satellite.[4]

Despite the multitude of obstacles that small providers face, their rural fiber deployment continues at an impressive pace. In the 2013 survey, 29 percent of respondents' customers were served by FTTH; in 2014, the percentage grew to 39 percent; and in this year's survey, almost half (49 percent) have access to FTTH service. This growth is all the more remarkable given the regulatory instability of recent years. Policies that encourage investments in and then sustain future-proof networks – such as fiber – will be most efficient in responding to consumer demand over the lives of those networks, particularly when compared to short-term strategies that focus on getting lower-speed broadband deployed quickly only to find that consumer demands outpace the capabilities of such low-speed networks in a few short years.

Clearly, smaller operators recognize the importance of fiber to their network both now and in the coming future, and are taking the necessary steps to include it in their plans. Fifty percent of those survey respondents with a fiber deployment strategy expect to offer FTTN to more than 75 percent of their customers by the end of 2018. Seventy-eight percent of respondents expect to be able to provide FTTH to at least half of their customers by year-end 2018. An additional 40 percent have already completed fiber deployment to all their customers.

---

[4] NTCA 2015 Broadband/Internet Availability Survey Report (2016), NTCA-The Rural Broadband Association, Arlington, VA.

Due in no small part to increased fiber deployment, broadband speeds offered by NTCA to customers continue to increase. Per the survey results, 85 percent of NTCA members' customers can get broadband at speeds of 10 Mbps or higher, including 71 percent who can get service at speeds above 25 Mbps, In the 2013 survey, 66 percent of respondents' customers could subscribe to broadband speeds of 10 Mbps or greater.

The story for Pioneer is very similar. Ninety-seven percent of our customers have access to 10 Mbps service. The remaining three percent of customers are served by long local loops that provide 7 Mbps or 8 Mbps service. We work with those customers on an individual basis to find solutions to their broadband needs. Twenty-one percent of our customers are served by FTTH. Another sixteen percent are currently part of a fiber build, and will be served by FTTH by mid-2017. The remaining 63 percent are served by FTTN, copper or coax, with many of those customers having more than one technology choice. We have deep fiber penetration throughout our service territory that allows us to provide more than the 10 Mbps to a vast majority of our customers.

But for (and likely because of) all this progress, our customers are demanding more and more speed. In 2016, we saw more than 1,000 customers move from the basic 10 Mbps speed to a higher-tier package. Due to this demand, we continue to utilize new technology in our FTTN, copper and coax networks to meet demand, but also continue to deploy fiber. I envision the fiber build to continue at a steady pace until we have reached our entire territory with FTTH. The speed and sustainability of deployment, however, will be predicated on reasonable access to capital and the availability of Universal Service Fund (USF) support – important points I will address further below.

But before moving on to discuss the essential complementary role that access to capital and sufficient and predictable USF play as cornerstones of rural broadband investment, this brings me to a final, critical point about broadband deployment – for all of the success I just described of Pioneer and other NTCA members, the job is far from done in rural America. Where fiber has already been built, we must maintain it over thousands of miles. Where customers already have high-speed broadband, we need to roll trucks many miles or have customer service representatives trained to deal with questions about router and device configurations in ways that were unimaginable when we were just a "telephone company." We also need to address the fact that even the best networks in rural markets are dependent upon so-called "middle mile" or long-haul connections to reach Internet gateways hundreds of miles away in places like Denver and Kansas City. Reaching those distant locations is expensive as well, and as our customers' bandwidth demands increase, so too does the cost of ensuring sufficient capacity on those long-haul fiber routes that connect rural America to the rest of the world.

And then there are all those places where fiber or other robust facilities have *not* yet been built. For the 85 percent of NTCA member customers who can subscribe to 10/1 Mbps services today, that means there are 15 percent of customers who cannot get even that basic level of broadband. For the 37 percent of Pioneer customers that we hope to have connected with fiber to their premises by the middle of this year, that means there are 63 percent who do not yet have such robust future-proof connections. In a country where the Federal Communications Commission (FCC) has indicated that 90 percent of Americans already have affordable access to 25/3 Mbps service and many urban consumers and businesses are already reaping the benefits of 100 Mbps or Gigabit speeds, broadband access in rural America remains far behind urban areas notwithstanding the best efforts of companies like Pioneer and other NTCA members.

Add onto all of this the fact that, on average, many rural Americans need to pay far more for broadband than urban consumers due to insufficient USF funding, and it becomes readily apparent that the job of getting rural America connected – and, just as importantly, keeping rural America connected – is far from done. The narrative of rural broadband deployment progress is therefore at once a story of success and a story of work still to be done.

The Role of Rural Utilities Service Funding

As noted earlier, the upfront financing of network construction is one of two complementary cornerstones necessary to achieve success in rural broadband deployment. In rural areas, the intensive capital costs of communications networks are compounded by the geographic distance over which facilities must be deployed and the often-challenging terrain characteristics. These areas also have relatively small number of users (as compared with more densely populated urban areas) to help recover the costs of deployment and ongoing operations. USDA's Rural Utilities Service plays a crucial role in addressing such rural broadband challenges through its telecommunications programs that finance network upgrades and deployment in rural areas.

RUS has been lending for broadband capable plant since the early 1990s at a net profit for taxpayers, and these programs have been a great success story. The agency has helped advance state-of-the-art networks to rural Americans left behind by providers unable or unwilling to serve low population density markets. Reliable access to capital helps rural carriers meet the broadband needs of rural consumers at affordable rates. While RUS financing is one of several sources of capital for rural carriers, as I noted earlier, there are in fact very few other sources – with rare exception, RUS, CoBank, and RTFC reflect the effective universe of lenders to which most small rural providers can turn for outside financing of substantial network construction projects.

Given the increased attention that has been paid by members of Congress and other policymakers to closing a "digital divide" and allowing rural America to keep pace with the rest of the country and the world from a technological perspective, it will be important therefore to continue providing RUS with the resources it needs to lend in support of rural broadband deployment. In fact, as Congress grapples with where to best direct scarce resources, it is important to note that the RUS Broadband Loan & Guarantees program and the traditional Telecommunication Infrastructure Loan &

Guarantees program make loans that must be paid back with interest – creating a win/win situation for rural broadband consumers and American taxpayers.

NTCA also supports the Community Connect Grants program; while limited funding restricts its reach, the grant mechanism makes the program popular with providers serving the highest cost areas where even loans may be difficult to justify. NTCA accordingly urges the committee to continue to support the RUS Broadband Loan program that is subjected to the Farm Bill reauthorization process at or above current funding levels as you formulate recommendations. Furthermore, we urge the committee to continue its long history of support for the Telecommunications Infrastructure and Community Connect programs that are also vital to the ongoing deployment and maintenance of advanced communications infrastructure throughout rural America.

The Complementary Role of the FCC's Universal Service Fund Programs

Unfortunately, the success, momentum, and economic development enabled by the RUS's telecommunications programs was stalled to some degree in recent years due to uncertainty in the Federal USF program that is so important to help justify the business case for initial construction and to sustain operations on networks once built. From time to time, some observers confuse or conflate RUS (or other lending programs) with USF, but the two in fact serve very different but complementary purposes; access to capital and ongoing USF support are each distinctly important in achieving rural broadband success of the kind seen to date. RUS lending programs, much like other lending programs, are focused on financing the substantial upfront costs of network deployment – but RUS programs and the few others I have mentioned are particularly important in high-cost, sparsely populated rural areas where once again many commercial banks are unlikely to lend.

By contrast, the USF programs do *not* provide substantial upfront financing for network construction. Instead, the USF programs represent a complementary cornerstone of rural broadband by helping to *justify the business case* for such construction. More specifically, the USF programs are aimed by law at ensuring "reasonably comparable" services are available at "reasonably comparable" rates. In this regard, the high-cost USF programs promote *both* availability *and* affordability. Without the cost recovery enabled by USF support, it would be difficult or often impossible to justify obtaining a loan and building a network in a high-cost area, precisely because the pricing of services would then need to be so high that no consumer or business could actually afford to buy those services. In fact, we are already seeing such concerns about affordability arise as it becomes increasingly apparent that USF programs are insufficiently funded, with many consumers still facing the prospect of paying hundreds of dollars per month for standalone broadband services even in the wake of recent FCC reforms intended to fix that problem.

In the wake of reform debates that stretched nearly a decade and created substantial uncertainty in recent years particularly, NTCA has made substantial efforts to restore regulatory certainty to the USF programs, both by working with the FCC on modernizing the programs to more directly support the delivery of broadband to consumers and by seeking more sufficient funding under a USF high-cost budget that had been held constant since 2010. Specifically, in March 2016, the FCC adopted an order that contained a series of reforms to the USF mechanisms upon which Pioneer and other small rural telcos rely to recover the costs of investment and ongoing operations in high-cost areas. The order defined options for telcos to elect either a "model-based" USF support mechanism that would provide carriers with additional support in exchange for incremental broadband buildout obligations or a reformed "non-model" USF support mechanism that would now provide support to enable more affordable broadband rates for rural consumers and businesses.

Unfortunately, even as the March 2016 order resolved some long-running reform debates and took several important steps to more directly orient the high-cost USF program toward broadband, the order did not address a fundamental concern – the lack of sufficient funding under a budget that effectively provides telcos with less revenue today than they had prior to reforms adopted in 2011. To be clear, the FCC thankfully did provide additional funding in the March 2016 order – $200 million per year – to help facilitate the "model option" as part of the reforms described above; these funds will certainly help enable the expansion of broadband in areas where it is lacking today. But demand for model support far exceeded supply, confirming the insufficiency of a budget that was otherwise held constant at 2010 support levels. In fact, even with the annual incremental infusion of $200 million in support, USF funding for the model remains approximately $110 million per year short of demand, meaning that tens of thousands of rural consumers will see lower speeds or no broadband at all as a result. The FCC is now seeking comment on whether and how to address this shortfall, and NTCA and a number of other stakeholders are urging the FCC to provide full funding to enable the business case for greater expansion of broadband.

But this unfortunately reflects only a portion of the USF funding shortfall that affect rural consumers. As noted earlier, the FCC also reformed the existing "non-model" USF mechanisms to more directly support consumer purchases of broadband services. While this was an important step that offers some promise and for which NTCA and its members were grateful, the fact is that the reforms only fixed the "mechanics" and did not address the underlying problem of insufficient funding. Indeed, due to the budget that has been flat since 2010, the non-model mechanisms look to be underfunded in the amount of at least $140 million this year, and as a result, the new budget control adopted as part of the reforms will cut an estimated 10 percent of USF support this year on average for companies like Pioneer – cutting recovery of costs that we have already incurred in deploying networks and delivering services to consumers. Moreover, the budget control can and will vary from period to period, undercutting the kind of predictability that is called for by law and needed when evaluating future investments. For Pioneer, for example, the unpredictability and impact of the budget control mechanism hits close to home, with our support having been reduced by approximately five percent of support in the last few months of 2016 and some estimates indicating that the budget control could increase to around nine percent this year. This loss of support due to the budget control will translate into higher prices for consumers for broadband, because the only other place we can turn to recover those costs are our consumers – and the unpredictable nature of the level of the budget control hinders our ability to plan for future investments in broadband networks.

Thus, as NTCA summarized in a recent filing with the FCC, "while much effort may have gone into rebuilding 'the engine' of non-model USF reforms, the ongoing lack of 'gasoline in that engine' (in the form of sufficient budget resources) risks rendering its operation inefficient at best and utterly ineffective at worst." This budget crisis – captured in the form of the new budget control mechanism – will deter customer purchases of standalone broadband and ultimately undermine additional deployment too, as small telcos will need to factor estimated support reductions into future planning efforts and scale back investments. Remedying this USF budget concern will be important if we are to achieve the kinds of network deployment progress and sustained delivery of affordable, high-quality broadband to consumers that this committee and many other members of Congress hope to see in rural America.

Rural Broadband Benefits the Entire U.S. Economy

For years, until uncertainty began to creep into the USF programs, the complementary cornerstones of RUS and other lending efforts on the one hand and the USF programs on the other hand worked well in concert to achieve substantial success in advancing rural telecommunications investments and sustaining rural telecom operations in the form of affordable rates for consumers. As discussed above, after years of reform debates and uncertainty, the FCC has taken steps to finally adopt and implement reforms as discussed above, but there is still much more work to be done to make sure the reforms and programs actually work as intended and that these cornerstones of access to capital and USF can once again operate in concert – and this is important because of what it means for the economy in rural America and nationwide.

Investing in rural broadband has far-reaching effects for both urban and rural America, creating efficiencies in health care, education, agriculture, energy, and commerce, and enhancing quality of life of citizens across the country. A series of studies confirms that significant benefits flow from rural broadband investment to broader urban and statewide populations. For example, a report released in April 2016 by the Hudson Institute in conjunction with the Foundation for Rural Service found that investment by rural broadband companies contributed $24.1 billion to the economies of the states in which they operated in 2015.[5] Of this amount, $17.2 billion was the direct byproduct of the rural broadband companies' own operations while $6.9 billion was attributable to the follow-on impact of their operations. In Kansas, the direct economic impact of rural telecommunications was $468 million with indirect impacts of $171.5 million.

The Hudson study also confirmed that while small telcos like Pioneer produce a range of telecommunications services in rural areas, the economic activity generated by such operations accrues both to the rural areas served and to urban areas as well. In fact, most of this benefit goes to urban than rural areas because many of the vendors, suppliers, and construction firms that rural telcos use are based in urban areas. Only $8.2 billion, or 34 percent of the $24.1 billion final economic demand generated by rural telecom companies accrues to rural areas; the other 66 percent or $15.9 billion accrues to the benefit of urban areas.

Additionally, the report found that the rural broadband industry supported nearly 70,000 jobs nationwide in 2015, including more than 1,200 jobs in Kansas, both through direct employment and indirect employment from the purchases of goods and services generated. Jobs supported by economic activity created by rural broadband companies are shared between rural and urban areas. Forty-six percent are in rural areas; 54 percent are in urban areas.

Other, earlier studies reinforce these findings. For example, the Center for Economic Development and Business Research at Wichita State University found that the total economic impact of Kansas rural telecom companies (in the form of direct wages and induced economic activity) averaged $137.2 million dollars a year between 2011 and 2014.[6] The companies included in the report spent an average of $98 million dollars per year on capital improvements to maintain and expand communication capacity in rural Kansas.

Of course, these referenced studies only look at the direct and indirect economic impact of the investments and operations of the telcos themselves. The broader socioeconomic benefits of broadband for *users* cannot be ignored. A Cornell University study, for example, found that rural counties with the highest levels of broadband adoption have the highest levels of income and education, and lower levels of unemployment and poverty.[7] A recent Pew Study further finds that among those Americans who have looked for work in the last two years, 79 percent utilized online resources in their most recent job search and 34% say these online resources were the most important tool available to them.[8]

---

[5] "The Economic Impact of Rural Broadband" (2016), The Hudson Institute, Washington, D.C.

[6] "Economic Impact of Kansas Independent Rural Telephone Companies" (2016), Center for Economic Development and Business Research, W. Frank Barton School of Business, Wichita State University.

[7] Broadband's Contribution to Economic Health in Rural Areas" (2015), Community & Regional Development Institute, Cornell University.

[8] Searching for Work in the Digital Era" (2015), Pew Research Center, Washington, D.C.

Access to healthcare is a critical issue for rural areas as well, where the lack of physicians, specialists, and diagnostic tools normally found in urban medical centers creates challenges for both patients and medical staff. Telemedicine applications help bridge the divide in rural America, enabling real-time patient consultations and remote monitoring, as well as specialized services such as tele-psychiatry. One study found that doctors in rural emergency rooms are more likely to alter their diagnosis and their patient's course of treatment after consulting with a specialist via a live, interactive videoconference.[9]

There is also a shortage of teachers in many areas of rural America and those public school districts rely on high-speed connectivity to deliver interactive-video instruction for foreign language, science and music classes. For example, students in rural Minnesota can attend online music classes offered through the MacPhail Center for Music in Minneapolis.[10] Broadband networks also enable farmers and ranchers to use the Internet to analyze weather data, manage nutrient application, map their crop yields, and adjust planting for the next season with modern precision agriculture tools, and gain access to new markets. Farmers are relying heavily on both wireless and wireline broadband technologies, resulting in monthly data usage of 30 to 40 Gigabytes.[11]

Retail e-commerce has benefited tremendously from sales in rural America as well, where consumers may lack access to local retail outlets, but through the availability of rural broadband networks, can access a variety of shopping options. According to the Hudson Institute, rural consumers generated $9.2 billion in online sales in 2015 and if all rural Americans had access to broadband networks, the authors estimate that Internet sales would be $1 billion higher.[12]

Conclusion

Entrepreneurial small rural carriers have leveraged public and private capital, universal service support, and public-private partnerships to lead a stunning technological revolution in many parts of rural America. These small businesses play an essential role in deploying broadband to rural areas, and the services enabled by broadband are essential to the startup, operation, and growth of other rural small businesses. Rural America is poised for a bright future powered by smart technologies that promote affordability, sustainability, and efficiency in the operation of rural industry and the delivery of essential services such as healthcare, education, and public safety – all key to sustaining and growing rural population. But such benefits will only be possible if robust broadband is available, affordable and sustainable. Rural telecom providers and lenders such as RUS must have regulatory certainty before they can justify greater investments in

[9] "Telemedicine Consultations and Medication Errors in Rural Emergency Departments" (2013), Center for Healthcare Policy and Research and Departments of Pediatrics, University of California Davis.

[10] "Bringing Broadband to Rural Minnesota" (2016), Center for Rural Policy and Development, Mankato, MN.

[11] "Farmers Harvest Gigabytes with Broadband and Wireless Technology" (2016), CoBank Rural Infrastructure Briefings.

[12] "The Economic Impact of Rural Broadband" (2016), The Hudson Institute, Washington, D.C.

the networks of the future, and providers like Pioneer need sufficient ongoing USF support to avoid the prospect of charging rural consumers tens or hundreds of dollars more per month to recover the costs of operating in such rural and remote locations.

Much of the focus in today's broadband policy debates is on what it takes to "get broadband out there." That is an essential question to be sure, and financing programs like those available through RUS and the few other lenders I have mentioned are the most time-tested, effective means of doing so. Yet, just as important is the question of what is needed to "keep broadband out there" – to ensure that rural broadband networks once built can be maintained, that the services atop them remain affordable, reliable, and of a quality comparable to what urban Americans can get. Thus, the mission of universal service – and the economic benefits it delivers locally and to the nation as a whole – requires the resourcefulness and entrepreneurship of small businesses like Pioneer, access to capital from programs like those offered by RUS, and the availability of sufficient and predictable ongoing cost recovery mechanisms like the USF program so that rural consumers and businesses can indeed obtain services that reasonably comparable in price and quality to those available in urban America.

Statement for the Record by Richard B. Myers, President Kansas State University, before the Senate Committee on Agriculture, United States Senate, February 23, 2017

Introduction

Chairwoman Roberts, it is indeed my pleasure to welcome you, on behalf of Kansas State University, to the campus of Kansas State University your Alma Mater. We are pleased to have you in Kansas and we thank you, and value your leadership in the work of this important committee. Senator Stabenow, welcome to Kansas and Kansas State University.

Today, I would like to also welcome our valued friends and stakeholders to this hearing today at Kansas State. Without question, this group represents a broad range of interests that are all, in one way or the other, impacted by the health and vitality of Kansas and US agriculture.

The Land-Grant System

There is another way in which it is fitting that testimony on behalf of the 2018 Farm Bill begins in Kansas. Kansas State and Michigan State maintain a friendly banter around which school was the first and which school the second land grant university. The Morrill Act which established of the land grant system was enacted in 1862. The Kansas Legislature on February 16, 1863 accepted the Morrill Act and designated Kansas State University as the Land Grant University in Kansas. At the time that federal legislation was signed by President Lincoln, little could he or the authors of the bill have imagined the implications of the act. The partnership that was developed between the states and the federal government with the enactment of the Morrill Act and the follow on Hatch and Smith-Lever Acts have been the backbone of agriculture, agriculture research and outreach for one hundred and fifty five years in our country.

Kansas State University

K-State Research and Extension serves as the front door to Kansas State University the state's land-grant university. We provide trusted, practical education to help individuals, businesses and communities solve problems, develop skills and build a better future. A few examples of the work performed on behalf of Kansas and American agriculture.

Wheat Breeding

The world's population is expected to reach 9.6 billion by 2050. To feed and sustain a growing population, we develop innovative practices that benefit Kansas, our nation and the world. Through cutting-edge research in areas such as genetics, disease prevention and food security, we help agriculture — Kansas' largest employer — be more profitable, sustainable and efficient.

With a name befitting its place at the summit of Kansas agriculture, the K-State-produced wheat variety called Everest just completed its fourth year as the top variety planted across the state — and the fifth time out of the last six years that a K-State variety has held the top spot. Everest was first released in 2009.

Sorghum Interests Cooperate to Promote Growth

As a global leader in sorghum research and promotion, K-State co-founded a unique coalition with industry leaders and producers. In early 2016, the Kansas Grain Sorghum Commission, United Sorghum Checkoff Program, Kansas Department of Agriculture and K-State formed the Collaborative Sorghum Investment Program. The program focuses on expanding markets for sorghum and increasing the average national sorghum yield from 62 bushels per acre to 100 bushels per acre by 2025 by funding research in such areas as plant breeding, genetics and field-level management.

In terms of national rankings, Kansas is the No. 1 producer of sorghum, but in terms of statewide acreage and return, it ranks behind wheat, corn and soybeans. K-State coordinates these efforts through the Center for Sorghum Improvement, which aims to achieve major advances because farmers have not seen private technology investments in sorghum for the last couple decades. Those advances will come from work currently being done in labs at K-State and in test fields across Kansas.

Along with seeking improvements on the front end of production, the center is also working on the back end: growing and opening markets for sorghum. This includes building the case for more sorghum use in livestock feed, entering the $24 billion pet food industry and creating products for people that capitalize on food-grade sorghum as a gluten-free, low-glycemic index product high in antioxidants.

Local Food Hub Benefits Farmers, Consumers

Five years ago, it seemed like a simple idea: find a way to help smallholder farmers in Kansas sell the food they grow to more people. K-State Research and Extension helps farmers become more efficient, more profitable and more self-sustaining. We also assist consumers and communities. Local food-system development is community vitality.

The food hub is a producer cooperative that goes beyond selling food at local farmers markets. The food hub helps farmers sell their products to larger buyers, such as restaurants, hospitals, schools and food companies.

Today, smallholder farmers in Kansas have numerous options for providing their goods through the food hub. This food hub allows K-State Research and Extension to think critically about how to grow the local food system in a way which invests back into Kansas farmers and also benefits Kansas communities and consumers.

Bio Agro Defense

As you know Senator Roberts thanks to your herculean effort the National Bio and Agro Defense Facility is under construction on the campus of Kansas State. Kansas State is steadfast in protecting agriculture. Last month the Blue Ribbon Study Panel held a hearing at Kansas State University. Panel member and former U. S. Senate Majority Leader Tom Daschle referred to K-State that day as "the Silicon Valley for biodefense" a designation we take seriously and will proudly accept and continue to strive to maintain.

Again Senators Stabenow and Roberts for traveling to Kansas State for this hearing in our nation's heartland. We are proud you chose our campus to gather important information on the future of agriculture.

Testimony of Kathleen O'Brien (Kathy), General Manager, Nemaha-Marshall Electric Cooperative, Senate Agriculture Committee Hearing, "Hearing from the Heartland: Perspectives on the 2018 Farm Bill from Kansas," February 23, 2017, Manhattan, KS

Thank you, Chairman Roberts and Ranking Member Stabenow, for inviting me to testify. My name is Kathy O'Brien. I am the General Manager of Nemaha-Marshall Electric Cooperative in Axtell, Kansas. I am here representing my own co-op, the Kansas

Electric Cooperative Association, and the National Rural Electric Cooperative Association.

Nemaha-Marshall Electric Cooperative delivers electricity to around 3500 homes, farms, and businesses in northeast Kansas. Nemaha-Marshall was incorporated in 1938 by rural residents to serve rural consumers in all of Nemaha and Marshall Counties and parts of Washington, Pottawatomie, and Jackson counties. Our co-op builds and maintains over 1500 miles of electric distribution line.

While our first business priority is to deliver reliable, affordable electricity to our members, our purpose is much greater than that. We exist to benefit the communities we serve. We are more than just a poles, wires, and electrons company. Our broader purpose is to provide the power that empowers our communities to thrive. We are much more than just small electric utilities - we are the engines that drive economic opportunity across the heartland and rural areas everywhere.

We've been keeping the lights on in rural America for almost 80 years, and that's as important a job today as it ever has been. Some parts of Kansas have actually become less densely populated since then. In fact, Nemaha-Marshall's service territory still averages only about two houses per mile. The cooperative business model is uniquely suited to meet the needs of these consumers.

Rural areas still grow most of the food, generate most of the power, and manufacture most of the goods that this country consumes. When rural areas suffer, electric cooperatives suffer and, more importantly, the country as a whole suffers. That's why the Farm Bill is *essential* for co-ops, for Kansas, and for the country. The Farm Bill contains important rural development tools that support our efforts to strengthen our communities. I want to talk about just a few.

Rural Utilities Service (RUS)

In the early 1900's, as urban areas began to electrify, rural areas lagged behind. Eventually, farmers and ranchers in remote areas took the initiative to form electric cooperatives and did it themselves. In 1936, the Rural Electrification Act formalized the partnership that allowed electric cooperatives to access affordable credit from the federal government to finance that infrastructure. In the past 80 years, a lot has changed, but the same fundamental challenge still exists – how to affordably connect those few customers in high cost rural areas. What was then called the Rural Electrification Administration is now the Rural Utilities Service and it's as relevant today as it was back then. REA and RUS loans have helped build, expand, and improve the infrastructure across rural America necessary to provide power, deliver clean water, and other necessities. It's been the most successful public-private infrastructure investment program in the history of the country.

RUS loans help electric co-ops reduce costs and improve reliability for our members by financing basic maintenance like replacing poles and wires. But it also helps us fund projects to make our systems more modern, efficient, and secure. It might be hard to believe, but as recently as ten years ago at Nemaha-Marshall, many of our member-customers read their own meters and figured their own bill using a rate chart. Today, thanks to RUS, we read our meters remotely, which is much more accurate, efficient, and cost effective.

RUS depends on a yearly appropriation from the Agriculture Appropriations bill. We have historically enjoyed strong support for robust funding for RUS, in large part because we're such a good investment for the federal government. The President's Budget request for 2017 estimates that the federal government could earn up to $300 million in net revenue from RUS loans. We ask that you help us maintain that support.

We also ask that you support policies that allow us to use RUS loans to address a broad set of co-op needs – whether for renewable generation, baseload generation, or for making environmental upgrades to existing generation. Just as the times have changed and the needs of rural America have changed, so too has the RUS loan program. We have appreciated working with the Committee over the years to help make the program more streamlined and efficient, and we look forward to exploring new ways to continue to improve the program. Modernizing the RUS loan program is good for both borrowers (electric co-ops) and taxpayers. The RUS annually reviews and approves billions of dollars of loans, and finding ways to more efficiently process those loans reduces burdens on taxpayers while meeting borrowers' needs more quickly as well.

Guaranteed Underwriter Program

Another important financing option available to electric cooperatives is loans from cooperative banks. Co-op banks add healthy competition to the marketplace. The Farm Bill contains a provision that allows those loans to be guaranteed by RUS for cooperative business purposes. We encourage you to continue that policy.

In addition to investing in the electric cooperative network, the fees paid on Guaranteed Underwriter Loans can be used to fund Rural Economic Development Loans and Grants – known as the REDL&G program.

Rural Economic Development Loans and Grants (REDL&G)

Under the REDL&G program, USDA provides zero-interest loans to utilities (including electric co-ops), which, in turn, pass the funds through to local businesses and other groups that create jobs in rural areas. This positive cycle of business development can strengthen both the co-op and the local communities by helping stabilize populations and the co-op's customer base.

During the last ten years, 81 REDL&G projects totaling $49 million were responsible for 2100 jobs in rural Kansas. Included among those projects are grocery stores, health care facilities, libraries, and new fire trucks just to name a few. We believe that the program is a valuable tool in offsetting population flight and job losses in rural Kansas.

Five years ago when I was here, I gave an example of how the REDL&G program works in my hometown of Seneca, Kansas. Back then, I described how a local employer, Koch and Company, a cabinet and door manufacturer, received a $450,000 REDL&G loan in 2004 for a cabinet plant expansion. The project created 55 new jobs and retained 185 jobs at that time. Since then, Koch has continued to expand and in 2016 had annual revenue of $85 million. That's up from $40 million when I was before the Committee back in 2011. They now employ 650 employees in multiple states, more than doubling during the last five years. That is an excellent return on investment.

Energy Efficiency

For years, electric co-ops across the country have provided information and advice to consumers to help them use electricity more efficiently and cost-effectively. The wide range of assistance includes rebates for energy-efficient appliances, switching to more energy efficient light bulbs, and time of day rates to encourage off-peak usage. Here in Kansas, Midwest Energy has pioneered an innovative partnership with its members to allow "on bill" financing of energy efficient improvements made to a customer's home. They call it the HomeSmart Program. In short, Midwest helps the consumer finance these improvements who then pays back that loan every month through their bill. Even with the loan payment, consumers' bills tend to go down because of the energy savings associated with these improvements.

The Rural Energy Savings Program Act included in the last Farm Bill was modeled in part on the Kansas HomeSmart program. We encourage you to maintain the Rural Energy Savings Program, the Energy Efficiency and Conservation Loan Program, and the Rural Energy for America Program. We believe these are all important tools that can help replicate Kansas's successes around the country.

Regulations

The federal government should have a reasonable regulatory philosophy that recognizes the stewardship that stakeholders like electric cooperatives have taken in the communities we serve.

For example, NRECA has concerns with the Waters of the U.S. rule issued by the EPA and the Army Corps of Engineers. Electric cooperatives conduct several activities associated with providing electric service which require Clean Water Act permits. We believe this rule could drastically broaden the types of work that trigger the need to get a permit, possibly including routine repair and replacement of poles and wires. That would result in increased costs and decreased reliability for our customers. We urge the EPA and the Corps to engage in a meaningful dialogue with all stakeholders to craft a new rule that takes into account the concerns of those who provide essential services to rural communities.

NRECA also recently filed comments with the U.S. Fish and Wildlife service opposing the listing of the Lesser Prairie Chicken under the Endangered Species Act. We believe that our work with state wildlife agencies to enact voluntary conservation measures is paying big dividends. We've helped manage more than ten million acres in five states which has helped the Lesser Prairie Chicken population to stabilize, without having to resort to a more burdensome bureaucratic approach.

Broadband

Just as with other types of infrastructure, rural America can't be competitive without access to high speed broadband service. Many comparisons are drawn between the lack access to robust broadband service today and the need for electrification in rural areas 80 years ago - with the urban areas of the country well-served, and rural areas being left behind. Some electric co-ops around the country are leading the way in connecting rural customers to high speed broadband. As Congress contemplates telecommunication and infrastructure policies in the farm bill and in other legislative packages, we believe that all potential providers including electric cooperatives should be eligible for programs designed to bridge the digital divide.

Conclusion

We are a healthy nation because we have vibrant, bustling urban cities AND because we have verdant, productive rural areas. Unfortunately, whether it's infrastructure or jobs or access to health care, it seems that too often rural America gets the short end of the stick. The Farm Bill is important legislation that helps to address some of those disparities.

Electric Cooperatives enjoy a productive partnership with the federal government and with the communities we serve to promote the health of rural America. We look forward to continuing to work with you toward that important goal. I'm happy to answer any of your questions.

Testimony of Gena Ott, Financial Officer, Frontier Farm Credit, before the Senate Committee on Agriculture, Nutrition & Forestry, Field Hearing, February 23, 2017

Mr. Chairman and Ranking Member Stabenow, thank you for the opportunity to testify today on behalf of Frontier Farm Credit. My name is Gena Ott, and I am a financial officer serving borrower-owners of our eastern Kansas cooperative lending Association, based in the Emporia, Kansas, office. I am a 32-year employee of the Farm Credit System, having served in both lending and crop insurance roles.

My testimony today will provide an overview of the credit conditions across the Frontier Farm Credit territory in eastern Kansas. I will share examples of some of the decisions producers are facing and the ways our Association is working with them to make the most of their options. I will highlight the role that crop insurance plays as a safety net for customers and provide information regarding the role of Frontier Farm Credit in serving diverse needs in agriculture and rural communities. Moreover, I will share the ways in which my Association collaborates with other organizations to fulfill our mission.

Frontier Farm Credit is part of the nationwide Farm Credit System, serving the eastern third of Kansas. The Association has $2 billion in loan volume, which increased by 3.4% in 2016. The Board of Directors declared a $9 million cash-back dividend from 2016 earnings that will be paid to cooperative members this spring. Loan repayment capacity in our portfolio is largely dependent upon income from corn, soybeans, wheat and cattle. Many of our customers are also dependent on off-farm income, though the level varies widely. Government program payments related to corn, soybeans, wheat, the Conservation Reserve Program, and the Conservation Stewardship Program are also a source of income for many customers.

As my colleagues in our risk management and credit roles assess the ag economy, they view Midwest agriculture conditions as follows. Generally, the upper 50 to 60 percent of our grain producers are and have been holding their own if not showing some level of profitability, though minor. The bottom 15 to 20 percent of grain producers are those with a combination of higher debt load, higher cost of production, and overall lack of profitability; they are having to make considerable adjustments to try to put them in a position of viability to weather this change in the ag cycle. The lower performing percent, after two to three years now of losses, are in a position of vulnerability and their adjustments are more significant – including major changes to the scope of their operation, selling of assets, and for some, considering exiting production agriculture. Those in between the upper 60 percent and lower 20 percent present a mixed bag of situations, but generally still have options due to their overall equity position.

Cattle producers continue to brace for the future. After a 3 percent increase last year, cow numbers are expected to grow another 3.5 percent by year-end – back up to 1995 levels. Fed cattle prices and margins will continue to be under pressure, although cattle feeders will continue to see relief from lower calf prices. Fed cattle prices in the $1 - $1.20/lb. range are most probable, and packer margins will narrow.

Those of us who work with farmers and ranchers have been in a mode of talking with our customers to help them assess their operations and have been encouraging them to manage their risk. In return, we hear from our customers the importance of strong markets and regulatory reform for the viability of their farms and ranches.

As a financial officer, I have been having conversations about the four "Rs" of overhead and/or fixed costs. When a producer owns land, it may be a good time to look to Re-amortize it. For machinery and equipment, now may be the right time to Refinance. With rented land, leases and terms of the lease may lead to conversations with landowners to Renegotiate. And, for family living expenses, it's a time to Re-assess.

For many customers, as the previous numbers would indicate, the cycle we are in will allow them room to adjust. However, some may make more far-reaching decisions. In all cases, these conversations are individual to the customer and to the operation, and we will work with them every step of the way.

Growing a farm or ranch is a significant financial commitment and can be especially challenging for less-established producers. Frontier Farm Credit makes extraordinary efforts to support young, beginning and small farmers and ranchers. There are 3,871 individual young, beginning and small customers at Frontier, comprising more than 58 percent of our customers and representing $630 million lent to this segment. Of those, 1,219 are young and beginning, representing $206 million in credit. Specialized lending programs, such as our AgStart program, include a full line of products with customized underwriting and modified credit approval standards for farmers age 35 or younger or with 10 years of experience or less.

Frontier Farm Credit also offers a unique Development Fund that provides both business planning assistance and working capital loans to young and beginning farmers and ranchers. Young producers haven't enjoyed earnings to build the working capital that is crucial in building an operation and sustaining a cushion for adversity.

The development fund injects cash (working capital) into an operation and requires only interest payments for five years. The customer at the end of five years then establishes a repayment plan for any balance remaining on the note. Participating producers have completed a five-year cash flow, a business and market analysis, and a detailed business plan complete with mission statement, objectives and strategies to achieve their objectives. The business plan also includes a risk management plan (including calculating break-evens and utilizing crop insurance Revenue Protection at a 75 percent level). Participants also establish a financial plan that helps keep them focused and includes working capital goals.

I recently met with one of our Development Fund customers. He's in the second year of the program, and we are about to update his five-year plan. He has picked up additional ground for 2017, which is exciting, and requires more working capital. It's our desire to be his financial partner and help him succeed by not only providing funds but also helping him develop business and financial management skills that will help him fulfill his dream to have a career in agriculture that provides for him and his family.

Mr. Chairman and Ranking Member Stabenow, I want to thank both of you for your commitment to crop insurance. It is an important public-private partnership, and a critical risk management tool for farmers. The strength of the current crop insurance partnership rests in the ability for a farmer, or rancher, to select products that meets their needs for individualized risk management.

As an example, the foresight of producers who purchased crop insurance in 2012 mitigated the direct financial impact on their operations even though final corn and soybean yields were significantly below trend lines for both crops as a result of drought that year. Farmers bought revenue protection coverage at levels of 70 percent or greater on more than 90 percent of insured corn acres within Frontier Farm Credit's territory. Of the 128 crops covered by crop insurance, the categories that suffered the most damage in 2012 were corn, wheat, cotton, soybeans, pasture, rangeland and forage.

Crop insurance performed as it was intended: though each case is different, farmers who purchased crop insurance generally received income that would at least cover their investment in the 2012 crop. That means most were able to plant again in 2013, continuing to produce feed, food and energy and averting consumer inflation. They also were able to make purchases at their neighbors' stores and other businesses, which helped support the economy in every local community. That insurance meant that producers were able to maintain obligations with their creditors. Finally, the insurance program also averted the need for ad hoc disaster assistance.

As a lender in the Flint Hills of Kansas, I would also call your attention to Livestock Risk Protection (LRP) and the Pasture, Rangeland and Forage Product (PRF). LRP and PRF have been important products for cattle producers. Frontier Farm Credit has been regionally active with these products in the marketplace.

The culture of Frontier Farm Credit encourages collaboration in the communities we serve and within the industry. Our Working Here Fund provides grants for projects and organizations that make a positive impact in the eastern Kansas counties we serve. Grants are focused on the areas of ag education, young and beginning producers, and hunger and nutrition. Grants are also considered for essential services and disaster relief needs in rural communities.

Recently, Greenwood County, Kansas, used this program to enhance their fairgrounds. When a storm damaged the livestock barns there in 2014, the aftermath revealed the need for not just repair, but new facilities altogether. Dollars helped spur additional fundraising, and assisted in growing not only the new building, but also excitement with two new 4-H clubs in the county.

Frontier Farm Credit also provided Working Here Fund support for the FFA garden in Marion, Kansas. Students there engage local residents and provide fresh produce to a local food pantry. Students are learning and helping to feed others in their community.

More than a decade ago, leaders from Kansas ag organizations and Kansas State University established the Women Managing the Farm Conference to encourage women to come together and develop the knowledge and skills needed for success in a competitive agricultural environment. Women represent central roles in the agricultural heritage that builds and sustains communities throughout the world. According to the 2012 Census of Agriculture, women are the principal operators of 6,783 farms in Kansas, and there are 25,611 total women farm operators in the state. Further, women have a variety of other roles in farming operations, including those who inherit ag land.

I've had the privilege with my Farm Credit colleagues to be involved on the steering committee and as a presenter for Women Managing the Farm. Demand for this statewide program remains strong, and local groups continue to emerge. We recognize the support and engagement of USDA in these programs and welcome their continued involvement.

Frontier Farm Credit assisted in formation of the Kansas Farmer Veteran Coalition, and provides credit education when needed for veteran training events. We welcome opportunities for involvement in future events and commend the veterans who have taken on leadership roles in these organizations. Similarly, Frontier Farm Credit has been a partner with the SAVE Farm (Service-member Agricultural Vocation Education). Financial Officers provide participants with credit training as they make decisions regarding their future opportunities in agriculture.

Collaborative opportunities are important, and we would hope that the spirit of public policy encourages federal agencies to be at the table as we engage with all segments of agriculture. Thank you for the opportunity to share the ways in which Frontier Farm Credit is involved in supporting the next generation of producers, rural communities, and diverse agriculture across Eastern Kansas.

We know that you, the leadership of this committee, understand the challenges facing rural communities and agriculture, the challenges that lie ahead with respect to the Farm Bill, the importance of crop insurance as a safety net to farmers and ranchers. We thank you for your support and ask that you share your knowledge and experiences with your colleagues to help them understand, too, as you work through the process of another Farm Bill.

Chairman Roberts, it is always great to have you back home and we are proud of the work you do every day on behalf of our state. Thank you, Ranking Member Stabenow, for coming to Kansas to listen. Thank you, again, for this opportunity to share the story of Farm Credit in eastern Kansas and I look forward to your questions.

Written Testimony Presented before the Senate Agriculture, Nutrition and Forestry Committee, Hearing from the Heartland: Perspectives on the 2018 Farm Bill from Kansas, February 23, 2017, by Derek Peine, Chairman, Renew Kansas, CEO, Western Plains Energy, LLC

Chairman Roberts, Ranking Member Stabenow, and distinguished members of the Senate Committee on Agriculture, Nutrition, and Forestry, thank you for the opportunity to testify before you today regarding the 2018 Farm Bill and the roll the ethanol industry in Kansas and America plays in the agriculture economy and rural communities.

My name is Derek Peine, and I am here today representing Renew Kansas. Renew Kansas is the trade association that represents the independent ethanol production facilities in our state and those who provide services to the Kansas ethanol production industry. Renew Kansas serves as a central contact for the Kansas ethanol industry, and as a clearinghouse for accurate, reliable information about the many benefits of using ethanol blends to power our vehicles.

I currently serve as chairman of the Renew Kansas Board, and I am also the CEO of Western Plains Energy, LLC, an ethanol plant located in Northwest Kansas. Western Plains Energy produces 50 million gallons of denatured ethanol annually and employs a team of 48 people.

Today I want to talk about the relationship between producers of agricultural products, the ethanol industry, the animal feed industry, and rural America in general. Each of these groups play a key role in the American economy, and the success of each group is directly linked to the success of the others.

Let me start by sharing a key point about the ethanol industry. Western Plains Energy, like most ethanol plants today, was founded with two goals in mind. First, an ethanol plant would provide additional value for the producer's grain by creating additional local demand. Second, an ethanol plant would provide needed jobs and additional economic value to the communities in region in Northwest Kansas. These two goals are as relevant and as important today as they have ever been.

Positive for Kansas and the United States Economy

There are 12 dry mill ethanol plants currently in operation in Kansas, producing about 550 million gallons of ethanol per year. This production creates a local market for approximately 200 million bushels of sorghum and corn, utilizing about 20 percent of corn and sorghum production in Kansas. Unlike many other areas in the country, ethanol produced in Kansas has the ability to utilize these two different feedstocks interchangeably in the ethanol production process. In addition, one-third of the grain used for ethanol returns to the food stream as wet or dry distillers grains, a valued, high-nutrient livestock feed.

These facilities provide a stable domestic market for agricultural producers during a time of volatile challenges such as weather and decreased commodity prices. The ethanol industry also provides a consistent supply of high quality distiller grains for Kansas feed yards and dairies. Each of the ethanol production plants in Kansas are located in a rural area, and they provide more than 380 direct jobs across the state with an average salary of over $50,000. Kansas ethanol production annually provides over $2 million in real property taxes, $100,000 in personal property taxes, and $53 million in trucking fees.[13] With regard to the United States economy, annually, the industry sustains nearly 400,000

[13] Source: Kansas Legislative Research Department Study.

jobs, contributes $44 billion to the US GDP, and added $24 billion to household incomes.[14]

Positive for American Agriculture

It is to the benefit of all Americans to ensure a healthy US agriculture sector that is able to consistently provide food and nutrition for all of us. I believe that the ethanol industry has provided the greatest contribution to agriculture profitability in my life time.

For years, producers were plagued with oversupply of their commodity products which resulted in stagnant pricing. In fact, corn carryout values peaked at nearly 5 billion bushels in 1986 from an 8.2-billion-bushel crop and an export value of nearly 1.5 billion bushels. Then there was a paradigm shift. With regulatory support from the Renewable Fuel Standard, the ethanol industry began to grow. This growth provided a localized end-use for corn and sorghum crops, which helped to provide pricing support of those crops. Each year, technology has improved to allow producers to obtain increasing grain production yields. And each year, the ethanol industry has consumed more and more of that grain. Data from the past 36 years (1980-2016) reveals that corn yields have improved an average of nearly 2 bushels per acre per year (based on a straight-line average), growing from around 91 bushels per acre in 1980 to the record-setting 174.6 bushels per acre in 2016. During this same time period, exports have been flat (based on a straight-line average). Corn demand, including distiller grain demand, by the feed sector has increased modestly during this same time frame.

When we talk with our nearly 200 local farmers who provide us corn and sorghum, we hear repeatedly how important a strong, predictable farm safety net is to their operations. Many of them cite the federal crop insurance program as something that greatly helps them be able to finance their capital intensive farming operations. In order for our business to be successful, a symbiotic relationship exists: we need a strong farm economy to keep productive and innovative farmers on the land, and they need us as a strong, consistent, local market for their grain.

Today, corn producers face the familiar situation of oversupply and depressed pricing. We have just experienced the largest corn crop in US history and the largest corn crop in Kansas history, and the projected carryout from this past harvest is expected to be 2.3 billion bushels. Looking ahead to the future, increasing yield numbers are likely to continue to create larger corn production numbers, putting even more downward pressure on commodity pricing.

The good news is that the ethanol industry stands ready to help. Our industry has been working hard to create additional demand on both ethanol, and subsequently on corn, and to actively position the industry for increased production capacity.

---

[14] Source: J. Urbanchuk, ABF Economics LLP.

First, Renew Kansas and the ethanol production industry have been actively developing additional domestic ethanol markets, namely markets for E15 (a mixture of 15% ethanol and 85% gasoline). We have worked successfully with the privately funded Prime the Pump program and USDA's Biofuels Infrastructure Program to provide E15 to consumers at 640 locations across 28 states.[15] By the end of 2017, these numbers are expected to grow to more than 1,000 locations.[16]

Within our state, Renew Kansas is a proud partner of the Kansas Better Blends Initiative (KBBI), which is an alliance of key partners in the ethanol industry that is utilizing USDA's Biofuels Infrastructure Program. In addition to our association, other KBBI partners include the Kansas Department of Agriculture, Kansas Corn Commission, Kansas Grain Sorghum Commission, United Sorghum Checkoff Program, and ICM, Inc. These organizations have committed matching funds and in-kind services to make this program a success. The USDA Grant is administered by the Kansas Department of Agriculture, and in total, KBBI will make available $2.23 million directly to retailers for installation of new or retrofit equipment here in Kansas.

We have also focused on increasing ethanol demand internationally. Ethanol exports have been growing, and we surpassed the 1-billion-gallon mark in 2016. And the trade programs authorized under the Farm Bill have been key in helping the ethanol industry unlock additional trading partners. Keeping USDA Foreign Ag Service trade promotion available to ethanol is a key component to ensuring we can expand our export opportunities.

While there is much optimism about foreign markets for ethanol, I would be remiss if I did not mention trade restrictions from China that have shut out American ethanol exports and have also reduced the demand for ethanol distiller grains. The recent increases from 5% to 30% tariff on US ethanol and approximately 70% total tariff on US distillers by China have significant impact on US exports. While not related to the Farm Bill, these restrictions will hamper the ethanol industry from helping farmers have a stronger marketplace for their grain.

The combination of increasing the ethanol concentration in our domestic fuel supply and increased exports can help relieve the current over-supply of domestic corn. This would also provide the country and the agriculture community a consistent solution for the increased crop production in future years.

The ethanol industry is also poised to increase production capacity. Innovation is driving plants to produce more ethanol from the same bushel of corn through both increased conversion yields and the addition of cellulosic ethanol. Yes, it is finally here. Cellulosic ethanol production is finally a commercially available option for existing ethanol plants. Not only are plants able to convert the starch in grain to ethanol, but they are now able to convert some of the fiber in the grain to ethanol as well. Beyond

[15] Growth Energy.

[16] Growth Energy.

cellulosic, there has also been considerable development to allow plants to get more throughput through the existing assets with nominal capital investments. These combined technological improvements make it possible to for us to expand production capacity to accommodate the expected increase in corn production.

Continued Support for Ethanol Provides Continued Support for Agriculture

The ethanol industry can provide immediate support to grain pricing by increasing ethanol production capacity. To support increased capacity, we must increase both domestic and international demand for ethanol. This is where you can help.

As committee members, and policy makers, we respectfully request that you advocate for policies supportive of renewable fuels – including those not related to the Farm Bill. Supportive policies will provide confidence to grain producers that there will be demand for their product, and it will provide confidence to existing ethanol producers and investors to continue to aggressively pursue innovation and improvements.

Specifically, we ask that you support E15 as an option for consumers. E15 is a federally approved fuel for all vehicles 2001 and newer, and there has been a strong commitment by both the industry and the government to build the refueling infrastructure needed to expand the availability of this fuel. To turn away from E15 now would mean reduced ethanol demand in both the short and long-term, hurting a key market for farmers.

I also want to touch on a regulatory hurdle and market barrier to entry that impacts the E15 marketplace. Due to a 26-year old legislative oversight, even though E15 is a less expensive, higher performing fuel, it cannot be sold like E10 during the summer months. This is because of statutory Reid Vapor Pressure (RVP) restrictions. And legislation will be introduced in the House and the Senate to address this issue.

RVP is a measurement of evaporative emissions from motor vehicles. Under the Clean Air Act, RVP is capped at 9 pounds per square inch (psi). E10 comes in at around 10 psi, but given the fuel's favorable environmental profile it was issued a one-pound waiver under the 1990 Clean Air Act Amendments. As the ethanol level in gasoline increases, the RVP decreases, resulting in a cleaner fuel. While the RVP of E15 is less than E10, measuring between 9 and 10 psi, it does not receive the same waiver as E10, making retailers comply with two separate RVP levels. Because of this, fuel retailers are not allowed to sell E15 in certain areas of the country during the summer months, even though it is a cleaner fuel than E10.

For retailers already selling E15, this causes confusion for their clientele who have become accustomed to using a less expensive and better performing fuel in E15. While they can purchase E15 the same way as E10 on May 31, from June 1 to September 15 they are advised that the exact same fuel they just purchased will not be available to them for several months. Most importantly, this acts as an illogical barrier to fuel retailers who are interested in offering E15, but shy away because of the implications of not being able to sell a fuel year-around. In all of this, it is the consumer who suffers. Americans should have the option to choose what kind of fuel they use, not be subjected to a "one size fits all" rule. By fixing this RVP issue, consumers will have the choice of using a cleaner, higher performing, less expensive fuel.

I also wanted to briefly touch on the Renewable Fuel Standard (RFS), the bedrock policy of America's ethanol industry. Corn ethanol is an earth-friendly biofuel that reduces greenhouse gas emissions by an average of 43 percent, while some advanced biofuels can reduce emissions by 100 percent or more over gasoline. It is because of the market access granted by the RFS that we have 12 ethanol plants in Kansas today. While this policy is not related to the Farm Bill, it is absolutely a critical component to the success of farmers here in Kansas and America.

I wanted to close by thanking the Chairman and the Committee for allowing me the opportunity to testify here today. We are proud of the work that America's ethanol industry does to help the American farmer and rancher succeed. We believe very strongly that a healthy farm and ranch sector is critical to our success. Farmers provide grain to our facilities, and ranchers utilize the feed product we produce.

The work you are doing today to develop a strong farm bill is critical to the work we do to produce feed and fuel, and we hope that our positive message will help you produce a solid, predictable Farm bill in Washington, D.C.

Again, thank you for your time today.

Respectfully submitted, Derek Peine

Statement of the Kansas Sunflower Commission, Farm Bill Field Hearing, February 2, 2017

Thank you Senator Roberts, Senator Stabenow and distinguished members of the Committee. Welcome to Kansas, my name is Cameron Peirce, I am from Hutchinson, Kansas in Reno County, I am so pleased you have chosen Kansas as one venue to listen to the impact of Farm Bill programs and funding on Midwestern producers. I currently serve as the Vice-Chairman of the Kansas Sunflower Commission; I hope to give you some insight into the importance of Farm Bill programs to sunflower growers and to all commodity producers in Kansas. It is a great honor for me to represents the thousands of farmers who produce these commodities.

First I will give you some quick facts about sunflowers in Kansas and nationwide. Annually, Kansas plants between 65,000 and 90,000 of oil seed and confection sunflowers. In 2016 USDA estimated 1.6 million acres of sunflowers were planted nationwide. Oil seed production makes up 1.4 million of those acres with non-oil about 200,000 acres. Almost all of those acres are planted in eight mid-western States. The US shipped over 70,000 metric tons of confection sunflowers overseas and nearly 39,000 metric tons of sunflower oil in 2016.

Similar to other commodities, the market price for sunflower has declined over the past three years while international production has increased, making it increasingly difficult for farms to be profitable. $18.65 million have been paid to sunflower base acres in the first to years of the current Farm Bill. In these challenging times, Farm Bill programs, and particularly the risk management programs, are a vital food security mechanism that keeps American food safe and affordable. I am sure you aware Farm Bill dollars are infused back into rural America through purchases of farm goods and services, agriculture inputs and everyday household needs. They are a part of the financial equation that keeps rural America whole. More importantly, these programs keep American agriculture successful and give producers a vital safety net. The volatility of weather and markets are unpredictable for the Kansas farmer, having a safety net in place ensures safe and affordable food can continue to be produced in Kansas and across the United States.

As we look at the future of the Farm Bill we hope you and your fellow Senators understand how important agriculture is to the success of the rural parts of our country. Volatility in agriculture markets is managed with good practices and farm diversification. The same principles apply when it comes to funding of programs within the Farm Bill. We sincerely hope the appropriators in Washington will allow your committee the opportunity to determine how funds will be distributed amongst the Titles and programs within the Farm Bill. The expertise and agriculture backgrounds of the Committee members will be extremely important as the limited resources are distributed.

As you look at priorities in this new Farm Bill please consider that producers still need a safety net for crop failure and disaster. Crop insurance has been and still is the best tool for these situations. Full funding for the crop insurance program is the highest priority for sunflower growers and I suspect that it is the case for all commodities. Both production and revenue protection insurance products are important options for producers. The flexibility these options offer is important as producers weigh input costs, planting decisions and premiums. I encourage the Committee to continue the flexibility currently found in federal crop insurance.

Conservation programs in the Farm Bill are an important part of crop production and sunflowers benefit from having those programs in place. Sunflowers are generally part of a robust no-till rotation, a practice that has gained wider acceptance and implementation through EQIP funding. USDA-NRCS's soil health initiative has been a big success in the last few years. Producers, agribusiness and commodity investors now understand how important soil health practices are to increasing productivity on the land and protecting our natural resources at the same time. Every effort should be made to encourage producers to adopt practices that improve our nation's soils. Programs like EQIP need to be maintained at current funding levels.

Some of the newer programs authorized in the last Farm Bill are also important for producers as revenue loss coverage programs as we have seen the last two years. Specifically the Agriculture Loss Coverage (ARC-CO) and Price Loss Coverage (PLC) are important tools for producers to maintain their businesses. Both of these programs were well intentioned when authorized, but could use some improvements with the next authorization of the Farm Bill. For example, the ARC-CO program uses county specific data from the National Agriculture Statistics Service to predict revenue from the covered commodity, which works in counties where sufficient data exists, but is ineffective where the county specific data is insufficient. I hope the Committee will examine some of the flaws in these programs as the discussion about reauthorization takes place.

The USDA Agriculture Research Service (ARS) conducts genetic, pest and disease control as well as alternative use research and is a vital component toward improving sunflower production and marketability for producers. Although ARS funding is not provided through the Farm Bill, members of Congress must understand how research helps producers keep up with the increasing demand for food. Sunflower producers have helped in this effort as well. The National Sunflower Association and the Kansas Sunflower Commission along with grower commissions from other states have provided $2.8 million over a three-year period to help fund the ARS Sunflower Unit, whose mission is to significantly increase yield production through improved genetics and increased pest resistance.

I understand there will be many more public interests lobbying your committee for other programs and overall debt reduction actions. So I will take this opportunity to remind you that American agriculture is the original industry that got this country started. We still produce the safest and most abundant food worldwide.

In Midwest States like Kansas, agriculture is still a major contributor to state and local economies. We need your support and leadership in Congress to continue our tradition and our way of life. With the utmost respect to you and the difficult decisions you have ahead, I would ask you remember those of us out in the country that put food on your tables as you make these decisions.

Thank you.

Kansas Cooperative Council Written Testimony, Greg Ruehle, February 23, 1917

The Honorable Senator Pat Roberts, Chairman, The Honorable Senator Debbie Stabenow, Ranking Member Committee Members, U.S. Senate Committee on Agriculture, Nutrition & Forestry.

Chairman Roberts, Ranking Member Stabenow and members of the U.S. Senate Committee on Agriculture, Nutrition and Forestry, thank you for conducting your first formal field hearing on the 2018 Farm Bill, *Hearing from the Heartland: Perspectives of the 2018 Farm Bill from Kansas*, here in our state. We are pleased to welcome you back home, Senator Roberts, for this important meeting.

Farmers, ranchers, agribusinesses and those serving these constituencies have a vested interest in federal farm policy. The agricultural industry is the backbone of our great state's economy, so we appreciate having this hearing in Kansas.

Our Association, Members, and our Members Involved in the Hearing Today

The Kansas Cooperative Council (KCC), founded in 1944, is a voluntary statewide trade association representing all types of cooperative businesses with operations in Kansas. Our members include agricultural marketing and supply cooperatives, rural electric and telecommunications cooperatives, members of the Farm Credit system, and insurance and risk management cooperatives. We are pleased that various co-op industries are represented here today and are taking part in the industry panel. Frontier Farm Credit is a direct member and Nemaha-Marshall Electric Cooperative is connected to our association through our member, the Kansas Electric Cooperatives, Inc. We appreciate their presence here and their willingness to share thoughts and concerns on behalf of their sectors of the Kansas cooperative community.

At the time we prepared this statement, we understood that one of our larger local farmer cooperatives, MKC, and DFA, one of our regional members, will be submitting written comments individually. MKC will share perspectives from a grain handling and ag supply cooperative, while DFA will share insights from the dairy sector. Other co-ops may comment, as well. Whether other cooperative entities appear as formal conferees today or provide written comments, we appreciate their contributions to the official record of today's hearing and we commend their testimony to you.

Our agricultural cooperative members include the traditional grain elevator and agriculture input providers. These local co-ops range in size from a single location operation to those with multiple facilities spread across several counties. Although the concrete silo is a popular image of "the co-op," our agricultural membership is broader than just that. Servi-Tech Laboratories is a technologically advanced agronomy and laboratory service provider. We are pleased that their President & CEO, Greg Ruehle, will be presenting additional comments today on behalf of Servi-Tech and the Kansas Cooperative Council.

As the committee knows, the provisions of the Farm Bill drive agriculture policy and influence on-farm operational decisions and related industry decisions. Components in past farm bills helped encourage the growth of the cotton industry in Kansas. Over time, cotton acreage has expanded to support four gins and one warehouse in our state. Two of the producer-owned gins in Kansas are members of the Kansas Cooperative Council, as is the regional marketing cooperative they participate in, Plains Cotton Cooperative Association (PCCA). The Kansas Cotton Association (KCA), an invited conferee for the hearing today, is an associate member of the KCC. With KCA's participation today, we will note that their comments, both Tom Lahey's presentation and their written testimony, will provide a more expanded description of their challenges with the existing Farm Bill and the cotton industry's needs moving forward than what we present today. As we noted in regard to other members above, we respectfully draw your attention to KCA's concerns, as cotton is an important segment of our Kansas agricultural cooperative landscape.

To further illustrate the diversity within the agricultural cooperative sector, we have the top three U.S. farmer-owned cooperatives in our membership. Their interests include, among other things, dairy production and marketing, animal feed, crop inputs and petroleum refining and distribution.

The industries represented within our membership all have connections of varying degrees to agriculture producers and agribusinesses, Thus they are, or can be, affected by federal agricultural and rural policies. That makes most all of our members a stakeholder, in some fashion, in the discussions regarding the next Farm Bill. Therefore, we are very appreciative of the opportunity to have a representative on the industry panel today and to submit these written comments, as well.

Need for Increased Emphasis on Working Lands Programs

Our agricultural cooperatives, which are owned and controlled by farmers and ranchers, have a particularly close connection to farm programs. As you know, our grain handling members rely on grain production to sustain their businesses. They need grain to handle, market or store. Obviously, weather or pest outbreaks can impact the quantity and quality of grain coming into the elevator. But, farm policy also impacts what is planted and the number of acres planted.

Historically, Kansas has been among the leaders in the number of acres enrolled in the Conservation Reserve Program (CRP). Initially, the program was designed primarily to address issues such as erosion. Over time, the CRP program has expanded beyond that initial framework to address other concerns including enhancement of wildlife habitat.

Our association has long-standing concerns with the CRP program's blanket requirement that enrolled land must be idled for the term of the contract. We believe a "working lands" model where stewardship concerns are addressed through integration into active production is a far better approach, as it achieves environmental benefit while preserving economic productivity. While we do acknowledge that idling certain acres may be the appropriate option for some ground, we would prefer a system where that determination is made on a field-by-field basis and not mandated.

We strongly advocate for addressing more of our environmental goals through working lands programs. We also encourage better cost-share opportunities for producers willing to participate in working lands programs under voluntary public-private partnerships which advance stewardship of our natural resources.

The stewardship goal should be the main driver for participation rather than payment/cost-share availability.

In late 2007, Kansas embarked on a targeted water conservation initiative and, to accomplish the program goal of reducing irrigation, entered into a Conservation Reserve Enhancement Program (CREP) agreement with the United States Dept. of Agriculture (USDA). As you know, CREP is a specialized program under the Conservation Reserve Program (CRP). As a specialized CRP program, producers enrolling in the CREP program had to quit farming that land and place it under a cover crop. The goal of Kansas' particular water quantity CREP was water conservation, and that goal could have been accomplished by converting to dryland production if the land was capable of sustaining that practice. But, under the terms of the CREP agreement, the land had to be idled no matter what. We do acknowledge that a significant portion, maybe even all the top tier acres actually enrolled, might not have been well suited for dryland production in most weather years. But, it is troubling to our members that there is not even the possibility to consider whether dryland farming could be appropriate on some acres.

The concern is magnified for us because the decision to enter into a CREP was largely driven by cost rather than stewardship. At the time, the cost-share available under the CREP program allowed the state to leverage federal dollars on an eight-to-one ratio. Kansas could draw down 80 percent of the funding through USDA with a 20 percent match. That match could include state dollars, local support and even state in-kind support to reach the 20 percent threshold. Nowhere near that amount of federal cost-share support was available under working lands programs, so Kansas pursued the CPEP, because that is where the money was.

We believe it is entirely possible for environmental programs, and the associated funding, can be designed so that stewardship goal, not the amount of matching funds drives decision making. We respectfully encourage your committee to keep this in mind as you work through the details of the 2018 Farm Bill and:

- Adjust conservation programs to allow for a greater degree of crop production where that is not significantly inconsistent with the conservation goal sought; and
- Channel conservation program funding more heavily toward working lands programs where conservation and crop production can co-exist.

We do recognize we are asking you to consider greater emphasis on working lands programs that continue agriculture production at a time when we have tremendous amounts of grain in this state still in temporary storage after bountiful 2016 harvests. And, we do recognize that conservation programs that idle land, in essence, can influence supply and thus commodity prices. So it may seem counter-intuitive to some that we place so much emphasis on working lands programs over those that take land out of production. But in a longer-term view, we think that a blanket policy to idle every acre enrolled in a program, no matter what the conservation goal of that particular enrollment may be, is an unnecessary restraint.

Importance of Farm Credit System to Cooperatives and the Need to Maintain Jurisdiction within the Ag Committees

The Kansas Cooperative Council membership includes Farm Credit associations in Kansas and their lending bank, CoBank. The Farm Credit System was created with a unique mission, ownership structure and authorizing legislation as compared to many other financial institutions. As you know, jurisdiction over the system rests in your committee and your House counter-part. We continue to believe that this is the proper venue as the Ag Committee is best suited to understand the challenges faced by the Farm Credit System owners – their farmers, ranchers, and cooperative members.

The Farm Credit System is an important financial partner in rural Kansas and rural America. The system is there to support our rural cooperatives, as well as individual producers.

Crop Insurance

Crop insurance is an important component of an overall risk management plan and safety net component for many producers. The additional economic stability that comes with that ripples beyond the farm gate to area agribusinesses and the rural economy when producers are still able to pay their bills at the co-op and buy groceries.

Rural Utility Service (RUS)

Rural Utility Service loans and loan guarantees are vital to our rural utility members, their local member-owners, and rural communities. The RUS serves as a reliable source of credit for rural electric cooperatives (RECs) and RLECs. Loans through RUS allow local RECs and RLECs to upgrade systems, improve capacity, increase efficiency, and meet the increasing demands of 21st century customers.

Rural Economic Development loans and grants link cooperatives with their local communities to spur economic development, retain jobs and create new employment opportunities. Adequate funding for RUS loan programs is important in sustaining rural Kansas and rural America.

Improvements to Rural Infrastructure

Improving our nation's infrastructure appears to be an important component of President Trump's agenda. Rural America has many needs that might be addressed under infrastructure improvement plans. In Kansas, our infrastructure needs include repairing roads and bridges and expanding broadband. Nationally, agriculture shippers are also active in seeking improvements to our nation's locks and dams. The Farm Credit system, RUS, and other USDA Rural Development program areas have a strong history of supporting rural community infrastructure improvements, and with the additional emphasis this administration seems ready to focus on infrastructure needs, such entities can become even more important players in this space.

Funding

Under the 2014 Farm Bill consideration, voluntary funding reductions resulted in an estimated $23 billion over 10 years, based on calculations at that time that would be redirected to deficit reduction. The January 2017 baseline estimates indicate that just nutrition and crop insurance alone will spend approximately $100 billion less than anticipated. So, it is vitally important that the budgetary savings coming out of the 2014 Farm Bill be recognized when we look at funding components of the 2018 bill.

Other Overall Concerns

In preparing these comments, our rural telecommunications interests noted the overarching paperwork burden associated with participation in government programs. We trust that many of our cooperative members would echo the same concern, whether they are participating in a program that falls under the Farm Bill or any other area. To that extent, where there are opportunities for this committee to encourage streamlining of processes and paperwork, whether in Farm Bill legislation or by direction to agencies administering Farm Bill programs, it would be helpful to our members.

Thank you for the opportunity to provide comments on in preparation for the 2018 Farm Bill. As a state heavily dependent on the broader agricultural economy, federal farm policy has a significant impact on many of our co-op members and their local cooperative member-owners.

Sincerely,

James L. Jirak,
Chairman of the Board Kansas Cooperative Council

Leslie J. Kaufman,
President/CEO Kansas Cooperative Council

Greg Ruehle,
President CEO Servi-Tech Laboratories

Clay Scott, Family Farm and Ranch Ulysses, Ks, Raising Irrigated/Dryland Corn and Hard White Wheat, Cattle and Boys, Testimony before the United States Senate Committee, on Agriculture, Nutrition, and Forestry, McCain Auditorium at Kansas State University, February 23, 2017, "Hearing from the Heartland: Perspectives on the 2018 Farm Bill from Kansas," Written Testimony

Introduction

Welcome to Kansas. Chairman Roberts -welcome home-, Ranking Member Stabenow and members of the committee. Thank You for the opportunity to speak about production agriculture and those issues concerning the development of the 2018 farm bill. My farm is located in far southwest Kansas-about 90 miles west of Dodge City- near where my great grandfather homesteaded years ago. We are home to several large beef feedlots, dairies and swine facilities. Including a group of dairymen near Sumner Michigan who have recently started a large expansion of their existing heifer facilities-north and west of Ulysses.

In addition to farming I am actively involved in water. I am a delegate to the Kansas Water Congress, a member of the National Water Resources Association (NWRA), and a board member and past president of the Southwest Kansas Groundwater Management District. Together members of the NWRA and Kansas Water Congress provide water to millions of individuals, families, and agricultural producers in a manner that supports communities, the economy and the environment. This connection between agriculture and water is clear and of growing importance. In the U.S. we are fortunate to spend less than ten percent of household spending on food, this is far less than many other developed countries. A key input to keeping food affordable is ensuring a reliable supply of water.

Infrastructure

As Congress and the Administration discuss a potential infrastructure package it is important that it considers the vital importance of water infrastructure. Water and food are both strategically important resources and without a strong commitment to water infrastructure our nation's ability to produce food will be hindered. Water infrastructure is key not only to food production. It is also vital for power generation, manufacturing, and human health and safety. Water infrastructure is one of the most important components of our nations infrastructure system. This importance needs to be recognized.

Technology

Technology in agriculture is changing our world at a rapid pace. Advancements in breeding and biotechnology are bringing improvement to our fields and when combined with new techniques and practices these stronger plant genetics are pushing our yields results higher while our inputs are being reduced. Mobile drip irrigation, soil moisture probes, and conservation tillage are practices that are delivering solid results and producing improved soil health and increasing sustainability.

I would like to note that proper environmental stewardship is critical to bringing this technology to the market at an affordable cost to the farmers. Streamlined review of technology guided by sound science and combined with a proper market acceptable release is absolutely imperative. USDA and congress have helped this immensely in last few years. Market disruptions from non-approved traits to the export supply are not acceptable. These non-approved traits create huge expenses for exporters, disrupt supply channels due to segregation, weaken farm revenue and feed the notions of those opposed to production agriculture. I would urge this committee to continue improvements upon these concerns.

Attached are the first year study results from a Natural Resources Conservation Service (NRCS) Conservation Innovation Grant (CIG).

Crop Insurance

The current crop insurance program is our most crucial risk management tool. It is the basis for our ag lending industry and farm credit. Improvements are needed. During the 2016 crop year, Kansas saw record production in many areas of the state. This exceptional production forced cash prices much lower. While futures prices did decline most of the losses occurred via the increased basis adjustments. Yet, farmers who rely on the revenue policy of their multi-peril insurance for price loss coverage were disappointed to see no losses paid because the pricing was done on the futures only side of the contract. None of Kansas grain elevators, coops, or farmers were able to deliver against the Kansas City Board of Trade wheat contracts due to logistics. Thus the cash price fell while the "hedged bushel" leveled off. I suggest that MPCI products have a method of correction to represent equivalent cash prices paid vs the Futures Contract of Record. If the price of Kansas City Futures contract doesn't represent the price of wheat, what is it really worth?

Limited Water Irrigation Coverage

My farms and region suffer from limited well yields. For several years we have incorporated water technology systems such as soil moisture probes to accurately access the root profile in our soils. Together with selected hybrids with the drought technologies, we are changing our production practices to produce very strong yields. One difficulty is we cannot report these fields as irrigated due to yield goal limitations/definitions nor do they fit a true dryland field. As a result, we are reporting on Farm Service Agency (FSA) and Multi Peril Crop Insurance (MPCI) reports as dryland with water applied. A third definition of coverage would be useful to areas where intensive water management are called for and do not force additional irrigation in challenged areas. RMA will be offering this needed policy for 2017 by written agreement only. Its inclusion into the next farm bill is needed for areas of intensive or expanded water management.

ARC/PLC Program

The current crop support plan is difficult to understand. Counties suffer from reporting errors that distort program payments. Some of these reporting errors may be self inflicted. The Risk Management Agency (RMA) requires acres where limited irrigation water is applied to fields yet have a yield goal below current Average Production History (APH) to be called dryland. The majority of the wet acres on my corn fields meet this definition. However, Farm Service Agency (FSA) declares acres with any water applied to be called irrigated. Thus, a confusing set of data that corrupts accurate results. The coordination of terms and practices between RMA and FSA must be revisited in the next farm bill.

Water Conservation

The greatest resource in western Kansas is water. Like all states in the west, we strive to increase efficiencies and improve on new technologies to extend and preserve this resource. The new mobile drip irrigation systems (a new technology and practice) are helping take these efficiencies to a maximum extent. Ultra low drops with mobile drip lines place the irrigation just inches above the root zone to provide the exact amount water needed and eliminate most evaporation and runoff possibilities.

Water conservation programs -like those found in the EQIP program- must reward those working towards conservation. Using historic usage only encourages maximizing usage prior to enrollment. Those who are already working to conserve have a larger burden to achieve the same gains. Conservation is a key to sustaining this resources and one which a robust partnership where Farm bill programs and Farmers and Ranchers can succeed.

Conservation Reserve Program

The conservation reserve program is probably the best practice for environmental stewardship in the farm bill. Approving quality lands to meet quotas over environmental needs in others is not serving the interest of it intended goal. As with all programming in the next farm bill, please look to the environmental return of enrollment and not to retirement. It is also important to ensure that USDA adheres to contract agreements when implementing CRP and CREP.

Grassland and Forest Health

Forest and grassland health are keys to protecting the water supply of many western states. The Committee took steps to improve forest health in the 2014 Farm bill and Chairman Roberts introduced the Emergency Wildfire and Forest Management Act in the last session of Congress. We greatly appreciate Chairman Robert's and the Committee's attention to this important issue. As the Congress works to address forest health issues NWRA believes it is critical that both forest management reforms and resolution of the "fire borrowing" issue are addressed in comprehensive legislation focused on improving the health and resiliency of our forests.

Duplicative Permitting

NWRA also encourages the Committee to clarify that a National Pollutant Discharge Elimination System (NPDES) permit is not required for pesticides already approved under the Federal Insecticide, Fungicide and Rodenticide Act (FIFRA). The judicious use of pesticides plays an important role in the United States economy and the livelihoods of countless individuals.

Pesticides help grow the food that feeds the world's growing population. They can also help improve the efficiency of water delivery and carbon free hydropower generation by keeping infrastructure free from invasive weeds that can reduce water delivery and impede power generation. It is unnecessary to require a NPDES permit in addition to FIFRA licensing. It creates an additional layer of unnecessary red tape.

I have three sons, two enrolled this last fall at Fort Hays State University with an eye to returning to the farm. It is a difficult and expensive transition. Support for the beginning farmer and rancher programs is a helpful resource and a great investment in sustaining new blood of our industry. I would encourage continued support that your committee has shown for these projects.

I appreciate the opportunity to provide testimony to your committee today. I would like to thank you for your diligence and honest effort to attend the Kansas segment of the 2018 Farm Bill Hearings and I thank you for hearing our prospective of agriculture Thanks again.

Respectfully submitted,
Clay Scott

NRCS Conservation Innovation Grant

2016 Annual Progress Report

Grantee: Southwest Kansas Groundwater Management District No. 3

Project Title: A Demonstration and Evaluation of the Potential for Mobile Drip Irrigation (MDl)

Technologies to Reduce Water Use and Extend the Usable Life of Groundwater Supplies

Project Directors:
Trevor Ahring
Clay Scott
Mark Rude

Project Status: There are 10 fields that have been equipped with mobile drip tape on the inner 3 spans or evaluation in the CIG project. These fields are located in the following sections, all within Stanton and Grant Counties. Kansas:

See Figure I for a complete project map, including land with fully-irrigated com, limited-irrigation corn, and irrigated wheat.

Each project field has been equipped with Dragon-Line® mobile drip irrigation technology on the inner three spans of a center pivot system. Irrigation was scheduled using soil moisture probes to maximize yield and minimize water use.

Field Inputs

- Seeding Rate: All fully-irrigated corn ground was seeded at a rate of 27,500 spa. Limited irrigation corn ground was seeded at a rate of 19,600 spa. Irrigated wheat was seeded at a rate of 90 lb/ac.

Sec 21-28-38
Sec 8-28-38
Sec 18-28-38
Sec 3-29-39
Sec 4-29-39
Sec 31-27-39
Sec 14-27-39
Sec 21-27-39
Sec 16-27-39

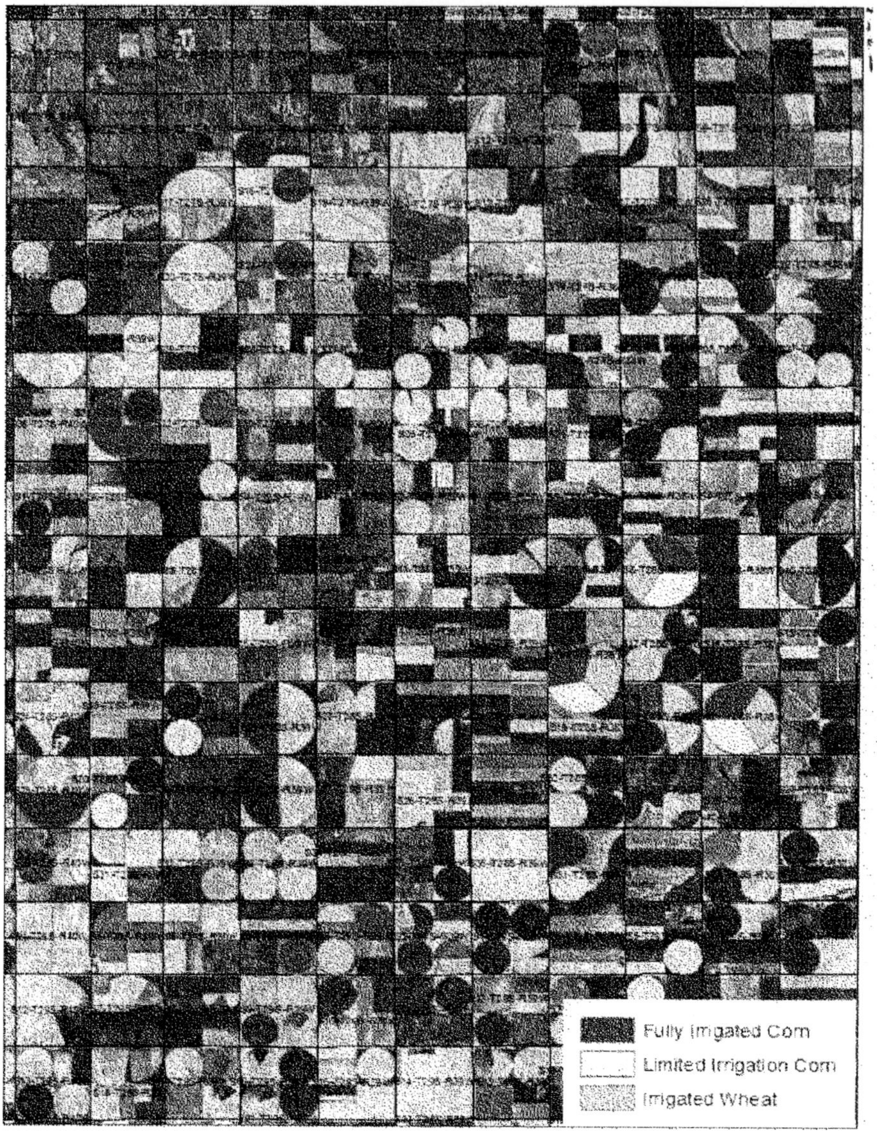

Figure 1. Project map. All fields located in Grant and Stanton Counties.

- Fertilizer: Fully-irrigated corn was fertilized with 225 lb N. Limited irrigation corn was fertilized with 160 lb N. Wheat was fertilized with 100 lb N.
- Water: The summer of 2016 was wetter than normal, producing 19" rain. This high rainfall, combined with good management, allowed for project wells to be shut off for 33 days in July and August. Fully-irrigated corn ground received 14.7" of irrigation water. Limited irrigation corn received 9.8" of irrigation water. Wheat received 8" of irrigation water.

Yields

Yields tor each project field were as follows (no hail loss unless indicated otherwise):

- Section 31-27-39: 241 bsh/ac (fully-irrigated corn)
- Section 14-27-39: 229 bsh/ac (fully-irrigated corn)
- Section21-27-39: 202 bsh/ac (w/29% hail damage) (fully-irrigated corn)
- Section 16-27-39: 203 bsh/ac (w/19% hail damage, 11% grain snap) (fully-irrigated corn)
- SW ¼ Section 3-29-39: 222 bsh/ac (fully-irrigated corn)
- NE ¼ Section 3-29-39: 98 bsh/ac (irrigated wheat)
- SE ¼ Section 4-29-39: 227 bsh/ac (fully-irrigated corn)
- Section 18-28-38: 231 bsh/ac (4% hail loss) (fully-irrigated corn)
- 220 bsh/ac (limited irrigation com)
- 100 bsh/ac (irrigated wheat)
- Section 8-28-38: 233 bsh/ac (fully-irrigated corn)
- 215 bsh/ac (limited irrigation com)
- 80 bsh/ac (irrigated wheat)
- Section 21-28-38: 228 bsh/ac (fully-irrigated corn)
- 226 bsh/ac (limited irrigation corn
- 48 bsh/ac (wheat streak mosaic virus) (irrigated wheat)

There were no significant yield differences on the acreage covered by mobile drip irrigation compared to the acreage covered by drop nozzles. This may have been because of the higher than average rainfall, or it might have been because the technology docs not significantly affect yield.

Water Savings

For each of the project fields, nozzles on the inner 3 spans were replaced with mobile drip irrigation, covering 196.4 project acres. Of these acres, 133.4 acres were fully irrigated corn, with 14.7" irrigation water applied. 42 acres were irrigated wheat, with 8" irrigation water applied. 21 acres were limited irrigation com with 9.8" irrigation water applied. The total water applied with mobile drip technology was 208.6 AF. All project wells are replacing nozzles in the inner towers that apply water at a rate 0.204 ac-in/hr with mobile drip irrigation that applies water at a rate of 0.126 ac-in/hr. The water use on those acres with the old drop nozzle packages would have been 337.5 AF. The total water savings for the 2016 project year were 128.9 AF.

Other Benefits

Replacing inefficient nozzles in the inner 3 spans improved the overall uniformity of pressure in the center pivot system, allowing nozzle size to be increased in the outer spans. This improved the rate of application without increasing the overall pumping rate, allowing the systems to be shut off for more days than they otherwise would have. This reduces operational cost and saves energy.

Budget

The overall project budget is $57.800, including $25,200 federal funds and $32,600 non-federal funds. To date, $15,076.65 of federal funds have been spent. This funding was used to help purchase mobile drip irrigation systems and soil moisture monitoring equipment. $12,564.35 of non-federal funding has been spent. This includes $9,064.35 cash for purchase of mobile drip irrigation systems and soil moisture monitoring equipment It also includes $3.500 in-kind contribution for reporting and creation of an informational video (can be seen at This leaves a remaining budget of $30,159. This includes $10,123.35 federal finding and $20,035.65 non-federal funding. Equipment costs to date have been less than anticipated, so it is likely that the project will be concluded without exhausting the remaining federal and nonfederal budget.

Work to Be Completed

There are still two years remaining for evaluation. Each project field will continue to be evaluated and GMD3 will create a final report, including cost-benefit analysis, as well as a recommendation to NRCS whether or not they should incorporate this practice into EQIP.

Written Testimony of the National Pork Producers Council, Hearing from the Heartland: Perspectives on the 2018 Farm Bill, before the Senate Committee on Agriculture, Nutrition & Forestry, Manhattan, Kansas, February 23, 2017

Introduction

The National Pork Producers Council (NPPC) is an association of 43 state pork producer organizations that serves as the global voice for the nation's pork producers. The U.S. pork industry represents a significant value-added activity in the agricultural economy and the overall U.S. economy. Nationwide, more than 60,000 pork producers marketed more than 118 million hogs in 2016, and those animals provided total cash receipts of nearly $240 billion. Overall, an estimated $23 billion of personal income and $39 billion of gross national product are supported by the U.S. pork industry.

Iowa State University economists Daniel Otto, Lee Schulz and Mark Imerman estimate that the U.S. pork industry is directly responsible for the creation of more than 37,000 full-time equivalent pork producing jobs and generates about 128,000 jobs in the rest of agriculture. It is responsible for approximately 102,000 jobs in the manufacturing sector, mostly in the packing industry, and 65,000 jobs in professional services such as veterinarians, real estate agents and bankers. All told, the U.S. pork industry is responsible for nearly 550,000 mostly rural jobs in the United States.

U.S. pork producers today provide 25 billion pounds of safe, wholesome and nutritious meat protein to consumers worldwide, and exports add significantly to the bottom line of each U.S. pork producer. U.S. exports of pork and pork products totaled 2.3 million metric tons – a record – valued at $5.94 billion in 2016. That represented almost 26 percent of U.S. production, and those exports added more than $50 to the value of each hog marketed. Exports supported approximately 110,000 jobs in the U.S. pork and allied industries.

Next Farm Bill

Obviously, pork producers have a strong interest in the next Farm Bill. NPPC has formed a Farm Bill Policy Task Force to gather input from producers from around the country. The task force will hold a number of meetings to review and evaluate many of the Farm Bill issues that will affect the U.S. pork industry. NPPC is committed to working with Congress to help craft the 2018 Farm Bill.

As it has requested in every Farm Bill on which it has weighed in, the U.S. pork industry asks that Congress in the next Farm Bill maintain the U.S. pork industry's competitive advantage, strengthen its competitiveness and defend the industry's competitiveness by supporting provisions that would be beneficial to agriculture and by opposing unwarranted and costly provisions and regulations that would negatively affect America's farmers and ranchers.

There are several issues pork producers would like Congress to address in the next Farm Bill that could help U.S. pork producers.

Foot-and-Mouth Disease Vaccine Bank

Foot and Mouth Disease (FMD) is one of the most economically devastating foreign animal diseases affecting animal agriculture. It is an infectious and sometimes fatal viral disease that affects cloven-hooved animals, including pigs and cattle. It is easily spread through a number of methods, including through the air, contact with contaminated equipment and by predators. An outbreak today of the disease, which last was detected in the United States in 1929, likely would cripple the entire livestock sector. In addition to causing harm to production animal agriculture, the economic consequences undoubtedly would ripple throughout the entire rural economy, from input suppliers to packers and from processors to consumers.

FMD is endemic in Africa, Asia, some South American countries and the Middle East. The FMD virus has seven viral serotypes and more than 60 subtypes, with wide strain variability. Sporadic outbreaks with different types continue to pop up in countries around the world.

Increased travel and trade between affected countries make the United States increasingly vulnerable to introduction of the disease. Now, the country has to confront the possibility of terrorists using FMD as a weapon to inflict significant damage to the U.S. economy and affect food availability.

In the U.S. Department of Agriculture's Foreign Animal Disease preparation strategy document on the phases and types of an FMD outbreak, Dr. James Roth, professor and researcher at Iowa State University, identified four phases of the disease: 1) confirmation of an outbreak (typically three days); 2) surveillance and epidemiological work necessary to provide timely evidence of the extent of an outbreak to support decision making by government officials; 3) recovery from the disease; and 4) freedom from the disease (possibly with vaccination).

He categorized FMD outbreaks as having six types: Small Focal, Moderate Regional, Large Regional, Widespread or National, Catastrophic U.S. and Catastrophic North American, which includes Canada and Mexico.

Given the structure of the U.S. livestock industry, the likelihood of having a Small Focal or Moderate Regional outbreak is remote. The livestock industry estimates there are approximately 1 million pigs and 400,000 cattle moved daily in the United States, some over long distances. In addition, there are numerous auctions, fairs and exhibits that concentrate large numbers of animals in a single location, providing the opportunity for one infected or exposed animal to spread the disease to many animals. Thus, it seems unlikely that, if the United States had an outbreak, it would be on the smaller end of Roth's scale.

The World Organization for Animal Health (OIE) sets standards for managing and determining a country's disease status. Those standards range from "stamping out" (killing all infected and exposed animals) to being free of FMD, or "free with vaccination."

After watching countries such as the United Kingdom, Korea and Japan, whose livestock populations pale in comparison to the United States, struggle to manage FMD outbreaks by killing large numbers of animals, USDA's Animal and Plant Health Inspection Service (APHIS) changed its policy on managing the disease from "stamping out" to using vaccine to limit the spread.

This policy change was endorsed by the U.S. livestock industry as a cheaper and more practical alternative given the enormous size of the U.S. livestock herd and the movement of livestock around the country. The United States simply cannot "kill" its way out of an FMD outbreak.

The problem, though, is the United States does not have enough FMD vaccine available nor could a sufficient quantity be obtained in time to implement an effective control program.

U.S. law prohibits storing live FMD virus on the U.S. mainland, so foreign production companies are the only source of finished vaccines. The United States is the only country in the world that maintains its own vaccine antigen bank, which is maintained at the Plum Island Animal Disease Center on Plum Island, N.Y., and which has a limited number of antigens.

Currently, if there were an FMD outbreak in the United States, antigen would be shipped to a vaccine manufacturer in either Pirbright, England, or Lyon, France, to be turned into finished vaccine and shipped back to the United States. After three weeks, the process would produce only 2.5 million doses of vaccine.

Iowa State's Roth estimates that at least 10 million doses would be needed during the first two weeks of an outbreak. Currently, there is no surge capacity to produce additional doses of vaccine; all the vaccine production capacity in the world is currently in use by other countries.

Additionally, it must be noted that the vaccine antigen bank serves as the North American Bank and thus includes Canada and Mexico.

Over the past several years, the United States has made significant progress in FMD preparedness through the development of secure supply plans for milk, pork and beef, and APHIS continues to work with the livestock industry to improve its preparedness capability. Fixing the antigen bank capacity and improving vaccine availability must be a priority in future preparedness efforts.

Establishing a more robust FMD vaccine bank will require a significant increase in budget outlays. (The current FMD efforts are funded at just $1.9 million.) But the cost pales in comparison to the economic cost of an FMD outbreak in the United States.

Because North America is free of FMD, an outbreak of the disease in the United States would immediately shut off all exports of U.S. livestock, meat and dairy products, creating a precipitous drop in livestock markets. Since U.S. consumers have little knowledge of the disease, which cannot affect people, there also likely would be serious disruptions in the domestic market because of decreased demand for those products. According to one recent study, prevention of FMD is estimated to be worth $137 million a year to the U.S. pork industry.

Iowa State University economist Dermot Hayes estimates the cumulative impact of an FMD outbreak on the beef and pork industries over a 10-year period would be $128.23 billion. The annual jobs impact of such a reduction in revenue would be 58,066 in direct employment and 153,876 in total employment. Corn and soybean farmers over a decade would lose $44 billion and nearly $25 billion, respectively, making the impact on those four industries alone almost $200 billion.

The history of government involvement in disasters like an FMD outbreak is that, once a problem occurs, unlimited resources are committed to getting control of the situation. In the case of FMD, there is a clear opportunity to invest in a robust vaccine bank that would limit the economic impact on producers, feed suppliers and consumers and reduce the government's cost for control and eradication of the disease.

A recent study by Kansas State University estimated the cost to the U.S. government of eradicating FMD would be $11 billion if vaccination is not employed. But costs could be cut significantly if vaccination is used, and, the study estimated – depending on the strategy – losses to consumers and producers could be cut by 48 percent.

Congress should work with the Trump administration to address the alarming gap in the government's preparedness for an FMD outbreak. Whether the disease introduction is the result of terrorism, careless travelers or carried on traded commodities, the calamitous result would be the same: devastation to the U.S. livestock industry and a significant hit to the U.S. economy.

NPPC urges Congress to provide the authority and $150 million a year in mandatory funding for USDA APHIS to protect the U.S. livestock industry from an FMD outbreak. Specifically, the Farm Bill should direct APHIS to:

- Contract for an offshore, vendor-maintained vaccine antigen bank that would have available antigen concentrate to protect against all 23 of the most common FMD strains currently circulating in the world.
- Contract for a vendor-managed inventory of 10 million doses – the estimated need for the first two weeks of an outbreak.
- Contract with an international manufacturer(s) for the surge capacity to produce at least 40 million doses.

Disease Surveillance

An adjunct to a robust FMD vaccine bank is a world-class disease surveillance system. Being able to detect and identify any disease that could affect the U.S. food supply is vital to the continued viability of the U.S. pork industry.

The United States faces an increasing threat from the introduction of a foreign animal disease (FAD) into the U.S. livestock herd, but there is evidence that the safety net in place to prevent such an introduction needs to be improved.

Late last year, the House Agriculture Committee held a hearing on American Agriculture and National Security, which highlighted the vulnerability of the U.S. food supply to the potential for FAD introduction by terrorists or by accident.

Additionally, in October 2015, the bipartisan Blue Ribbon Study Panel on Biodefense, co-chaired by former Department of Homeland Security Secretary Tom Ridge and former Sen. Joe Lieberman, released a report that highlighted the need for improving the U.S. system for protecting the U.S. livestock herd and the nation's food supply from FADs.

Disease surveillance is the foundation of disease prevention and preparedness. The threat of new and emerging diseases continues to grow, with scientists continually warning the public and animal health authorities about the increasing risks. In May 2013, for example, the first case in the United States of Porcine Endemic Diarrhea virus was identified on an Ohio hog farm. That disease, which USDA determined likely came from China, spread quickly throughout the Midwest and killed between 8 million to 10 million mostly young pigs over an 18-month period.

Other bacterial and viral diseases are lurking around the world, and that is the reason the U.S. pork industry has devoted significant resources to endemic and foreign animal diseases, funding more than 120 research projects and spending more than $5 million for studying, monitoring and addressing swine diseases over the past 10 years.

The outbreak of H1N1 influenza in 2009 demonstrated the interrelationship of human and animal health when combating new and emerging diseases. From that experience, the U.S. pork industry learned that a Comprehensive and Integrated Surveillance System (CISS) is needed to ensure the capture of data about a broader range of diseases.

The industry has been working with USDA APHIS and the Centers for Disease Control and Prevention (CDC) to develop a CISS, including continuation and expansion of ongoing swine influenza surveillance. Completion of this is critical to maintaining the pork industry's known disease status, which, in turn, is vital to maintaining and expanding U.S. pork exports. The CISS is designed to provide an "early warning system" and to allow for development of response plans in advance of an epidemic.

The U.S. pork industry is collaborating with APHIS to test implementation of a CISS and to determine how it can be connected to an animal traceability system. Currently, the most significant shortcoming is funds to build the infrastructure to accommodate a more robust system of surveillance.

The ability to expand and strengthen surveillance to include other diseases will help increase exports. Reducing surveillance, however, would give other countries justification to restrict U.S. exports because of inadequate surveillance data.

U.S. pork producers also support USDA's animal traceability system. An effective traceability system is critical to the national animal health infrastructure and is required for certification by the OIE. The ability to quickly trace diseased and exposed animals during a foreign animal disease outbreak would save millions of animals, lessen the financial burden on the industry and save the American taxpayer millions of dollars.

With support from all sectors of the pork industry, approximately 95 percent of U.S. pork producers' premises already are registered under the USDA livestock identification program. Premises identification is the key to meeting a goal of tracing an animal back to its farm of origin within 48 hours, which would allow animal health officials to more quickly identify, control and eradicate a disease; prevent the spread of a disease; and make certifications to trading partners about diseases in the United States.

NPPC requests that Congress include in the Farm Bill authority for $30 million a year for the National Animal Health Laboratory Network, which conducts diagnostics on animal diseases, and $70 million a year for block grants to the states for disease surveillance and other support.

Agricultural Research

NPPC supports expanding federal funding for research, education and extension programs by improving the quantity and quality of USDA research through the agency's Agriculture and Food Research Initiative (AFRI). Basic, competitive agricultural research allows America's farmers to remain globally competitive in the face of a growing world population, improves public health and strengthens national security.

AFRI is the USDA's premier competitive research program and makes peer-reviewed, competitively-awarded research grants. The grants fund basic and applied research, education and extension to colleges and universities, agricultural experiment stations and other organizations conducting research in priority areas that are established partially in every Farm Bill.

The 2008 Farm Bill required AFRI to make available 60 percent of grant funds for basic research and 40 percent for applied research. Despite being authorized for $700 million in the 2008 Farm Bill and reauthorized in the 2014 Farm Bill, the program never has received anywhere near full funding in the appropriations process. In fact, USDA's overall research funding has decreased by 30 percent since 2009.

While other federal research and development budgets have grown over time, agricultural research funding has stagnated. This stagnation has occurred despite studies consistently reporting high social rates of return – between 20 percent and 60 percent annually. The United States is falling behind developing nations in its commitment to funding agricultural research, which has created rapid increases in the country's productivity. Amid growing challenges, such as the threat of new diseases, maintaining the position as the world leader in agricultural research and technology should be an overarching goal.

NPPC supports increasing the funding for agricultural research to ensure that the U.S. livestock industry maintains its competitiveness in the global marketplace.

Production and Marketing Regulations

NPPC works on behalf of America's pork producers to ensure that laws and rules don't impose unnecessary costs on the U.S. pork industry, restrict it from meeting consumer demands in an economical manner or prevent market-based solutions to issues. The structure of the pork production and packing sectors should be allowed to change with the demands of the growing global marketplace. This includes allowing producers and packers to adopt new technologies and pricing and marketing mechanisms that enable the former to reduce their risks and the latter to capture economies of scale.

The U.S. pork-packing sector is the envy of the world in terms of efficiency and food safety, and legislation and regulation should not take away or hamper that source of international advantage. Allowing producers and packers the freedom to develop new ways of doing business will enhance the value of U.S. pork products at home and abroad and reduce costs and risks.

The U.S. pork industry, which has developed a wide variety of marketing and pricing methods, including contracts, to meet the changing needs of a diverse marketplace, strongly opposes any provision that would eliminate or restrict such mechanisms. Limiting producers' options could force the livestock markets to revert to an inefficient system used more than half a century ago in which animals were traded in small lots and at prices determined in an open-market bid system.

Dictating how U.S. pork producers sell and raise their animals and how packing companies buy livestock would severely cripple the competitiveness of the U.S. pork industry. Mandates – whether pushed by lawmakers or activists – must not stand in the way of the free market.

Of particular and immediate concern to the U.S. pork industry is the Farmer Fair Practices Rules, specifically an Interim Final Rule, which was issued in the final weeks of the Obama administration.

Written by USDA's Grain Inspection, Packers and Stockyards Administration (GIPSA), the Interim Final Rule broadens the scope of the Packers and Stockyards Act (PSA) of 1921 related to the use of "unfair, unjustly discriminatory or deceptive practices" and "undue or unreasonable preferences or advantages."

USDA in 2010 proposed a number of PSA provisions – collectively known as the GIPSA Rule – which Congress mandated in the 2008 Farm Bill. But the agency was blocked by Congress through amendments to annual agricultural spending bills from implementing a provision that would eliminate the need to prove a competitive injury to win a PSA lawsuit. Protecting competition is the heart of the PSA. In fact, eight federal appeals courts have held that harm to competition must be proved for an action to be a violation of the PSA.

The Interim Final Rule would eliminate the need to prove injury to competition, which would prompt an explosion in PSA lawsuits by turning nearly every contract dispute into a federal case subject to triple damages.

The inevitable costs associated with increased lawsuits and the legal uncertainty they would create likely would lead to further vertical integration of the pork industry and drive packers to own more of their own hogs – reducing competition for producers of all sizes, stifling innovation and providing no benefits to anyone other than trial lawyers and activist groups that will use the rule to attack the livestock industry.

(An Informa Economics study found the GIPSA Rule, including the Interim Final Rule, now would cost the pork industry more than $420 million annually, with most of the costs related to PSA lawsuits brought under the "no competitive injury" provision.)

The U.S. pork industry right now is enduring its fair share of headwinds. It does not need more of them in the form of the Interim Final Rule of the Farmer Fair Practices Rules.

NPPC urges Congress to work with the Trump administration to rescind the Interim Final Rule and to ensure that any USDA rule to amend the Packers and Stockyards Act not restrict producers' ability to sell or packers' ability to buy animals and not limit their ability to use technologies and pricing and marketing mechanisms that work for their mutual benefit.

Likewise, federal mandates on production practices, including ones that would dictate animal housing systems, would add to producers' costs and weaken the U.S. pork industry's competitiveness vis-a-vis foreign competitors.

Nearly three decades ago, the U.S. pork industry developed and implemented strict standards for animal care and judicious use guidelines for use of animal drugs. These standards and guidelines are part of the industry's Pork Quality Assurance Plus and Transport Quality Assurance programs, which require producers and handlers to be trained and certified in caring for and transporting animals.

Pork producers do not support Congress including animal care and handling provisions in the Farm Bill – a piece of legislation that has been aimed for more than 80 years at maintaining the competitiveness of the U.S. agriculture and livestock sectors.

USDA Export Programs

Expanding foreign markets for U.S. pork products increases producers' bottom line and contributes significantly to the U.S. economy, fostering job growth and increasing the U.S. gross domestic product. Pork represents 37 percent of global meat protein intake, more than beef and poultry, and world pork trade has grown significantly over the past decade or so. The extent of the increase in global pork trade in the future will hinge heavily on continued efforts to increase agricultural trade liberalization.

The U.S. pork industry in 2016 exported nearly $6 billion of product, which supported more than 50,000 jobs. It is estimated that U.S. pork prices were $50.20 per hog higher last year than they would have been in the absence of exports.

It is important to strengthen the ability of U.S. agriculture to compete in the global marketplace. But the downside of growing exports is, of course, the larger economic impact on producers and the U.S. economy should there be any disruption in trade. Pork producers understand this dynamic and recognize that it would be devastating for the U.S pork sector.

While the best way to increase U.S. pork exports is through free trade agreements that eliminate all tariff and non-tariff barriers on pork, programs run by USDA's Foreign Agricultural Service and authorized under the Farm Bill also are important to U.S. agricultural exports.

The Market Access Program (MAP) uses funds from the Commodity Credit Corporation to help producers, exporters, private companies and other trade organizations finance promotional activities for agricultural products of the United States. The Foreign Market Development Program, also known as the Cooperator Program, helps create, expand and maintain long-term export markets for U.S. agricultural products.

NPPC supports funding levels that will sustain those important programs.

Environment

Protecting the environment is a top priority of the U.S. pork industry. Pork producers are committed to running productive pork operations while protecting the environment and meeting or exceeding environmental standards. Pork producers have fought hard for science-based, affordable and effective regulatory policies that meet the goals of today's environmental standards. To meet strict environmental criteria while maintaining production, they support the federal government providing through conservation programs within the Farm Bill cost-share support to help defray some of the costs of compliance.

For many farmers, USDA conservation financial assistance funds through the Environmental Quality Incentives Program (EQIP), the Conservation Stewardship Program (CSP) and the Conservation Reserve Program (CRP) are integral to making investments in environmental protection practices and technologies possible. Certainly there will be advances made by many farmers without federal funding assistance, but conservation financial assistance is critical for many, and it will help build a foundation of practices that can sustain conservation improvements for the long term.

Under the EQIP program, however, pork producers have not received enough support to meet all the challenges they face related to conservation and the environment. Producers who use EQIP would like to see the scope of projects covered by the program widened.

NPPC wants in the next Farm Bill funding maintained for EQIP and the other critical working lands conservation programs, and on CRP, it supports the current limit on acreage that may be enrolled in the program.

Conclusion

The U.S. pork industry is the lowest-cost producer and No. 1 exporter of pork in the world, and U.S. pork producers continue to produce the most abundant, safest, most nutritious pork in the world. Pork producers have proved very resilient over the past years, weathering financial crises and diseases as well as the vagaries of a supposedly free-market economy pushed and pulled in various directions by government intervention and regulation. All the while, they have invested in and adopted new technologies that have promoted animal health, protected the environment and added thousands of jobs and billions in national income to the American economy.

For America's pork producers to continue as leaders in the international and domestic economies, for them to take advantage of the opportunities and meet the challenges presented to them, Congress and the administration, through the next Farm Bill, should pursue policies and regulations that support the U.S. pork industry rather than hinder its ability to continue producing safe, lean and nutritious pork and pork products for the global marketplace.

Testimony to the United States Senate Committee on Agriculture, Nutrition, and Forestry, Mrs. Cherise Tieben, City Manager, Dodge City, Kansas, February 23, 2017, Manhattan, Kansas

Mr. Chairman and members of the Committee, welcome to Kansas. I am Cherise Tieben, City Manager of Dodge City, Kansas, the proud home community of Senator Pat Roberts. Thank you for allowing my testimony about a rural housing challenge with a positive outcome. In 2008, Dodge City community leaders recognized, the lack of quality affordable housing and the resulting impediment to recruiting, retaining and expanding the local workforce. At the time, the local housing supply was limited, including an inadequate stock of affordable and moderate housing available for purchase by first-time homebuyers. In the preceding five years, only 64 newly constructed residential homes had been built. Local stakeholders saw the need for a housing assessment which was subsequently commenced to evaluate the existing housing stock and quantify the long-range housing demand for our community. There were many inputs to the study including, evaluation of current federal, state and local government policies and incentives. The results of the housing study were beneficial and identified several obstacles while also projecting a need to build 568 single family homes and 379 multi-family homes, in varying price ranges in the following 5 years. The housing assessment highlighted the serious lack of inventory of starter homes for first-time homebuyers. And, banking regulations were tightening, making it more difficult for first-time home buyers to qualify for a conventional residential home loan. Young families and people moving into the community needing to utilize USDA RD loans to purchase affordable to moderate market range homes were encouraged to buy or build outside of Dodge City due to the population restrictions of the loan program. The City of Dodge City and three other southwest Kansas communities brought to the attention of Senator Roberts, the stifling impact of the USDA RD loans population limit. Senator Roberts saw the need for an upward adjustment to the population limit and led the effort for a change, which became effective in May, 2014. The impact is measurable - 94 USDA guaranteed loans, totaling $9.9 million dollars have been underwritten. The other southwest Kansas communities also share a similar success. The positive results allow the retention of existing businesses, the ability of existing businesses to grow and improves opportunities to recruit new business to our community. Again, Senator Roberts thank you for being our champion on this and so many other issues. Thank you for the opportunity to testify today. I am pleased to answer any questions.

Testimony of Kent Winter, before the U.S. Senate Committee on Agriculture, Nutrition & Forestry, Manhattan, Kansas, February 23, 2017

Chairman Roberts, Ranking Member Stabenow and members of the Committee, I would like to thank you on behalf of Kansas grain sorghum farmers for the opportunity to share our views on discussions surrounding the upcoming farm bill.

I farm near Andale in south central Kansas, producing grain sorghum, wheat, soybeans, corn and alfalfa, and I currently serve as president of the Kansas Grain Sorghum Producers Association.

Kansas is the nation's leading producer of grain sorghum. Last year we produced 55 percent of the nation's grain sorghum crop, above our normal production rate between 40 and 50 percent of the U.S. grain sorghum crop. Sorghum is used as a feedstock for ethanol, for livestock feed and is exported to other countries. There is also a growing market for sorghum as a consumer food choice and in the distilled spirits industry. Grain sorghum has great rotational benefits for many Kansas farmers because it will often grow in challenging conditions, especially where water supplies are short.

Times are tough on the farm. Prices for most commodities have collapsed the last year, and lenders and farmers are very worried about producers staying in business. This means farm programs are critical in our day-to-day business decisions in Kansas. When producers apply for a farm operating loan, the banker asks two questions; What are your crop insurance guarantee levels, and what do you anticipate in other farm program safety net support? The ability to secure annual operating loans directly depends upon the stability of farm programs. Strong farm programs provide certainty and stability that is vital for growers to be able to obtain operating capital from their banks. That operating capital is what bolsters local rural economies.

We appreciate your leadership in maintaining and strengthening farm programs. The current Price Loss Coverage program is working for sorghum. In the first year of this farm program, strong cash sales from export demand held our prices above the reference price level set for sorghum in the last farm bill.

However, as prices dropped significantly in the last year, needed support has kicked in for sorghum farmers, and it is a simple program to understand. Agriculture Risk Coverage (ARC) has been very confusing and somewhat frustrating for some of our membership because it is hard for growers to understand why one county gets payments and the adjacent county does not. Therefore, having a robust risk management system in place is vitally important to my farm, and that includes a PLC program that today fills the gap between the level of risk management coverage I need compared to the level of coverage I can get through crop insurance today.

Mr. Chairman, in regards to the conservation of our natural resources, sorghum is not only the nation's premier water saving grain crop, but it also offers valuable conservation characteristics such as drought and heat tolerance, high residue stubble, expansive root systems, carbon sequestering capacity, and wildlife habitat and food. Sorghum is drought tolerant and well suited for arid conditions and is especially important in areas that draw water from the Ogallala Aquifer to support agriculture. As the Ogallala has struggled to maintain adequate levels and recharge, sorghum's ability to produce grain with significantly lower water requirements is critical for the long-term existence of the Ogallala. Sorghum is a proven water-sipping crop and will be a solution, I think, many farmers will embrace.

As sorghum producers finalize our priorities for the conservation title, we want to ensure that the title works better for dryland farmers in the western plains. Whether that is water conservation practices in EQIP or resource-conserving crop rotation practices in CSP, we want the conservation title to work for all producers in all regions of the country. Sorghum producers support a variety of conservation programs and believe working lands conservation programs are vital to increasing productivity while also protecting our natural resources.

In Kansas, sorghum is used mainly for ethanol production and livestock feed. While most think of ethanol as a product made from corn, most Kansas ethanol plants use both feed grains to produce this renewable fuel Having both grain sorghum and corn available allows ethanol plants more flexibility and better pricing opportunities. This ensures a strong and viable ethanol industry in our state, and also ensures a good value-added market for sorghum producers.

Finally, trade by way of exports remains vital for our industry. Therefore, we support increased funding for Market Access Program and Foreign Market Development programs in this farm bill as well as even better trade agreements around the world.

While I have focused on the use of grain sorghum for ethanol, I would like to mention the potential for the use of sweet sorghum and high biomass sorghum. As technology continues to advance in this area, discussions continue with major energy companies on the use of different types of sorghum as feedstocks, so maintaining energy title programs that continue to create opportunities and reduce risks for producers is important.

One last item that I would like to address is research. Unfortunately our industry is being plagued by a new insect called the sugarcane aphid, which has created significant financial and management challenges for our farmers. Research remains the answer for a long-term solution to this growing challenge, and we need help to deal with it and the damage it is causing.

In closing, I would like to underline the importance of stable and viable farm programs, especially to smaller crops like grain sorghum. Sorghum provides many benefits to conservation and crop rotations for our growers. Sorghum also plays an important role in a dependable feedgrain supply for our ethanol and livestock producers. However, as a crop that is planted to make the most of difficult growing conditions, it is also uniquely exposed to risk. Well thought-out farm programs that address risks and the potential of grain sorghum will benefit our growers as well as our local, state and national economies.

Testimony of Ken Wood, before the Senate Committee on Agriculture, Nutrition and Forestry, 2018 Farm Bill Field Hearing in Manhattan, Kansas, February 23, 2017

Mr. Chairman, Ranking Member Stabenow, and Members of the Committee, thank you for the opportunity to address you today. My name is Ken Wood, and I farm about 2,500 acres here in central Kansas, just outside of Chapman, Kansas. I produce wheat, corn, soybeans and grain sorghum. I serve as President of the Kansas Association of Wheat Growers, and am honored to have the opportunity to submit comments regarding the future of our country's farm policy.

Wheat is an important crop for Kansas. On average, Kansas plants 9.2 million acres of wheat.[17] For reference, that is 2,000 square miles larger than the state of Maryland.[18] In 2016 over 15 percent of all the land area in Kansas was covered with wheat.[19] In the fall of 2015, farmers planted eight and a half million acres of wheat and that 2016 crop yielded a record 57 bushels per acre, up 20 bushels per acre from the previous year.[20] This resulted in Kansas wheat production of 467 million bushels, about 1.5 times as much as 2015 harvest, and nearly double the 2014 harvest.[21]

---

[17] http://kswheat.com/producers/10-year-average-kansas-wheat-production.

[18] https://factfinder.census.gov/faces/tableservices/jsf/pages/productview.xhtml?pid=DEC_00_SF1_GCTPH1.US01PR&prodType=table.

[19] *Id.*

[20] https://www.nass.usda.gov/Statistics_by_State/Kansas/Publications/Crops/whthist.pdf.

[21] *Id.*

With these record yields, came stockpiles and bunkers of wheat on the ground. As of December 1, 2016, wheat stored in all positions totaled 420 million bushels, up 29 percent from a year ago and a record high.[22] In fall 2016 Kansas farmers planted almost 1 million fewer acres of wheat than the previous year, just under seven and a half million acres.[23] This represents the second lowest planted wheat acres in Kansas in over a century.[24] Many feel that low prices and a struggling farm economy have resulted in lower planted wheat acres. Although we were blessed with a bountiful harvest in 2016, 2017 is shaping up to be a tough year for Kansas wheat farmers. Farm income levels are at their lowest point since 1985. Between 2014 and 2015, net farm income dropped 95%, and net farm debt levels have increased 25% over the last three years.[25]

According to USDA, farming is still overwhelmingly comprised of family owned businesses. 99% of U.S. farms are family farms, and they account for 89% of farm production.[26] Low prices, coupled with rising costs, are placing even more stress on the Kansas wheat farmer, forcing them to cut costs and find efficiencies in order to be profitable. This situation highlights the need for federal programs like crop insurance and illustrates the vital importance of a farm safety net.

Crop insurance, for me, is the most important segment of the "Farm Safety Net." When a natural disaster looms on the horizon, whether it is a drought, flood, hail storm, or in my case, a tornado, we know that crop insurance will help keep us in business.

On May 25, 2016, at about 8:00 p.m., my farm, home, vehicles, most of my machinery, and approximately 300 acres of my crops were totally destroyed by an EF 4 tornado. The availability of crop insurance was not *the* deciding factor, but certainly a contributing factor in my decision to rebuild and re-establish my business. I honestly don't think that I would have had the courage to start over without having the protection that crop insurance offers. I had buildings and machinery to invest in, and I certainly made sure that they were insured. Similarly, I had ongoing investments to make in seed, fertilizer, and crop protection products. I really didn't want to leave that investment uninsured. For most of us, crop insurance will not guarantee a "good year," but it offers the promise of "another year."

I am old enough to remember vividly the circumstances that the ag community lived through during the decade of the 1980's. I believe that if we would have had crop insurance available then, like it is now, the 1980's wouldn't have been nearly as devastating. We had a glut of grain, which drove down prices. Then we had 4 years of drought, which eventually helped the price situation, but in the meantime, we had little to sell at very low prices. While I think that having a stronger safety net back then wouldn't have solved the problem, I have to think that it would have softened the blow.

---

[22] http://usda.mannlib.cornell.edu/usda/nass/GraiStoc//2010s/2017/GraiStoc-01-12-2017.txt.
[23] https://www.nass.usda.gov/Statistics_by_State/Kansas/Publications/Crops/whthist.pdf.
[24] *Id.*
[25] http://www.agmanager.info/kfma/state-summaries.
[26] https://www.ers.usda.gov/webdocs/publications/eib164/eib-164.pdf.

Despite passage of a five year Farm Bill, some in Congress continue to come after Title 1 farm programs and the federal crop insurance program. Some say that we are giving handouts to farmers and that farm programs cost us too much money. However, 72% of all farms received no farm-related Government payments in 2015[27] and all together, agriculture spending makes up less than three tenths of one percent of overall federal spending.

A budget exercise in the fall of 2015 showed how crop insurance is continually under attack. It was only after heavy pushback from the ag community and our champions on the Hill when Congressional leadership agreed to reverse the cuts as part of a highway bill a couple of weeks later. We are always on notice that when Appropriations bills reach the floors of the House or Senate, it's very possible that we'll see anti-crop insurance amendments being offered. In the past, efforts to cut crop insurance have come after the federal share of premium support, either through hard caps or through establishing AGI limitations on eligibility. Such caps would limit participation and make crop insurance more expensive for all producers. As was evident in my story, crop insurance is vital to protecting farmers and is a resource to keep us farming. Without it, we would be vastly limited in who is able to afford to farm.

In addition to disaster insurance, Agriculture Risk Coverage (ARC) and Price Loss Coverage (PLC) programs provide key support for farmers. The 2014 Farm Bill allowed producers a choice between revenue protection and price protection, programs which replaced the former direct payment program. One improvement to the current programs that we would like to see in the future would be to increase the reliability of the data collected. This has been specifically impactful in the administration of the ARC-County program. The ARC guarantee is based on county yields that use NASS data; however, many don't trust the accuracy of NASS data, particularly since returning surveys isn't specifically required, and the accuracy of the data isn't necessarily verified. Additionally, if NASS doesn't receive sufficient responses for a particular county, USDA has a cascade of other sources in place for determining county yield, which includes RMA and regional data. This process has led to situations with significant differences in payment rates between neighboring counties.

The last Farm Bill was written at a time when economic conditions were much different than what farmers are currently facing. Wheat prices have dropped below loan rates, which has only happened a couple of times in the last two decades. The low prices triggered the availability of Marketing Assistance Loans (MALs) and Loan Deficiency Payments (LDPs). These programs are critical to helping producers with short-term cash-flow needs. The fact that they were triggered at all is an indicator of the bad economic conditions in rural America.

---

[27] https://www.ers.usda.gov/webdocs/publications/eib164/eib-164.pdf.

The financial situation in the agricultural economy has changed considerably over the last two years, and we are in the beginning of what is going to be a tough stretch for Kansas agriculture. As I stated earlier, farm income levels are at their lowest point since 1985. Net farm income dropped 95% from 2014 to 2015, and net farm debt levels have increased 25% over the last 3 years.[28] This downturn has largely been caused by low commodity prices, which are due to record highs in both local and worldwide production over the past two years.[29] These production levels have increased supply, while overall demand has waned, due to a strong U.S. dollar and decreasing exports.[30] In short, we have a lot of product and nowhere to go with it. Another major factor is that while revenues have only gone down, the cost of production and expenses have gone up. From 2009 to 2015 the cost of production has increased almost 50%.[31]

As the situation continues to deteriorate in rural America, it is small and beginning farmers that are going to be affected the most. Small and beginning farmers are the most vulnerable to changes in the marketplace, because they do not have the ability to absorb losses or tough conditions like some of the more established producers do. The USDA estimates that small farms make up 90% of the farm count and operate nearly half of America's farmland.[32] If conditions continue to worsen, we could see a lot of those farmers going out of business.

One way to help turn the agricultural economic situation around would be to help create demand for wheat products. This could be done by increasing food aid and supporting international trade.

Food aid has long been a point of pride for American farmers as we continue the more than 60-year tradition of Food for Peace. Lest we forget, the McGovern-Dole program was cofounded by one of Kansas' native sons. Last year we received reports from a trip to the Middle East and Africa examining the use of U.S. food aid. Members of that trip reviewed a dam project in Jordan being funded by the sale of donated U.S. wheat. We also heard about efforts being made about 130 miles from the Somalian border, in eastern Ethiopia, where U.S. wheat is being donated in response to the 50-year drought gripping the eastern part of the nation. It is programs like these that help farmers, through their bountiful harvests, to feed the world.

Last year the United States sent a total of 592,000 metric tons (21.8 million bushels) of Hard Red Winter wheat in food aid, which accounted for almost 10% of all Hard Red Winter wheat exports. Additionally, the only markets that purchased more Hard Red Winter wheat than the total of food aid donations were Nigeria, Japan, and Mexico.

---

[28] http://www.agmanager.info/kfma/state-summaries.

[29] https://www.wsj.com/articles/whats-behind-the-glut-in-agricultural-commodities-1476670020.

[30] https://www.wsj.com/articles/the-next-american-farm-bust-is-upon-us-1486572488.

[31] http://www.agmanager.info/kfma/state-summaries/2015-state-summary-detailed-cost-summary.

[32] https://www.ers.usda.gov/webdocs/publications/eib164/eib-164.pdf.

Perhaps the easiest and most effective way to increase commodity prices and improve the rural economy is to increase trade. Wheat is one of the most heavily exported crops grown in America and is the 7th most valuable crop in terms of export value.[33] Kansas ranks as the 8th largest state in terms of exports of agricultural products.[34] In 2015, Kansas wheat exports alone were valued at over 800 million dollars.[35] When considering all export production in the state of Kansas, wheat is the 2nd largest export, falling behind only aircrafts in terms of value.[36]

Because of our heavy dependence on exports the Kansas Association of Wheat Growers has been a major supporter of international trade deals such at NAFTA, CAFTA, and TPP. Although we were disappointed with how things ended with TPP, we would encourage Members of the Committee to help spread the message about how vital international trade is to the agricultural industry. On average, half of the wheat grown in Kansas is exported, and without trade, the Kansas farmer will continue to struggle.

For wheat, Mexico is a particularly important market. It was once a country that charged high tariffs on wheat. NAFTA instead created a duty-free wheat trade which moved Mexico into a top 5 export market for U.S. wheat. It is the largest consistent market and the largest total market over the past couple years. Kansas farmers certainly want to see good relationships maintained with our Mexican trading partners and obviously want to do no harm to wheat market access. If the U.S. decided to leave NAFTA or extract painful concessions, it is likely that Mexico will target the most sensitive sectors, and agriculture in particular. Mexico has alternatives when it comes to wheat. In 2010 the U.S. had over 80% of the wheat market there; last year it was only 55%. Russia, Ukraine, and EU in particular have all increased their market share.

We would also urge you to support ending the trade embargo with Cuba, or at the very least, support legislation in the House and Senate that would ease financing restrictions on the purchase of American agricultural products. Cuba's 11 million people consume close to one million metric tons (36.7 million bushels) of wheat each year. It is the largest wheat market in the Caribbean, but it currently purchases almost all of that wheat from the European Union and Canada. Cuba could import at least 500,000 metric tons (18.35 million bushels) of wheat from the United States each year but has not purchased U.S. wheat since 2011. Under the current embargo, the United States can export agricultural products to Cuba through the use of third-party banking institutions, which makes facilitating trade burdensome and often more expensive.

---

[33] https://www.ers.usda.gov/data-products/state-export-data/.
[34] *Id.*
[35] *Id.*
[36] https://www.census.gov/foreign-trade/statistics/state/data/ks.html.

Finally, once we do have trade deals, we need to make sure we are taking action to enforce them. The National Association of Wheat Growers and U.S. Wheat Associates recently rolled out a study conducted by Iowa State University economist Dr. Dermot Hayes showing that the support system used by China has led to U.S. wheat farmers losing out on over $650 million in lost revenue in one year. A study by DTB Associates last year demonstrated that China has been heavily exceeding the trade commitments it agreed to when it acceded to the WTO. Particularly given the low commodity prices farmers are receiving, there has been more and more attention paid to the fact that U.S. farmers aren't on a level playing field because of the subsidies employed by other countries.

As you know, nobody understands the need for good stewardship and conservation better than Kansas wheat farmers. This is what we do every day. We depend on clean water and healthy soils to make a living and feed the world. However, wheat farmers also need regulatory certainty so they know how to stay in compliance with the law. Costs of compliance have grown increasingly cumbersome over the last few years. Rules such as the EPA's Waters of the United States rule, duplicative environmental regulations, and ill-advised additions to the endangered species act, have made farming and ranching more difficult and more expensive for Kansans. I believe that reducing these burdens, and streamlining them into a reasonable, affordable, and manageable regulatory structure will help our bottom lines and keep farming profitable.

The agricultural economy is at a crossroads right now, with depressed prices, increased costs and many additional challenges. It is our duty, as stewards of the land, to leave the soil and environment in better shape for our next generation than it was when we received it. Along that same line, a strong safety net provides for the future of food production in the United States. We ask that you make decisions that will allow us the ability to sustain our livelihoods and provide for future generations of farmers. When a natural disaster looms on the horizon, whether it is a drought, flood, hail storm, or in my case, a tornado, we know that we have a safety net to help keep us in business.

I would like to thank you for coming to our state to hold this farm bill field hearing. Field hearings show your commitment to hearing firsthand from farmers and ranchers about the effects of farm legislation on individuals across the country. It has been an honor to submit testimony and speak on behalf of wheat producers. I look forward to any questions you may have.

Documents Submitted for the Record, February 23, 2017

Addendum to Written Statement by Secretary McClaskey

Kansas Agricultural Growth
Federal Policies and Programs Limiting Growth in Agriculture
February 23, 2017

Farmers, ranchers and agribusinesses must balance a lengthy list of challenges and variables, many of which they cannot control, as they work to grow and raise food for families across the globe. Kansas needs to be poised to work collaboratively to help craft quality legislation aimed at serving our farmers and ranchers in the next Farm Bill and other federal policy initiatives.

While challenges exist, the opportunity for growth and the willingness of the agriculture industry to work together to address these challenges is far greater. Following are issues related to federal policy and programs identified by industry stakeholders that limit growth potential of the agricultural industry. Working together, these challenges can be overcome.

Domestic and International Markets

- Access to international markets for agricultural products is key to growing the agriculture industry. Resistance to free trade agreements at the federal level can hinder this access.
- Regulatory approval of new seed technology around the world is important as Kansas farmers look to take advantage of the latest advancements to improve yield and meet worldwide demand. A reliance on non-science-based standards in some trade partner nations disrupts the ability of U.S. farmers to access critical international markets.
- The U.S. dairy industry is becoming increasingly affected by international dairy markets. A current surplus of milk supply worldwide has greatly suppressed domestic milk prices. While the U.S. must become more competitive on the world market, risk management strategies are needed to help protect the U.S. dairy industry from major price swings. The U.S. must also counter protectionist milk policies, such as a potential U.S. milk protein concentrate ban from Canada, poor dairy-specific Trans-Pacific Partnership negotiations, or Russian bans on dairy and agricultural products.
- It can be challenging to get U.S. Department of Agriculture meat inspectors to rural meat processing operations on a schedule that matches the needs of all parties. Only those facilities inspected by USDA are allowed to sell meat outside of the state borders even though state-inspected facilities must meet the same requirements for food safety.

Consumer Awareness

- Ever-increasing food safety expectations from the public and the government result in a growing regulatory burden on food processing businesses to implement processes, upgrade equipment, sample product, document activities and hire additional employees to complete all of this work.

- The U.S. has an antiquated view of poultry meal and poultry by-products as the only country in the world with split definitions. Other species don't have split definitions.
- USDA Animal and Plant Health Inspection Service is currently working on a biotech policy which may include double haploids as biotech versus traditional breeding. This type of process regulation is ineffective and unjust. Attention should be paid to the end product and whether genetic modification has actually occurred or not.
- Recent increase in demand for gluten-free products by consumers has the potential to decrease demand for wheat products at retail. Gluten-free has moved beyond health needs for a small percentage of the population into a dietary fad resulting in much misunderstanding about gluten, where it comes from and what advantages it brings to food. Standardized marketing claims for advertised characteristics such as gluten-free, natural, organic, local, etc. could help consumers better understand the products they are buying.

Workforce Development

- The temporary and seasonal guest worker programs do not work for many sectors of agriculture, such as the livestock and dairy industries, which require year-round labor.
- A lack of adequate housing in rural areas compounds the issue of a shortage of agricultural workers. The opportunity exists to engage with USDA Rural Development and local-level contacts to identify solutions to housing needs in rural communities.

Critical Infrastructure and Transportation

- Having the transportation infrastructure necessary to move agricultural commodities and products is critical. Ports such as the Port of Catoosa in Oklahoma where Kansas products are loaded on barges need to be maintained such that shipping capacity isn't delayed or reduced due to aging infrastructure.
- The beef industry relies solely on trucks and the highway system to transport live animals and beef products. Federal regulations can make it challenging to transport live animals or beef products in a manner that is safe for drivers and animals alike.
- Federal agricultural exemptions, such as hours of service for livestock haulers, are based on temporary exemptions, creating long-term uncertainty for the industry.

Access to Capital and Taxation

- Maintaining the flexibility farmers have in how they depreciate capital purchases as it relates to federal income taxes is critical for management and planning. Any changes that reduce that flexibility, or threaten to reduce it, compromise farmers' ability to plan for expenses.
- Farm families work their whole lives to build and maintain the family farming operation including the acquisition of land. Being forced to sell hard-earned assets to satisfy estate taxes is a devastating blow to family farmers, particularly beginning farmers.

Animal Health and Welfare

- Antibiotics are an important tool to prevent, treat and control disease in animals. Despite efforts to ensure that animal antibiotics do not affect public health, there are some lawmakers who continue to call for increased scrutiny and regulation on the use of antibiotics in food-producing animals.
- The lack of traceability system inhibits export growth potential and could potentially create animal health threats.
- In the past, some federal laboratories have been managed in a manner that does not fully integrate with the regional economy or capitalize fully on the potential to partner with private industry, especially small- and medium-sized enterprises, on research initiatives. It will be critical to work alongside the Department of Homeland Security and USDA in the development of strong partnerships with state government, private industry and universities to maximize potential of the National Bio and Agro-Defense Facility (NBAF).
- According to the World Health Organization, about 75 percent of emerging diseases are zoonotic. Currently, there is not a laboratory in the United States that can research and work on zoonotic diseases, and also develop vaccines and countermeasures to those zoonotic diseases, which affect livestock.
- Since the last horse slaughter facility was closed in the United States, the market for horses has crashed along with an explosion of unwanted horses that cannot be disposed of in any other manner. This also creates animal welfare issues for those unwanted, old and neglected animals. Federal appropriations are encouraged for horse slaughter facilities.

Natural Resources

- Burning the Flint Hills is a critical range management tool to improve prairie grass production and prevent intrusion from weeds and woody plants. Despite the Flint Hills Smoke Management Plan, there is concern that the federal government may propose regulations that may result in challenges to the ability of Flint Hills ranchers to burn rangeland.
- Threatened and endangered species reduce the pace or viability of new projects and expansions. An example of this includes the lesser prairie chicken, which until late 2015 was listed as a threatened species under the Endangered Species Act. While a court order vacated the listing of the chicken, the renewed review of the listing criteria by the U.S. Fish and Wildlife Service has the potential to delay or stop construction of new and expanding agriculture operations.
- Allowing limited haying, grazing and vegetative management on acres enrolled in federal cost share conservation programs would likely increase landowner interest and participation in these programs without compromising the natural resources benefits of the practices. In addition, some requirements of the cost-share programs disincentivize participation from growers of alternative crops such as sorghum.

Federal Policy and Regulations

- Though not unique to Kansas, there exist significant challenges due to federal laws and regulations, including: food labeling, dietary requirements, Waters of the U.S., the Endangered Species Act, burdensome Occupational Safety and Health Administration regulations and more.
- Cotton is not a covered commodity under the Farm Bill so it lacks the Price Loss Protection or Agricultural Risk Coverage afforded to other commodities such as corn, soybeans and wheat. Cotton growers have to rely on insurance products (Stacked Income Protection [STAX] Program) in the absence of other Farm Bill support mechanisms. While restoring cotton as a Title I commodity under the next Farm Bill is a more long-term resolution to this issue, designating cotton in the "other oilseed" category offers an alternative for improved coverage under existing commodity programs.
- There exist significant challenges due to federal laws and regulations that affect technology, including Federal Aviation Administration regulations that largely restrict Unmanned Aerial Vehicle use.
- Renewable Fuel Standard is a regular unknown when it comes to understanding the requirements for ethanol in U.S. gasoline. More transparency and predictability would bring increased stability to the ethanol market.

QUESTIONS AND ANSWERS, FEBRUARY 23, 2017

Senate Committee on Agriculture, Nutrition, & Forestry
Hearing from the Heartland: Perspectives on the 2018 Farm Bill from Kansas
February 23, 2017
Questions for the Record
Mr. David Clawson

Chairman Pat Roberts (R-KS)

1. Mr. Clawson, you mention the importance of USDA's conservation programs in your testimony. The 2014 Farm Bill significantly consolidated and streamlined the suite of conservation programs available to producers. Gearing up for the 2018 Farm Bill, what policy recommendations would livestock producers suggest Congress consider for the Conservation Reserve Program?

First, I would caution against increasing the number of new acres that could be enrolled in traditional CRP. KLA believes the program should focus on the most sensitive areas instead of taking entire fields out of production. Further, KLA supports rules to allow periodic haying and grazing as an important management tool as part of an NRCS management plan. We also support the flexibility to utilize CRP acres in emergency situations. KLA encourages the committee to consider ways in which CRP acres can be made available more quickly in emergency situations.

2. Mr. Clawson, I hear often that regulatory burdens are directly impacting farm operations both in Kansas and across the country. During these tough economic times, I'm sure these costs can be crippling. Can you elaborate or share with the Committee the regulatory challenges impacting your farm's profitability?

To begin, I would highlight the crippling effects of the GIPSA interim final rule on competitive injury. Implementation of that final rule would put an end to the value-based marketing programs that reward cattle producers for their investment in genetics and management practices that lead to beef products that better meet consumer needs.

The EPA Waters of the U.S. (WOTUS) rule is another example of a potentially devastating regulation. If implemented, WOTUS would represent an unprecedented expansion federal authority over private property. Compliance costs are difficult to determine, but certainl would add significantly to our cost of production. KLA strongly supports President Trump's action to withdraw this onerous rule.

The EPA is a source of many regulations that increase costs for my business. Numerous rules have increased the cost of energy, increasing the cost of many inputs and transportation. Our farming and ranching operations constantly strive to be more efficient, but producing food for people around the world is an energy-intensive effort. We need EPA to recognize the stewardship of land and water resources provided by farmers and ranchers. Far too often, EPA regulators have treated farmers and ranchers as the problem when it comes to protecting the environment.

Trucking regulations often ignore the type of product being hauled. For the well-being of the animal, cattle need to arrive at their destination as soon as possible. Livestock producers need flexibility in the hours-of-service rules. Neither standing on the truck nor being off-loaded during required rest periods is optimal for cattle health and well-being. Livestock producers need an exemption from hours-of-service rules to minimize the time in transit.

The time value of complying with trucking regulations also is substantial. While there are some exemptions for private not-for-hire haulers, the remaining regulations still are costly and require significant time for compliance. Complying with the Unified Carrier Registration (UCR) and the Interstate Fuel Tax Agreement (IFTA) requirements can be confusing and costly for private haulers. Most private haulers only cross state lines a few times a year but still must apply and pay the UCR fee and report fuel use. While this is normal for motor carriers, many farmers and ranchers are not experienced in wading through trucking regulations.

Also, many pickup truck and trailer combinations crossing state lines are required to get a USDOT number and again must pay the UCR fee and comply with IFTA. These vehicles are not semi-trucks and should not be treated like them. The weight threshold for these regulations needs to be increased to allow farmers and ranchers to operate their farm pickups as needed.

Senate Committee on Agriculture, Nutrition, & Forestry
Hearing from the Heartland: Perspectives on the 2018 Farm Bill from Kansas
February 23, 2017
Questions for the Record
Ms. Amy France

Chairman Pat Roberts (R-KS)

1. Ms. France, you mention the importance of USDA's conservation programs in your testimony. The 2014 Farm Bill significantly consolidated and streamlined the suite of conservation programs available to producers. Gearing up for the 2018 Farm Bill, what policy recommendations would you suggest Congress consider for the Conservation Reserve Program?

Chairman Roberts, thank you again for the opportunity to provide input into the 2018 Farm Bill development process. In western Kansas, where I live, the Conservation Reserve Program (CRP) represents a vital partnership connecting federal, state and farmer partners to protect sensitive land from degradation and improve environmental quality; and that is where the program should remain: protecting marginal and highly erodible lands (HEL). The CRP program has been extremely beneficial to producers, wildlife and the ecosystem throughout Kansas since its inception. In fact, Kansas (37,582 contracts on 21,966 farms totaling 2,074,491 acres) and Texas (19,264 contracts on 13,967 farms totaling 2,909,928 acres) are the only two states with more than two million acres enrolled in CRP as of December 2016. Every program though, could use some improvement and CRP is no exception. My suggestions include:

- Allow for additional management practices on CRP land: As mentioned in my written testimony, Farm Bureau strongly supports working lands conservation programs. Any effort to incorporate additional management practices as part of traditional or continuous CRP contract management and expansion of the CRP Grasslands Program would be a positive policy direction. As our friends at the National Resources Conservation Service (NRCS) often say, "what's good for the herd, is good for the bird," meaning careful inclusion of grazing practices in established CRP lands are beneficial to upland ground birds such as the lesser prairie chicken (LPC). Studies show improved habitat following grazing events thanks to increased forb diversity and seasonal changes within forage mixes. Likewise, for those farms where grazing is not easily employed, additional opportunities to incorporate haying into CRP contract management would be highly sought by Farm Bureau members. Over the course of the past decade Kansas has experienced record drought. In trying to assist fellow producers who were severely impacted by drought, and after jumping through multiple hoops, it was determined in most cases producers who were required to actively "manage" the CRP acreage could not bale and donate the bales to a drought stricken producer; rather, the bales taken from CRP acreage were required to be burned or destroyed. In limited cases, the bales could be donated but no reimbursement could be given to offset transportation, hauling or labor costs. Additionally, CP25 CRP acres in Kansas have not been allowed to be touched by hoof or swather; any assistance to allow at least grazing on CP25 acres would be much appreciated. Incorporating higher levels of management of CRP lands, and allowing for reasonable access to the growth of CRP grass during times of severe weather events as part of the next Farm Bill not only provides greater environmental incentive to keep these acres in land to conserve grass and provide wildlife habitat but also assist in managing the fuel load that CRP acres might provide to wildfires. As evidenced both in 2016 and again this year in Kansas, wildfire is both dangerous and devastating to rural communities. Carefully managed haying and grazing of CRP lands can play a key role in limiting the available fuel load as well as assist in the recovery efforts of areas burned if allowed to be baled and transported to areas impacted by fire.

- Continue efforts to ensure CRP rental rates accurately mirror local rental rates: To best balance the desires to enroll sensitive lands, yet also ensure that acreage is accessible to young and beginning farmers, both CRP and Conservation Reserve Enhancement Program (CREP) rental rates should be examined annually at enrollment to ensure they accurately reflect the rental rates of comparable land in the immediate area.

- Maintain the current 24 million acre cap for CRP: As farmers, Clint and I strive to maintain, build and restore the soil, water and air so we can pass our farm on to the next generation in better shape than when we began farming it. We believe proper funding of working lands conservation programs such as the Environmental Quality Incentives Program (EQIP) and the Conservation Stewardship Program (CSP) is the best way to achieve that goal. I know the CRP cap of 24 million acres will be thoroughly debated in Congress and I cannot tell you today if 24 million acres is the appropriate number or not. What I can tell you is as a farmer, USDA programs and dollars have a lot more bang for the buck within the crop insurance, Title 1 programs and even the EQIP and CSP programs of Title 2 than in increasing CRP payment rates or increasing the national CRP acreage cap.
- Transitional payments on expiring CRP contracts: Over the coming years Kansas will experience the following CRP contract expirations:
  - 2017 = 137,464 acres
  - 2018 = 106,413 acres
  - 2019 = 50,300 acres
  - 2020 = 503,483 acres
  - 2021 = 368,933 acres
  - 2022 = 298,148 acres
  - 2023 = 133,123 acres
  - 2024 = 476,627 acres

  With this amount of acreage expiring at some point over the course of the next Farm Bill, it is imperative some sort of workable transition mechanism be in place. Some of the expiring CRP acreage would be best suited to remain in grass and utilized for grazing or haying purposes, some will end up being returned to production agriculture. Yet some acreage should have the opportunity to reenroll in the CRP program to protect the sensitive nature of the soil. Farm Bureau looks forward to working with policy makers on ways to successfully transition large contract expirations into future programs and production practices that best suit the productivity of the soil and protect natural resources.
- Standardize management of CRP across the contracts: A lot of the producer activity and management issues with CRP stems from a lack of standardization among the multiple General CRP practices. For

example, CP25 is extremely restrictive while CP2, CP4 and CP10 are similar in the management practices allowed. When signing up for a CRP contract, the length of the underlying contract should not sway producers into agreeing to more restrictive land management activities. Standardization of management activities within all CRP contracts regardless of the practice chosen will help alleviate neighborly disputes (where one neighbor has grazing access to his CRP but the adjacent tract grazing is not allowed), help USDA service center employees better communicate the benefits of the program and ensure the most environmentally sensitive lands are placed in the program. The type of covers established (introduced grass, native grass, high forb mix, etc.) would still differentiate the practices and allow for a simplified ranking of applications.

- Greater emphasis on Continuous CRP: Enhanced payment rates provide incentives to put the most erosive, ecologically sensitive, or least productive land into grass, wetlands or timber. Doing so maximizes environmental benefits, provides the greatest return on investment, both by reducing payments associated with Title I programs and crop insurance on the lowest quality land. Furthermore, the highest quality and most productive lands continue to produce food, fiber, energy and forage.

Again, it was an honor to testify on behalf of Kansas Farm Bureau and our more than 30,000 farm and ranch family members across Kansas as you plan for the next Farm Bill. I appreciate the opportunity to provide more input regarding CRP and look forward to continuing the discussion.

Senate Committee on Agriculture, Nutrition, & Forestry
Hearing from the Heartland: Perspectives on the 2018 Farm Bill from Kansas
February 23, 2017
Questions for the Record
Mr. Lucas Heinen

Chairman Pat Roberts (R-KS)

1. Mr. Heinen, you mention the importance of USDA's conservation programs in your testimony. The 2014 Farm Bill significantly consolidated and streamlined the suite of conservation programs available to producers. Gearing up for the 2018 Farm Bill, what policy recommendations would soybean growers suggest Congress consider for the Conservation Reserve Program?

   The American Soybean Association's (ASA) voting delegates, this past week, have approved a resolution supporting an unspecified increase in the cap for the Conservation Reserve Program. Policymakers appear to be interested in many aspects of the Conservation Reserve Program, including rental rates, pollinator habitat incentives, and water quality benefits. ASA looks forward to joining in those policy discussions as the farm bill advances.

Senate Committee on Agriculture, Nutrition, & Forestry
Hearing from the Heartland: Perspectives on the 2018 Farm Bill from Kansas
February 23, 2017
Questions for the Record
Mr. Kent Moore

Chairman Pat Roberts (R-KS)

1. Mr. Moore, you mention the importance of USDA's conservation programs in your testimony. The 2014 Farm Bill significantly consolidated and streamlined the suite of conservation programs available to producers. Gearing up for the 2018 Farm Bill, what policy recommendations would corn growers suggest Congress consider for the Conservation Reserve Program?

The Kansas Corn Growers Association (KCGA) recognizes the important role that USDA programs contribute to maintaining and improving stewardship of our land, air and water resources.

The Conservation Reserve Program is a time-tested success story of the federal government and farmers and ranchers working together to improve soil health, water quality and wildlife enhancement. Kansas Corn supports the continuation of the CRP program in its current capacity as a tool that producers can utilize to address highly erodible acres. KCGA is currently working with other corn state associations and National Corn Growers Association to analyze current CRP policy and to consider more specific recommendations to improve the program.

At this point, our policy on CRP is unchanged from the 2014 Farm Bill.

In general, we support voluntary enrollment into the Conservation Reserve Program and renewal of contracts targeted to the most environmentally sensitive acres. We believe CRP rental rates should be adjusted to ensure that environmental or significant wildlife habitat sensitive land remain in the CRP program. We support voluntary enrollment under the continuous CRP provisions for wildlife habitat and food plot areas; filter strips and buffer strips; established waterways and turn rows, and other partial field enrollments impacting water quality.

Senate Committee on Agriculture, Nutrition, & Forestry
Hearing from the Heartland: Perspectives on the 2018 Farm Bill from Kansas
February 23, 2017
Questions for the Record
Mr. Michael Springer

Chairman Pat Roberts (R-KS)

1. Mr. Springer, since 2013 pork producers have struggled as Porcine Epidemic Diarrhea Virus crept onto hog farms in 39 states. The disease had a devastating impact and roughly 10% of the swine herd perished at the peak of the outbreak. Looking back on that experience, can you describe specific measures or needs related to disease preparedness and prevention that will equip producers so they can be prepared to address emerging disease threats?

Thankfully, our farm did not have to deal with PEDV, but we've had our share of other swine health challenges. For our farm, our first line of defense is our veterinarians. To keep them effective, they rely heavily on the federally-funded research performed at institutions such Kansas State University's College of Agriculture and Veterinary Medicine. These agricultural research projects have real-life application on our farm.

As an example of this, our farm recently built a building designed to "bake" or dry our trucks and trailers before they are allowed to enter our farm. Hopefully, this drying process limits one avenue of bringing diseases onto our farm. The building cost about $200,000 to construct and it costs about $50 per load to operate. This was an expensive addition to our biosecurity measures, but I see it as another form of insurance for our farm.

Senate Committee on Agriculture, Nutrition, & Forestry
Hearing from the Heartland: Perspectives on the 2018 Farm Bill from Kansas
February 23, 2017
Questions for the Record
Mr. Ken Wood

Chairman Pat Roberts (R-KS)

1. Mr. Wood, you mention the importance of USDA's conservation programs in your testimony. The 2014 Farm Bill significantly consolidated and streamlined the suite of conservation programs available to producers. Gearing up for the 2018 Farm Bill, what policy recommendations would wheat growers suggest Congress consider for the Conservation Reserve Program?

Response

2. KAWG's policy is to support maintaining the current level of CRP acres and the current CRP policy. As we look forward to the next farm bill, KAWG does not want CRP acres to be expanded and would want the current cap maintained. We would like to see a larger focus and emphasis on enrolling acres based on soils, specifically targeting less productive land that may currently be used in production. In the future, we would like to see the program allow for increased flexibility in management decisions by producers enrolled in the program. This will allow producers to make decisions in a time of need, such as following natural disasters, etc., and may also encourage more active producers to utilize CRP, in addition to the program's traditional usage by producers who are taking a less engaged role in farming operations.

In: The Farm Bill: Review, Background, and the WTO ISBN: 978-1-53615-272-2
Editor: Katie M. Harrison © 2019 Nova Science Publishers, Inc.

Chapter 2

PREVIEWING A 2018 FARM BILL*

Renée Johnson, Katie Hoover, Randy Alison Aussenberg, Mark A. McMinimy, Tadlock Cowan, Jim Monke, Joel L. Greene, Randy Schnepf, Sonya Hammons and Megan Stubbs

SUMMARY

Congress periodically establishes agricultural and food policy in an omnibus farm bill. The 115th Congress faces reauthorization of the 2014 farm bill—the Agricultural Act of 2014 (P.L. 113-79, H.Rept. 113-333)—because many of its provisions expire in 2018.

The 2014 farm bill is the most recent omnibus farm bill. It was enacted in February 2014 and succeeded the Food, Conservation, and Energy Act of 2008 (P.L. 110-246, "2008 farm bill"). In recent decades, the breadth of farm bills has steadily grown to include new and expanding food and agricultural interests. The 2014 farm bill contains 12 titles encompassing farm commodity revenue supports, farm credit, trade, agricultural conservation, research, rural development, energy, and foreign and domestic food programs, among other programs. Provisions in the 2014 farm bill reshaped the structure of farm commodity support, expanded crop insurance coverage, consolidated conservation programs, reauthorized and revised nutrition assistance, and extended authority to appropriate funds for many U.S. Department of Agriculture (USDA) discretionary programs through FY2018.

When the 2014 farm bill was enacted, the Congressional Budget Office (CBO) estimated that the total cost of mandatory programs would be $489 billion over the five years FY2014-FY2018. Four titles accounted for 99% ($483.8 billion) of anticipated farm bill mandatory program outlays: nutrition, crop insurance, conservation, and farm commodity support. The nutrition title, which includes the Supplemental Nutrition Assistance Program (SNAP), comprised 80% of the total, with the remaining 20% mostly geared toward agricultural production across other titles.

* This is an edited, reformatted and augmented version of Congressional Research Service, Publication No. R44784, dated March 15, 2017.

Traditionally, a primary focus of omnibus farm bills has been commodity-based revenue support policy—namely, the methods and levels of federal support provided to agricultural producers. The 2014 farm bill amended U.S. farm safety net programs by expanding crop insurance provisions and modifying counter-cyclical support while eliminating direct payments to growers of grains, cotton, and peanuts. Upland cotton was removed from eligibility for participation in the new revenue support programs as part of compliance with a World Trade Organization dispute settlement case with Brazil. Instead, cotton producers were offered an insurance-like support program that protects against within-season revenue shortfalls. Another major change involved dairy: Previous support programs were replaced with a new insurance-like margin program that insures against shortfalls in the difference between milk prices and feed costs. Most farm program proponents agree that the new cotton and dairy programs have performed ineffectively and are likely to see proposals for change.

Other farm interest groups, however, continue to point to competing policy priorities—covering a range of equity concerns across the entire farm sector—and call for enhanced support for small and medium-sized farms, specialty crops, organic agriculture, local and regional food systems, healthy and nutritious foods, research, conservation, and rural development, among others.

One of the principal drivers of a new farm bill debate will be the federal budget. According to CBO estimates, if ongoing programs were to continue under current law, mandatory farm bill spending by the four largest titles—nutrition, crop insurance, farm commodity programs, and conservation—is projected to be about $435 billion over the next five years (FY2018-FY2022), with domestic nutrition assistance accounting for nearly 77% of the total. This compares with actual costs for the first three years of the 2014 farm bill and projections for its last two years, which suggest that these four titles may cost $456 billion over FY2014-FY2018.

INTRODUCTION

The farm bill is an omnibus, multi-year law that governs an array of agricultural and food programs. Although agricultural policies are sometimes created and changed by freestanding legislation or as part of other major laws, the farm bill provides a predictable opportunity for policymakers to comprehensively and periodically address agricultural and food issues. The farm bill is renewed about every five years.[1]

The Agricultural Act of 2014 (P.L. 113-79, H.Rept. 113-333), referred to here as the "2014 farm bill," is the most recent omnibus farm bill. It was enacted in February 2014 and generally expires in 2018. It succeeded the Food, Conservation, and Energy Act of 2008 (P.L. 110-246, "2008 farm bill"). The 2014 farm bill contains 12 titles encompassing farm commodity revenue supports, agricultural conservation, international food aid and agricultural trade, nutrition assistance, farm credit, rural development, agricultural research, forestry, bioenergy, horticulture and organic agriculture, crop

[1] There have been 17 farm bills since the 1930s (2014, 2008, 2002, 1996, 1990, 1985, 1981, 1977, 1973, 1970, 1965, 1956, 1954, 1949, 1948, 1938, and 1933).

insurance and disaster assistance, and livestock issues. Provisions in the 2014 farm bill reshaped the structure of farm commodity support, expanded crop insurance coverage, consolidated conservation programs, reauthorized and revised nutrition assistance, and extended authority to appropriate funds for many U.S. Department of Agriculture (USDA) discretionary programs through FY2018.

The omnibus nature of the bill can create broad coalitions of support among sometimes conflicting interests for policies that individually might not survive the legislative process, but it can also stir competition for available funds, particularly among producers of different commodities or between those who have differing priorities. Such competition often results in farm state lawmakers seeking urban legislators' backing for commodity price supports in exchange for votes on domestic food assistance programs—and vice versa. In recent years, a more diverse range of groups has become involved in the debate, including national farm groups, commodity associations, state organizations, nutrition and public health officials, and advocacy groups representing conservation, recreation, rural development, local and urban farming facilities, faith-based interests, land-grant universities, and certified organic production.

This report provides background on each of the major titles of the current farm bill and previews of some of the potential issues that could factor into the debate.

FARM POLICY CONSIDERATIONS FOR THE 115TH CONGRESS

Since the 1930s, periodic farm bills have traditionally focused on farm commodity program support for a handful of staple commodities—corn, soybeans, wheat, cotton, rice, dairy, and sugar. In recent farm bills, however, the breadth of the farm bill has steadily grown to include new and expanding food and agricultural interests. Titles have been added to address emerging issues, and the farm bill has become increasingly omnibus in nature. Prominent additions to the farm bill have been nutrition assistance, farmland conservation, agriculture-based biofuels, and horticulture (specialty crops, such as fruits and vegetables, and organic agriculture). Farm bill titles have also become increasingly integrated. For example, the conservation and commodity titles both include provisions that affect land use and markets. Support for specialty crops, despite its stand-alone title, includes a series of provisions contained in other farm bill titles. The text box below briefly describes provisions in these titles. See the Appendix at the end of this report for a complete list of titles and subtitles of the 2014 farm bill.

The 2014 Farm Bill (P.L. 113-79): Functions and Major Issues, by Title

- Title I, Commodity Programs: Provides farm payments when crop prices or revenues decline for major commodity crops, including wheat, corn, soybeans, peanuts, and rice. Includes disaster programs to help livestock and tree fruit producers manage production losses due to natural disasters. Other support includes margin insurance for dairy, marketing quotas, minimum price guarantees, and import quotas for sugar.
- Title II, Conservation: Encourages environmental stewardship and improved management practices through various working lands programs, as well as changes in land use through land retirement and easement programs.
- Title III, Trade: Provides support for U.S. agricultural export promotion and export credit guarantee programs as well as international food aid programs that provide emergency and nonemergency foreign food aid. Other provisions address issues related to the World Trade Organization (WTO) obligations.
- Title IV, Nutrition: Provides nutrition assistance for low-income households through programs, including the Supplemental Nutrition Assistance Program (SNAP, formerly known as the Food Stamp Program) and emergency food assistance programs. Also supports the distribution of foods in schools.
- Title V, Credit: Offers direct government loans to farmers and ranchers and guarantees loans from commercial lenders. Sets eligibility rules and policies.
- Title VI, Rural Development: Supports rural business and community development programs. Establishes planning, feasibility assessments, and coordination with other local, state, and federal programs. Programs include grants and loans for infrastructure, economic development, broadband, and telecommunications.
- Title VII, Research, Extension, and Related Matters: Offers a wide range of agricultural research and extension programs that expand academic knowledge about agriculture and food and help farmers and ranchers become more efficient, innovative, and productive.
- Title VIII, Forestry: Supports forestry management programs run by USDA's Forest Service.
- Title IX, Energy: Encourages the development of farm and community renewable energy systems through grants, loan guarantees, and feedstock procurement initiatives. Also facilitates the production, marketing, and processing of advanced biofuels and biofuel feedstocks and research, education, and demonstration programs.
- Title X, Horticulture: Supports specialty crops—fruits, vegetables, tree nuts, and floriculture and ornamental products—through a range of initiatives, including market promotion, plant pest and disease prevention, and public research. Also provides support to certified organic agricultural production and locally produced foods.
- Title XI, Crop Insurance: Enhances the permanently authorized federal crop insurance program.
- Title XII, Miscellaneous: Covers other types of programs including livestock and poultry production and limited-resource and socially disadvantaged farmers.

As the 115th Congress considers a new farm bill, it does so in an economic setting of generally lower farm prices and income for the main commodity crops as well as continued focus on the overall cost of nutrition assistance programs. The largest of these programs—the Supplemental Nutrition Assistance Program (SNAP, formerly the Food Stamp Program)—accounts for the overwhelming majority of total farm bill spending. At the same time, some groups continue to call for further expansion of the farm bill to create and/or expand support for other competing policy priorities and to address equitability concerns across the nation's farm sectors. These include enhanced support for small and medium-sized farms, specialty crops, cottonseed, organic agriculture, local and regional food systems, urban farming, healthy and nutritious foods, food waste reduction, research, conservation, and rural development, among others. Efforts to reduce overall farm bill costs, given overall constraints on federal spending, may create heightened competition and tension among a range of U.S. farm policy stakeholders. There is also general uncertainty regarding priorities for farm policy under the new Trump Administration.

Potential expiration of the current farm bill and the consequences of allowing it to expire may also motivate legislative action.[4] When a farm bill expires, not all programs are affected equally. Some programs cease to operate unless reauthorized, while others might continue to pay old obligations, as provided under current law. For example, the farm commodity programs would not only expire but revert to permanent law dating back to the 1940s. Nutrition assistance programs require periodic reauthorization, but appropriations can keep them operating. Many discretionary programs would lose statutory authority to receive appropriations, though annual appropriations could provide funding and implicit authorization. Other programs have permanent authority and do not need to be reauthorized (e.g., crop insurance).[5]

Whether to retain the nutrition title in a new farm bill or to consider nutrition programs separately was debated during consideration of the 2014 farm bill. In 2013, after a farm bill with a nutrition title was defeated on the House floor, the House passed the bills separately—a farm bill without a nutrition title and a nutrition-only bill. After the conference committee negotiations began, the bills were joined together.[6] The enacted law included a nutrition title. Some continue to argue for a separate SNAP reauthorization, but many farm and nutrition policy stakeholders argue for retaining the nutrition title in a new farm bill.[7] Farm bills since 1973 have included reauthorization of

---

[4] For example, in 2012, the 112th Congress did not complete a new farm bill to replace the 2008 law, requiring a one- year extension for 2013. The 113th Congress passed reintroduced and revised bills, culminating in the 2014 farm bill. Some programs, though, still ceased to operate during the 2013 extension because they had no funding. For background, see CRS Report R41433, *Programs Without a Budget Baseline at the End of the 2008 Farm Bill.*

[5] For more information on the consequences of expiration, see CRS Report R42442, *Expiration and Extension of the 2008 Farm Bill.*

[6] For more background information, see CRS Report R43076, *The 2014 Farm Bill (P.L. 113-79): Summary and Side- by-Side.*

[7] For further review of this issue, see Parke Wilde, "The Nutrition Title's Long, Sometimes Strained, but Not Yet Broken, Marriage with the Farm Bill," *Choices*, Quarter 4 (2016). See also recommendations by The Heritage

the Food Stamp Program (renamed SNAP by the 2008 bill). This partnership between nutrition programs and farm programs is generally understood to generate rural and urban support for the farm bill. (For more information, see "Food and Nutrition").

BUDGET SITUATION AND OUTLOOK

Budget Basics

As with all areas of the federal budget, agriculture faces spending constraints. Budget issues are usually an important element when debate on a new farm bill begins. Federal spending is divided into two main categories: mandatory and discretionary spending. In the farm bill, mandatory spending—which does not require a separate appropriation—is authorized primarily for the farm commodity programs, crop insurance, nutrition assistance programs, and some conservation and trade programs.[8] Discretionary spending is authorized for everything else that is not considered mandatory spending, including most rural development programs, research and education programs, and agricultural credit. Research, bioenergy, and rural development programs sometimes secure both types of funding, but most of their funding is discretionary. Programs with discretionary spending are authorized in the farm bill but are paid for separately in annual appropriations under the jurisdiction of the appropriations committees.

Mandatory spending programs often dominate the farm bill debate and its budget. The farm bill "pays" for mandatory spending in addition to determining its policy. These procedures follow a framework of budget enforcement laws that use projected "baseline" and "scores" from the Congressional Budget Office (CBO).[9] An earlier pivotal decision may be whether the multi-year baseline projection, described below, is the appropriate amount for the farm bill or whether more or less spending should be built into the farm bill budget.

The CBO baseline is a projection at a particular point in time of what future federal spending on mandatory programs would be assuming current law remains intact. This baseline is the *benchmark* against which proposed changes in law are measured. When a new bill is proposed that would affect mandatory spending, the impact (score) is measured in relation to the baseline. Changes that increase spending relative to the

---

Foundation, *Blueprint for a New Administration: Priorities for the President*, chapter on the "Department of Agriculture."

[8] The Commodity Credit Corporation (CCC) is the funding mechanism for most of the various agriculture-related mandatory spending programs, though crop insurance and the nutrition programs and not funded by CCC. The CCC is a wholly owned government corporation that has the legal authority to borrow up to $30 billion at any one time from the U.S. Treasury. For more background, see CRS Report R44606, *The Commodity Credit Corporation: In Brief*.

[9] See CRS Report 98-560, *Baselines and Scorekeeping in the Federal Budget Process*.

baseline have a *positive* score; those that decrease spending relative to the baseline have a *negative* score. Increases in cost above the baseline may be subject to budget constraints such as pay-as-you-go (PAYGO) requirements.[10] Reductions from the baseline may be used to offset other provisions or reduce the deficit.

Having a baseline essentially gives programs built-in future funding if policymakers decide that the programs should continue. Straightforward reauthorization would not have a scoring effect. However, programs without a continuing baseline beyond the end of a farm bill do not have assured future funding.[11] Reauthorization would have a positive score that increases the bill's cost.

2014 Farm Bill Spending

When the 2014 farm bill was enacted, four titles accounted for 99% of anticipated farm bill mandatory spending: nutrition, crop insurance, conservation, and farm commodity support (Table 1). The nutrition title, which includes SNAP, comprised 80% of the total. Commodity support and crop insurance combined to be 13% of mandatory spending, with another 6% of costs in USDA conservation programs. The trade title was next in size, providing less than 0.5% of the total.

In dollars, the projected cost of the 2014 farm bill when it was enacted was $484 billion for the largest four titles and $489 billion for all 12 titles (Table 1).[12]

In the years since enactment of the farm bill, CBO has updated its projections of government spending based on new information about the economy and program participation.[13] However, reductions in projected farm bill spending since enactment do not generate savings that can be credited elsewhere, and higher-than-projected costs do not imply insufficient resources. Three years after enactment, the current projected cost of the 2014 farm bill is $456 billion for the four largest titles (FY2014-FY2016 actuals, and updated projections for FY2017-FY2018; Table 1, Figure 1). For the FY2014-FY2018 period, this is $28 billion less (-6%) than what was projected at enactment. Lower farm commodity prices have reduced the projected cost of crop insurance and increased the cost of the counter-cyclical farm subsidies, while lower-than-expected enrollment in SNAP has reduced nutrition title costs. These changes reflect shifts in the underlying economy—that is, the farm bill is costing $28 billion less than initially expected.

[10] See CRS Report R41157, *The Statutory Pay-As-You-Go Act of 2010: Summary and Legislative History*.
[11] See CRS Report R44758, *Farm Bill Programs Without a Budget Baseline Beyond FY2018*.
[12] CBO cost estimate of the Agricultural Act of 2014, January 28, 2014, http://www.cbo.gov/publication/45049.
[13] CBO, *Budget and Economic Outlook*, "10-Year Budget Projections," various updates, https://www.cbo.gov/about/products/budget_economic_data.

Table 1. Projected 2014 Farm Bill Outlays, by Title

Five years FY2014-FY2018, millions of dollars

		At enactment, February 2014		**Most recently, January 2017**	
	Farm Bill Titles (sorted)	Projection for FY2014-18	Share	Actual FY14-16; Proj. FY2017-18	Change since enactment
IV	Nutrition	390,650	79.9%	364,837	-25,813
XI	Crop Insurance	41,420	8.5%	30,533	-10,887
II	Conservation	28,165	5.8%	24,378	-3,787
I	Commodities and Disaster	23,555	4.8%	36,040	+12,485
	Subtotal, 4 largest titles	483,789	99.0%	455,787	-28,002
III	Trade	1,782	0.4%	1,530	-251
XII	Miscellaneous, including NAP	1,544	0.3%	na	na
X	Horticulture	874	0.2%	na	na
VII	Research	800	0.2%	na	na
IX	Energy	625	0.1%	na	na
VI	Rural Development	218	0.0%	na	na
VIII	Forestry	8	0.0%	na	na
V	Credit	-1,011	-0.2%	na	na
	Total, Direct Spending	488,629	100.0%	na	na

Source: CRS, using the CBO cost estimate of the Agricultural Act of 2014 (January 28, 2014) and the CBO *Budget and Economic Outlook*, "10-Year Budget Projections," January 2017.

Notes: "na" indicates sufficient detail is not available to compile projections for all titles in non-farm-bill years.

Future Baseline

For a new farm bill, there is presently no official baseline covering all titles. The official "scoring baseline" during 2017 would likely be the March 2017 CBO baseline, and a farm bill enacted in 2018 would likely use the March 2018 CBO baseline for the FY2019-FY2028 period. However, early baseline projections indicate a continuation of the economic changes above. The January 2017 CBO baseline projection for the four largest titles of the farm bill (assuming current law continues) is $435 billion over the next five years FY2018-FY2022 and $870 billion for the next 10 years FY2018-FY2027 (Table 2). The nutrition title is about 77% of these amounts, compared to about 80% when the 2014 farm bill was enacted. Beyond these four titles, other farm bill programs with baseline can be expected to add about another $4 billion of baseline over the five-year period.

Figure 2 shows how the relative proportions of farm bill spending have shifted over time. The figure combines actual USDA spending data (FY1990-FY2016) and CBO projections for those programs (FY2017 through FY2027). Since 1990, conservation and crop insurance spending have steadily risen as policy and enrollment have increased participation. Farm commodity program spending has risen and fallen with changing market price conditions and policy responses, though costs have generally decreased recently as counter-cyclical payments were smaller due to higher market prices. This trend, however, has reversed at least temporarily in the current projections for future spending. Nutrition assistance rose sharply after the recession in 2009 but began to decline during the economic recovery and is expected to continue to decline in the near future.

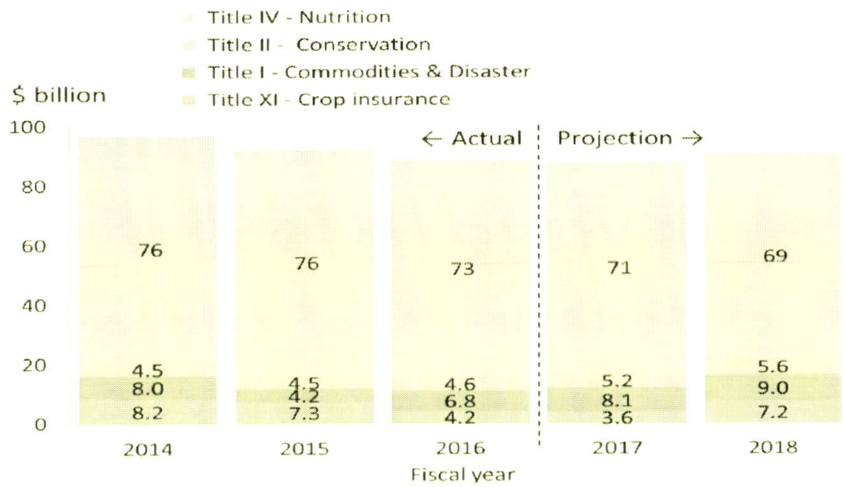

Source: CRS, using CBO *Budget and Economic Outlook*, January 2017.

Figure 1. Projected 2014 Farm Bill Outlays, by Title. January 2017 CBO baseline (FY2014-FY2016 actual, FY2017-FY2018 projected).

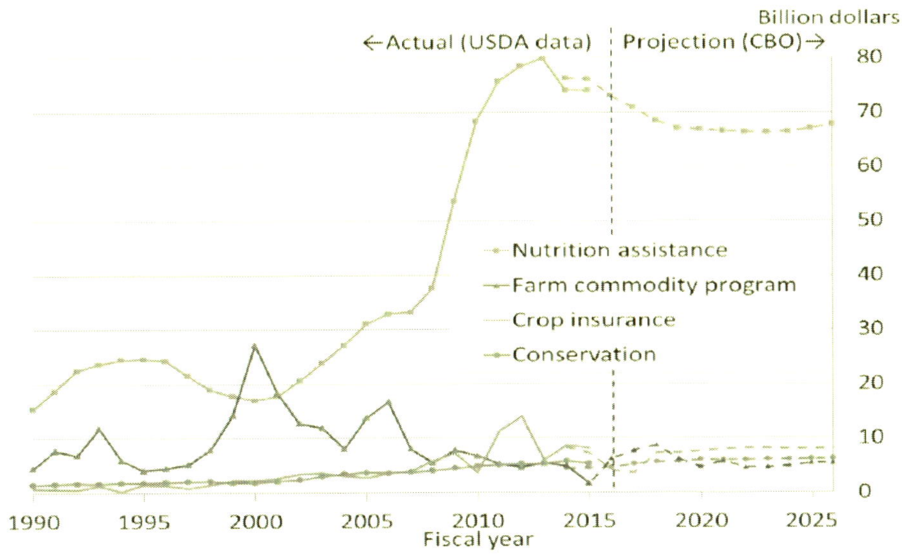

Source: CRS, using USDA data through 2016, and CBO *Budget and Economic Outlook*, January 2017. Break in line reflects difference between actual and projected values.

Figure 2. Actual and Projected Farm Bill Spending by Major Mandatory Programs. Actual FY1990-FY2016 USDA and CBO data; projected FY2017-FY027 CBO baseline.

Table 2. Baseline Projection for Farm Bill Programs, FY2018-FY2027
Estimate as of January 2017, budget outlays, millions of dollars

	FY 2018	FY 2019	FY 2020	FY 2021	FY 2022	FY 2023	FY 2024	FY 2025	FY 2026	FY 2027	FY2018-FY2022	FY2018-FY2027
Title I: Farm Commodity Programs												
Agricultural Risk Coverage	4,755	3,204	1,973	521	426	442	471	550	550	540	10,880	13,433
Price Loss Coverage	3,721	3,058	2,335	4,898	3,778	3,859	4,131	4,512	4,481	4,102	17,789	38,873
Marketing loans	63	88	59	55	53	53	57	46	53	58	318	585
Dairy	33	68	97	57	96	49	71	77	108	93	351	749
Disaster Payments	348	318	322	326	324	320	315	318	319	331	1,638	3,241
Other, incl. announced sequestration	62	-220	249	204	208	211	209	209	210	226	503	1,569
Subtotal	8,983	6,516	5,035	6,061	4,885	4,934	5,254	5,712	5,722	5,350	31,479	58,450
Title II: Conservation												
Conservation Reserve Program	1,884	1,873	1,987	2,026	2,057	2,102	2,144	2,183	2,199	2,179	9,827	20,634
CRP Technical Assistance	87	48	32	75	72	147	106	169	91	95	314	922
Conservation Security Program	1,626	1,831	2,046	1,889	1,840	1,820	1,771	1,768	1,810	1,812	9,232	18,213
Environmental Quality Incentives Program	1,483	1,549	1,567	1,620	1,661	1,692	1,728	1,741	1,748	1,750	7,880	16,539
Agricultural Conservation Easement Program	369	293	267	262	250	250	250	250	250	250	1,441	2,691
Regional Conservation Partnership Program	108	118	111	99	100	100	100	100	100	100	536	1,036
Agricultural Management Assistance	9	10	10	10	10	10	10	10	10	10	49	99
Other, incl. announced sequestration	42	-25	-26	-26	-12	-6	-8	-7	-7	-7	-47	-82
Subtotal	5,608	5,697	5,994	5,955	5,978	6,115	6,101	6,214	6,201	6,189	29,232	60,052
Title IV: Nutrition (SNAP)	68,525	67,061	66,823	66,579	66,415	66,352	66,498	67,050	67,773	69,282	335,403	672,358
Title XI: Crop Insurance	7,244	7,388	7,673	7,987	8,102	8,113	8,053	8,077	8,168	8,229	38,395	79,033
Subtotal, Four Largest Titles	90,360	86,662	85,525	86,582	85,380	85,513	85,905	87,053	87,864	89,050	434,508	869,894

	FY 2018	FY 2019	FY 2020	FY 2021	FY 2022	FY 2023	FY 2024	FY 2025	FY 2026	FY 2027	FY2018-FY2022	FY2018-FY2027
Other Programs Not Included Above												
Title III: Trade Market Access Program	199	200	200	200	200	200	200	200	200	200	999	1,999
Export Donation Ocean Transportation	100	100	100	100	100	100	100	100	100	100	500	1,000
Foreign Market Development	34	35	35	35	35	35	35	35	35	35	173	345
Specialty Crop Technical Assistance	9	9	9	9	9	9	9	9	9	9	45	90
Title VII: Research Specialty Crop Research Initiative	80	80	80	80	80	80	80	80	80	80	400	800
Title IX: Energy Rural Energy for America Program	50	50	50	50	50	50	50	50	50	50	250	500
Title X: Horticulture Plant Pest and Disease Management	75	75	75	75	75	75	75	75	75	75	375	750
Specialty Crop Block Grants	85	85	85	85	85	85	85	85	85	85	425	850
Organic and Christmas Tree Promotion	7	5	9	10	16	16	16	16	16	16	47	127
Title XII: Miscellaneous Miscellaneous (including NAP)	246	230	220	200	200	200	200	200	200	200	1,096	2,096
Subtotal, Other Programs	885	869	863	844	850	850	850	850	850	850	4,310	8,557

Source: Compiled by CRS using the CBO *Budget and Economic Outlook*, "10-Year Budget Projections," January 2017, https://www.cbo.gov/publication/52370; the text of the **Agricultural Act of 2014 (P.L. 113-79); and the CBO score of the Agricultural Act of 2014, January 28, 2014,** https://www.cbo.gov/publication/45049.

Notes: There is no official total yet for the baseline across all titles of the farm bill. The official scoring baseline for legislation during 2017 would likely be the March 2017 CBO baseline, and a farm bill enacted in 2018 would likely use the March 2018 CBO baseline for a different period. The January 2017 CBO baseline used here covers the projection for the farm commodity programs, conservation, trade, crop insurance, and nutrition programs. CRS compiled this table by grouping programs in the available baseline by title and augmenting it with programs from other titles of the 2014 farm bill that are known to have baseline beyond FY2018. It excludes projected outlays during the period for expiring farm bill programs that do not have a continuing baseline beyond FY2018 (see CRS Report R44758, *Farm Bill Programs Without a Budget Baseline Beyond FY2018*).

FARM ECONOMY AND INTERNATIONAL ENVIRONMENT

The U.S. agricultural sector experienced a golden period from 2010 to 2014, driven largely by strong commodity prices and agricultural exports. This period included a four-year run of record farm income and land values that culminated with the enactment of the 2014 farm bill. Since 2014, the U.S. farm economic outlook has changed dramatically. Bountiful U.S. crop harvests and fading international demand prospects have put downward pressure on commodity prices, farm incomes, and asset values while raising farm sector debt and debt-to-asset ratios. USDA projects that U.S. net farm income—a key indicator of U.S. farm well-being—will fall to $62.3 billion in 2017, down 9% from 2016 and down 50% from 2013's record of $123.7 billion. The 2017 forecast would represent the third year of decline and would be the lowest national net farm income since 2002.

The forecast for lower net farm income is primarily the result of the outlook for both lower crop and livestock receipts. Record grain, oilseed, and meat supplies in 2016 have depressed prices for most commodities—especially when compared with the period of 2011-2013, when prices for many major commodities experienced record or near-record highs. Agricultural exports were projected higher in 2017 at $134 billion, up 3% from 2016 but well below 2014's record $152.3 billion—due largely to a strong U.S. dollar coupled with a continued weak economic outlook in several major foreign importing countries. Despite the year-over-year decline, U.S. agricultural exports are still projected to account for over 30% of farm sector gross earnings in 2017.[12]

Farm wealth is also projected to decline for a third year in 2017 (down about 1% from 2016) to $2,836 billion. Farm asset values reflect farm investors' and lenders' expectations about long- term profitability of farm sector investments. The outlook for lower commodity prices and the expected decline from the past four years' strong outlook for the general farm economy have reversed the growth of farmland values. Because they comprise such a significant portion of the U.S. farm sector's asset base, change in farmland values is a critical barometer of the farm sector's financial performance. Farm credit conditions also appear to be deteriorating: Loan delinquencies and requests for loan extensions are increasing, and interest rates are rising.

Despite the downturn in the U.S. agricultural sector's financial outlook, it is still outperforming U.S. households in general. At the farm-household level, average farm household incomes have been well ahead of average U.S. household incomes since the late 1990s. In 2015 (the last year with comparable data), the average farm household

---

[12] ERS, *Outlook for U.S. Agricultural Trade*, AES-98, February 23, 2017; 2017 is a projection.

income (including off-farm income sources) of $119,880 was about 51% higher than the average U.S. household income of $79,263.[13]

The outlook for lower commodity prices and farm income and wealth suggests a weakening financial picture for the agricultural sector heading into 2017 but with substantial regional variation. Relatively weak prices for most major program crops and livestock products signal tougher times ahead for agricultural producers and are expected to trigger substantial payments under the new safety net programs of the 2014 farm bill. However, actual 2017 agricultural economic well-being will hinge on crop harvests and prices, as well as domestic and international macroeconomic factors, including economic growth and consumer demand.

FARM SAFETY NET PROGRAMS

The federal government supports farm income and helps farmers manage risks associated with variability in crop yields and prices through a collection of programs often referred to as the "farm safety net."[14] These programs include (1) commodity-based revenue support programs, which are reauthorized by periodic farm bills (most recently by Title I of the 2014 farm bill); (2) disaster assistance programs, which were permanently authorized by the 2014 farm bill; and (3) federal crop insurance, which is permanently authorized under the Federal Crop Insurance Act of 1980. Each of these three components is covered in this section and summarized in Table 3.

Through the first three years of the 2014 farm bill (2014 to 2016), USDA estimates the cost of farm safety net programs at $14.2 billion per year ($5.2 billion for commodity programs, $2.4 billion for disaster assistance, and $6.6 billion for crop insurance).[15]

Most of the cost for the farm safety net is traditionally attributed to a few major crops. For example, CBO projects that corn (48%), wheat (14%), soybeans (13%), rice (7%), peanuts (7%), and sorghum (3%) will cumulatively account for 91% of commodity program payments under revenue support programs in FY2017. Similarly, in 2016 four crops accounted for 77% of crop insurance premium subsidies: corn (38%), soybeans (20%), wheat (12%), and cotton (8%).[16]

---

[13] ERS, "2017 Farm Income Forecast," February 7, 2017; 2015 is the last year with comparable data.

[14] While many critics of farm subsidies take issue with what does and does not constitute a safety net and whether current farm programs actually perform as such, the term *safety net* is used here for all farm commodity and risk management programs as a catchall descriptor rather than as an assessment of the merits.

[15] Farm program outlays are from ERS, "Farm Sector Income and Finances: 2016 Farm Sector Income Forecast," November 30, 2016. Crop insurance outlays are from USDA, Risk Management Agency (RMA), Program Costs and Outlays; and CBO, USDA budget baseline, January 2017.

[16] Crop value and area planted are key determinants of total premium values. RMA, Summary of Business data, downloaded January 23, 2017, http://www.rma.usda.gov/data/sob.html.

Although these seven crops receive a majority of farm program support, they do not constitute a majority of farm output value: From 2010 to 2016, these crops accounted for 32% of total farm receipts (including fruits and vegetables, livestock, dairy, and poultry).

Farm support began with the 1930s Depression-era efforts to generally raise farm household income when commodity prices were low because of prolonged weak consumer demand. While initially intended to be a temporary effort, the commodity support programs survived but have been modified away from supply control and management of commodity stocks to direct revenue support payments. Similarly, federal crop insurance has expanded over the decades, with expanded commodity coverage and increased producer subsidies.

Effectiveness of the Current Farm Safety Net

Many policymakers and farmers consider federal support of farm businesses necessary for financial survival, given the unpredictable nature of agricultural production and markets. Yet some producers have criticized farm safety net programs for being too slow to respond to disasters, for not being well integrated, or for not providing adequate risk protection.

In contrast, long-time farm program critics question the need for any farm subsidies, contending that government funding could be better spent advancing environmental goals or improving productivity. Many environmental groups argue that subsidies encourage overproduction on environmentally fragile land. Others cite economic arguments against the programs—that they are a market-distorting use of taxpayer dollars, capitalize benefits to the owners of the resources, encourage concentration of production, favor large-scale farming at the expense of small or beginning farms, pay benefits to high-income recipients or when there are no losses, and harm farmers in lower-income foreign nations.

Congressional limits on the federal budget, particularly constraints on new spending, could play an important role in the policy design of the farm safety net in a new farm bill. Several other critical policy issues and options have emerged that are also likely to factor into the debate shaping a new farm bill. These issues include the general perception that the current suite of safety net programs is failing to provide a sufficient safety net for both cotton producers and dairy operations. In addition, the current policy design favors planting peanuts on generic base acres despite market incentives to the contrary: In the past, policymakers have expressed their intent to avoid such market distortions in the farm safety net design. Also, large county-level variations in Agricultural Risk Coverage at the county level (ARC-CO) program—attributable to county yield data shortcomings—have emerged in 2014 and 2015 payments and could be addressed by a new farm bill. Additional issues and options for a new farm bill are discussed in the report sections titled "Budget Considerations" and "Commodities Covered Under Safety Net Programs."

Program Design and Operation

Commodity Programs

The commodity provisions of the 2014 farm bill provide support for 26 farm commodities including food grains, feed grains, oilseeds, upland cotton, peanuts, pulse crops, and milk.[17]

Producers of program commodities are eligible for a variety of payments, much of which is financed through mandatory funding by USDA's Commodity Credit Corporation (Table 3).

Revenue support programs include ARC and the Price Loss Coverage (PLC) programs created under the 2014 farm bill. PLC is a revamped version of the counter-cyclical price support program from the 2008 farm bill, but it relies on elevated support prices. ARC is a shallow-loss revenue program that uses five-year Olympic moving averages of historical data[18] for national farm prices and county yields to determine a revenue guarantee. The ARC program is available at either the county level for individual commodities (ARC-CO) or the farm level (ARC-IC) on a whole farm basis for all program crops. Both ARC and PLC make payments on a delayed basis, because their payment formulas require an entire marketing year worth of monthly price data. For example, for corn grown and harvested in 2016, complete data for the season-average farm price are not available until September 2017, and payments are made after October 1, 2017.

In addition to ARC and PLC, producers of an expanded list of other "loan commodities"[19] are eligible for benefits under nonrecourse marketing assistance loans (MALs).[20] Current farm law also mandates that raw cane and refined beet sugar prices are

---

[17] Food grains include wheat and rice, and feed grains include corn, sorghum, barley, and oats. Oilseeds include soybeans, sunflower seed, rapeseed, canola, safflower, flaxseed, mustard seed, crambe, and sesame seed. Pulse crops include dry peas, lentils, small chickpeas, and large chickpeas.

[18] Refers to removing data for the high and low years then averaging the remaining three years of data.

[19] The additional "loan-only" commodities are extra-long staple and upland cotton, wool, mohair, and honey.

[20] A MAL provides interim financing in the form of a nonrecourse government loan for up to nine months for participating producers following harvest of their crops. The loan rates, which vary by program crop, are statutorily fixed prices per unit of production (7 U.S.C. 9032) as set by periodic farm bills. Under a nonrecourse loan, farmers have the option of forfeiting their collateral (i.e., the underlying crop) in payment of the loan rather than repaying the loan's principal and interest.

supported through a combination of limits on domestic output that can be sold for human use, nonrecourse loans for domestic sugar, and quotas that limit imports.

The 2014 farm bill made significant changes to the structure of U.S. dairy support programs, including the elimination of several major farm revenue support programs from the 2008 farm bill and their replacement by two new support programs: the Margin Protection Program (MPP) and the Dairy Product Donation Program (DPDP). The MPP is a voluntary program that makes payments to participating farmers when a formula-based national margin—calculated as the national average farm price for all milk[21] minus a national-average feed cost ration[22]—falls below a producer-selected insured margin that can range from $4.00 per hundredweight (cwt.) to $8.00/cwt. Milk producers must pay an annual administrative fee of $100 for each participating dairy operation and statutorily fixed premiums that rise steadily for higher margin protection levels and greater volumes of insured milk.

Table 3. Farm Safety Net Programs (authorized under the 2014 farm bill and other legislation)

Program Instrument	Commodity Coverage	Program Description and Projected Outlays ($13.9 bil./yr.)
Commodity Programs		Projected Avg. Outlays FY2017-FY2027: ($5.7 bil./yr.)
1. Price Loss Coverage (PLC)[a]	Wheat, corn, grain sorghum, oats, barley, long grain rice, medium grain rice, pulse crops (dry peas, lentils, small chickpeas, and large chickpeas), soybeans, sunflower seed, rapeseed, canola, safflower, flaxseed, mustard seed, crambe, sesame seed, and peanuts. Excludes upland cotton.[b]	Payments made if national season-average farm price (SAFP) is below statutory reference price (PLC). The per-unit payment rate equals the PLC minus the higher of the SAFP or the crop market loan rate (fixed in statute by the farm bill). Payments made on 85% of historical program (base) acres times historical program yield. No participation fee. ($3.7 billion/yr.)
2. Agricultural Risk Coverage (ARC-CO) county-level program	Same crops as PLC.	Payments made if actual crop revenue based on national SAFP and county yield is below a guarantee (equal to 86% of historical revenue using previous five-year Olympic moving averages of national SAFP and county yield). Per-unit payment rate equals difference between the actual crop revenue and the guarantee. Payments made on 85% of base acres. No participation fee. ($1.7 billion/yr.)

[21] "All milk" represents the average price for all milk sold by producers irrespective of the end use—whether for fluid milk consumption or for processing into butter, cheese, powder, or soft products such as ice cream or yogurt.

[22] The feed-cost ration is determined by a statutorily fixed formula set by the 2014 farm bill that uses USDA national average farm prices to calculate a value.

Program Instrument	Commodity Coverage	Program Description and Projected Outlays ($13.9 bil./yr.)
3. Agricultural Risk Coverage (ARC-IC) farm-level program	Same crops as PLC.	Payments made if cumulative farm revenue (as defined by ARC- CO) for all program crops is below guarantee based on 86% of historical cumulative revenue for each crop. Payments made on 65% of base acres. No participation fee. ($21 million/yr.)
4. Marketing Assistance Loan benefitsc	Same crops as for PLC and ARC, plus upland cotton, extra-long staple cotton, wool, mohair, and honey.	Nine-month nonrecourse loaned at a per-unit loan rate (fixed in statute), based on actual production. Producers may repay loan at below value if crop's market price is lower than its loan rate (called a market loan gain) or take a cash payment equal to difference (loan deficiency payment). Farmer chooses timing. ($65 million/yr.)
5. Nonrecourse loans, marketing allotments, and import quotas	Refined beet sugar and raw cane sugar.	Price guarantee for refined beet sugar and raw cane sugar; limits on sales of domestically produced sugar. ($0, designed to be no-net cost to federal budget; instead costs are borne by consumers.)
6. Dairy Margin Protection Program (MPP)	Milk.	MPP payments made if actual two-month average margin (milk price minus feed cost) is below producer-selected threshold ranging from $4/cwt. to $8/cwt. Signup fee of $100 plus statutorily fixed premium for coverage selected by producer. ($74 million/yr.)
6. Dairy Product Donation Program (DPDP)	Milk.	DPDP requires USDA to procure and distribute (to low- income groups) certain dairy products when the MPP margin falls below $4/cwt. for two consecutive months. DPDP purchases end after three months or if the U.S. price for certain dairy products is significantly above world prices. ($7 million/yr.)
Crop Insurance, STAX, SCO, and NAP		Projected Avg. Outlays FY2017-FY2027: ($7.9 bil./yr.)
7. Crop insurance	More than 100 crops, including commodity program crops, specialty crops (fruits, tree nuts, vegetables, and nursery crops), pasture, rangeland, and forage crops, and livestock margins.	Indemnities paid when yield or revenue drops below guarantees established prior to planting. Coverage level (50%-85%) selected by producer and based on expected prices, farm and/or area yield, and farm revenue. Loss is at field or county level, depending on policy. Insurance premiums are subsidized at an average 62% rate. ($7.9 billion/yr.)
8. Stacked Income Protection Plan (STAX)	Upland cotton.	A revenue-based, area-wide crop insurance policy that may be purchased as a stand-alone policy for primary coverage or purchased in tandem with an individual farm loss policy or area policy. STAX indemnifies losses in county revenue of greater than 10% of expected revenue (up to an underlying policy's insurance deductible if coupled) but not more than 30%. Insurance premiums are subsidized at 80% rate. ($86 million/yr.)

Table 3. (Continued)

Program Instrument	Commodity Coverage	Program Description and Projected Outlays ($13.9 bil./yr.)
9. Supplemental Coverage Option (SCO)	Program crops enrolled in PLC.	SCO must be purchased in conjunction with a traditional crop insurance policy. Indemnities are triggered by losses greater than 14% up to the underlying policy's insurance deductible on an area-wide basis only. SCO mimics the coverage, either yield or revenue, offered by the underlying insurance policy. Insurance premiums are subsidized at 65% rate. (No cost estimate.)
10. Noninsured Crop Disaster Assistance Program (NAP)	Crops not covered by crop insurance.	Payments for losses in excess of 50%. Participation fee of $250 per crop plus a charge for higher coverage. (No cost estimate.)
Disaster Assistance		Projected Avg. Outlays FY2017-FY2027: ($0.3 bil./yr.)
11. Supplemental Agricultural Disaster Assistance Programse (no disaster designation required)	Beef/dairy cattle, bison, poultry, sheep, swine, horses, other livestock, honeybees, farm-raised fish, and trees/bushes/vines producing an annual crop.	Payment for excess livestock mortality (LIP), grazing losses (LFP), other losses (ELAP), and excess fruit tree/vine mortality (TAP). No participation fee
12. Emergency Loans (EM) (requires disaster designation)	Crops and livestock (also physical losses to real estate).	Low-interest loans for producers in a disaster county and not eligible for commercial credit. Producers repay interest/principal in one to seven years (longer for real estate).

Source: CRS, using outlays from January 2017 CBO baseline for FY2017-FY2027.

Notes: The term *safety net* is used broadly here and does not assess the merits of the various programs. Not shown is additional support for dairy and sugar producers through import restrictions.

[a] Producers were give a one-time choice—to last for the duration of the 2014 farm bill (2014-2018)—for how to allocate their historical base acres by program crops and by either PLC or county-level ARC for each crop or individual ARC, which covers all crops with a single farm-level revenue guarantee.

[b] Upland cotton was removed from eligibility for Title I revenue support programs by the 2014 farm bill. However, upland cotton remains eligible for support under both the marketing assistance loan and crop insurance programs including STAX.

[c] Four types of benefits are obtainable under the marketing assistance loan program: loan deficiency payments (LDPs), marketing loan gains (MLGs), gains derived from use of commodity certificates, and benefits derived from forfeiting to USDA the quantity of a commodity pledged as collateral for a nonrecourse loan.

[d] Under a nonrecourse loan, farmers have the option of forfeiting their collateral (i.e., the underlying crop), in payment of the loan rather than repaying the loan's principal and interest.

[e] The four additional disaster programs cited above include the Livestock Indemnity Program (LIP); the Livestock Forage Disaster Program (LFP); the Emergency Assistance for Livestock, Honey Bees, and Farm- Raised Fish Program (ELAP); and the Tree Assistance Program (TAP).

In contrast to producers of traditional farm bill commodities, producers of specialty crops (e.g., fruits, vegetables, and tree nuts) and livestock have generally received little or no direct government support through commodity programs. Instead, these commodities benefit from federal investments in agricultural research and extension programs and from federal support for food and nutrition programs. These farms may manage risks through business diversification, purchase of federal crop insurance, and participation in federal disaster assistance programs.

Crop Insurance

The federal crop insurance program provides risk management tools to address losses in revenue or crop yield—revenue policies represent about 77% of total premiums; yield policies about 23%. Federally subsidized policies protect producers against losses during a particular season, with price guarantee levels established early in the year using the preplanting values of harvest-time futures contracts. This is in contrast to commodity programs, where protection levels are fixed in statute (e.g., PLC reference prices and MAL loan rates) or use five-year Olympic moving average data for national farm prices and county yields to determine a revenue guarantee (e.g., ARC-CO).

Federal crop insurance has grown in importance as a farm risk management tool since the early 1990s, due in large part to increasing federal subsidy intervention.[23] The federal government pays about 62%, on average, of the farmer's crop insurance premium. Thus, as both participation in crop insurance programs and the value of insured crops have grown over time, so too has the absolute level of federal premium subsidies. From 2006 through 2015, the federal crop insurance program cost taxpayers, on average, $7.2 billion per year, including premium subsidies of $5.6 billion, administrative and delivery support of $1.4 billion, and other costs of $0.2 billion.[24]

Crop insurance has perhaps the widest commodity and regional coverage of any federal farm program. In 2016, crop insurance policies covered 290 million acres and more than 100 commodities including fruit trees, nursery crops, dairy and livestock margins, pasture, rangeland, and forage. Major field crops such as corn, soybeans, wheat, and cotton are covered in most counties where they are grown, and crop insurance covers at least 85% of planted acres for each of these crops. Crop insurance is also available for over 80 specialty crops. In 2014, specialty crop policies covered more than 7.7 million acres, which constituted 53% to 75% of specialty crop area, depending on how total area is calculated.

A prominent crop insurance feature of the 2014 farm bill is the authorization of two new policies designed to reimburse "shallow losses"—an insured producer's out-of-pocket loss associated with the policy deductible—STAX and SCO. STAX is made available for upland cotton producers, while SCO is made available for other crops. STAX, or the Stacked Income Protection Plan, was created in response to upland cotton's removal from eligibility for Title I revenue support programs as the result of a final ruling

[23] Insurance policies are serviced through approved private insurance companies. Independent insurance agents are paid sales commissions by the companies. The insurance companies' losses are partially reinsured by USDA, and their administrative and operating costs are reimbursed by the government. The program is administered by the Risk Management Agency (RMA) and financed through USDA's Federal Crop Insurance Corporation (FCIC). Separately, the Noninsured Crop Disaster Assistance Program (NAP), administered by USDA's Farm Service Agency (FSA), attempts to fill in the gaps in catastrophic coverage in counties where crop insurance policies are not offered.

[24] RMA, Program Costs and Outlays, "Crop Year Government Cost of Federal Crop Insurance," June 27, 2016, http://www.rma.usda.gov/aboutrma/budget/costsoutlays.html.

from a World Trade Organization (WTO) dispute settlement case successfully brought by Brazil against U.S. cotton support programs.

To address conservation concerns, the 2014 farm bill links eligibility for crop insurance premium subsidies to compliance with wetland and conservation requirements for highly erodible land. Also, crop insurance subsidies are reduced for plantings on native sod acreage in certain states.

Disaster Assistance

The 2014 farm bill permanently authorized four agricultural disaster programs for livestock and fruit trees: (1) the Livestock Indemnity Program (LIP); (2) the Livestock Forage Disaster Program (LFP); (3) the Emergency Assistance for Livestock, Honey Bees, and Farm-Raised Fish Program (ELAP); and (4) the Tree Assistance Program (TAP). The programs provide compensation for a portion of lost production following a natural disaster. These programs, originally established in the 2008 farm bill for only four years, were authorized retroactively (with no expiration date) to cover losses beginning in FY2012.

All programs except ELAP receive uncapped mandatory funding via the CCC. That is, LIP, LFP, and TAP receive "such sums as necessary" to reimburse eligible producers for their losses. ELAP is capped at $20 million per year, and loss payments are reduced in order to fit under the cap.

The four permanent disaster assistance programs (LIP, LFP, ELAP, and TAP) in combination with federal crop insurance and the Noninsured Crop Disaster Assistance Program (NAP) cover nearly the entire U.S. farm sector with a permanent disaster program. This broad array of disaster support reduces the potential need for emergency assistance that Congress previously provided to farmers and ranchers in the form of ad hoc disaster payments.[25]

Budget Considerations

CBO periodically undertakes 10-year baseline projections for the total cost of mandatory USDA programs under the assumption that current legislation remains intact for the projection period. The 2014 farm bill expires at the end of 2018 (calendar year for dairy and marketing year for program crops) unless it is reauthorized. If a new farm bill is

[25] Agricultural disaster assistance programs are discussed in CRS Report RS21212, *Agricultural Disaster Assistance*.

finalized by 2018, then the CBO baseline budget projection for FY2019-FY2028 produced in March 2018 would provide the official benchmark used to write such a new farm bill.

The CBO score establishes a baseline against which policy proposals are measured for their budgetary impact. The CBO baseline score for agricultural programs is particularly important under current PAYGO restrictions,[26] because it represents the pool of money available for farm safety net programs including both commodity and crop insurance programs. Under PAYGO, any changes to the farm bill—including the farm safety net and other programs—must either fit within the CBO baseline score or find equivalent offsets within the larger federal budget score.[27]

As with most farm bills, a critical factor in determining the baseline budget for a new farm bill will be the price outlook for the program crops. Since payments under both the revenue-support programs—ARC and PLC—and the marketing assistance loan program are counter-cyclical to market conditions, an outlook for low commodity prices relative to program support levels could result in CBO projections of higher annual farm program outlays. A large CBO projected baseline could provide policymakers with greater flexibility in redesigning the farm safety net if they are so inclined.

Currently, CBO projects farm program outlays for FY2017-FY2027 at about $14 billion per year on average—including $5.5 billion for commodity programs, $7.9 billion for crop insurance, and $0.3 billion for annual disaster assistance.[28] These projections compare with the final CBO score for the 2014 farm bill of $13.4 billion in average annual outlays for the farm safety net, including $4.4 billion annually for commodity programs (plus disaster assistance) and $9.0 billion for crop insurance.[29] Thus, commodity programs are currently costing about $1 billion more per year on average than projected, while crop insurance is averaging about $1 billion less. Actual historical outlays during FY2006 to FY2014 were higher still at $15.4 billion per year on average—$6.7 billion for commodity programs, $7.1 billion for crop insurance, and $1.7 billion for disaster assistance.[30] The highest combined outlay for USDA safety net programs was recorded in FY2005 at $24.8 billion.

---

[26] PAYGO generally requires that direct spending and revenue legislation enacted into law not increase the deficit. It does not address deficit increases that are projected to occur under existing law, nor does it apply to discretionary spending. See CRS Report R41157, *The Statutory Pay-As-You-Go Act of 2010: Summary and Legislative History*.

[27] The concepts of a CBO score, PAYGO, and budget offsets are described in more detail in CRS Report R42484, *Budget Issues That Shaped the 2014 Farm Bill*.

[28] CBO, USDA baseline for mandatory programs, January 2017.

[29] CBO, USDA baseline for mandatory programs, January 2014.

[30] Calculations by CRS using data from ERS, "Farm Sector Income and Finances: 2016 Farm Sector Income Forecast," November 30, 2016; and RMA, Summary of Business data, downloaded January 23, 2017, http://www.rma.usda.gov/ data/sob.html.

Commodities Covered under Safety Net Programs

The extent of current commodity coverage of the farm safety net is primarily a result of the historical and evolving nature of farm policy. Producers of major commodities have benefited the most from farm programs because farmers and policymakers representing those commodities shaped the programs from their inception. Since then, other commodity advocates have not had the interest or sufficient political support to add their commodities to the mix. Coverage could be increased by enhancing crop insurance for nonprogram crops, developing a new whole-farm revenue support program that would encompass all crops grown on a farm or revising the current whole-farm insurance product so it would be more widely accepted by producers.

Role of Cotton in the Next Farm Safety Net

Perhaps the most notable omission from eligibility for the Title I revenue support programs (ARC and PLC) is upland cotton, which, as mentioned earlier, was removed from eligibility under the 2014 farm bill in response to a WTO dispute settlement case. Instead, cotton producers were given their own insurance-based program—STAX. In contrast to the revenue guarantees available under ARC and PLC, which have a statutorily fixed lower bound, the revenue guarantee under STAX is recalculated each year. Thus it decreases following consecutive years of market declines—as has been the case since 2014. Many cotton producers contend that STAX is both expensive and ineffective, since the STAX revenue guarantee has fallen below their cost of production and, thus, no longer serves as a useful safety net. This perception has contributed to low participation: In 2016, only 25% of cotton-planted acres were insured under STAX.

In 2016, the U.S. cotton sector requested that USDA designate cottonseed as an "other oilseed," thus allowing cottonseed to be eligible for the ARC and PLC payments. However, then-Secretary of Agriculture Tom Vilsack contended that he did not have such authority. Furthermore, some argued that designating cottonseed as a program crop would constitute reopening the 2014 farm bill and could have substantial costs associated with such a decision. According to news reports, USDA's internal estimates in early 2016 projected related costs in excess of $1 billion (or about $100 per acre) annually. Such potentially large support payments could significantly affect producer crop choices and could attract the attention of other WTO members, including Brazil.

Generic Base Issue and Peanuts

In response to the removal of cotton from eligibility for ARC and PLC payments, the 2014 farm bill reclassified former cotton base acres from the 2008 farm bill as "generic" base acres. Generic base acres are added to a producer's total base for potential payments but only if a program- eligible crop is planted on them. In other words, ARC and PLC payments on generic base acres are coupled to actual plantings. As a result, a combination of market conditions and government program incentives determine producer planting choices on generic base. Because of a favorable advantage stemming from peanuts' disproportionately high PLC reference price relative to both other program crop reference prices and to current market conditions, peanut production is favored on generic base acres over other crops. This unintended outcome has resulted in the outlook for large government payments to peanut producers relative to other crops: CBO projects annual USDA peanut program outlays (ARC, PLC, and MAL combined) of $580 million, or $349 per harvested acre, through 2027.[31] This compares with CBO projected program payments of $30 per harvested acre for corn, $7 for soybeans, $32 for wheat, and $199 for rice.

Dairy Margin Protection Program (MPP)

The U.S. dairy industry, like the agriculture sector in general, has experienced a sharp downturn in both market and financial conditions the past two years. Despite a significant drop in milk prices, minimal support payments have been made under MPP through the first three years of operation (and these have been largely offset by producer-paid premiums). By June 2016, farm- level milk prices had fallen by 42% from their September 2014 high. However, this output price decline was largely offset by a similar decline for major feed grain prices, thus preventing the MPP margin from falling below meaningful program payment triggers. As a result, the dairy sector has expressed widespread dissatisfaction with the program. In 2016, 54% of dairy operations were enrolled in MPP, and most of those (77%) were enrolled at the minimum $4.00/cwt. catastrophic level, thus missing out on MPP payments made when the margin briefly fell below the $6.00/cwt. threshold in May-June 2016.

ARC Yield Calculation Issue

Significant discrepancies in county-level payments for 2014 and 2015 were discovered under the ARC-CO program due, in part, to how USDA's National Agricultural Statistics Service (NASS) calculates average county yields. NASS relies on a cascading sequence of prioritized county-level data for its calculations. With respect to ARC-CO revenue calculations, the top data priority is based on NASS surveys of producers in counties with production of major program crops to obtain estimates of planted and harvested area, yields, and production. USDA currently requires that the NASS survey yield estimate be used if there are at least 30 producer survey responses or when survey responses represent at least 25% of a county's harvested acreage. If neither of these conditions is met, then the NASS county yield estimate is based on crop insurance data held by RMA. A comparison of the two estimates suggests that RMA yields are frequently higher than NASS yields. As a result, payments to producers in

[31] CBO, USDA baseline for mandatory programs, January 2017.

counties where RMA yields are used can be substantially lower than payments in counties using NASS yields. USDA is under no legislative requirement or guidance for this cascade policy. With no short-term fix in sight, the issue of substantial disparities in payment rates may reemerge for ARC-CO crop payments in future years. Barring any near-term fix by USDA, lawmakers could address county-to-county payment disparities in the context of a new farm bill.

Farm Program Reallocation: ARC versus PLC

Under the 2014 farm bill, producers were give a one-time choice that would last for the duration of the 2014 farm bill (2014 through 2018) for how to allocate their historical base acres across crops and by program: ARC or PLC. Most corn (93%) and soybean (97%) base acres opted for ARC-CO, while most rice (99%), peanut (100%), and barley (75%) base acres were placed under PLC. Wheat base acres were divided: 56% selected ARC-CO, 43% PLC. Less than 1% of all farms selected ARC-IC. It is unknown if a new farm bill will retain the ARC and PLC programs and, if so, whether farmers will be given a new opportunity to reallocate their base acres between the two revenue programs. However, current market conditions and the long-term outlook for relatively low prices tend to favor PLC for all program crops. CBO projections assume that participating farmers can reallocate their base acres among PLC, ARC-CO, and ARC-IC in 2019 and that most farmers significantly expand their base acres signed up under PLC: corn producers shift from a 7% share to 82%, soybeans from 3% to 49%, and wheat from 43% to 82%, according to CBO's January 2017 baseline. As a result, the CBO projections show PLC outlays exceeding ARC outlays by 2020.

Sugar Program

Unlike other commodity programs in the 2014 farm bill, Congress reauthorized the sugar program with no changes. Also, in contrast to dairy and other commodity programs, Congress structured the sugar program to operate at no cost to the federal government—an objective that has been largely achieved over the last decade with the exception of the 2012/2013 crop year, when low sugar prices triggered forfeitures under the program, resulting in federal outlays of $259 million. An issue that is currently outside the purview of the farm bill but could influence the debate over the U.S. sugar program is trade in imported sugar from Mexico. Subsequent to the enactment of the 2014 farm bill, the United States and Mexico reached agreements that regulated bilateral trade in Mexican sugar, including setting volume limits and minimum export prices and other parameters around this trade that are unique in the U.S. sugar market.

The U.S.-Mexico sugar suspension agreements are controversial. A broad cross-section of participants in the U.S. sugar market have asserted that the agreements are not working as intended and may not have succeeded in entirely eliminating the injury caused to U.S. sugar interests. These stakeholders also contend that these agreements could undermine various objectives of the U.S. sugar program—including that it operate at no cost—if market distortions created by these agreements trigger forfeitures of domestic sugar leading to government outlays. Given the importance of Mexican sugar as a source of supply to the U.S. sugar market, revising the agreements, withdrawing from them, or allowing them to remain in force as agreed upon in December 2014 could each have implications for the program.

As concerns the sugar program itself, sugar producers and processors—as represented by the American Sugar Alliance—have favored retaining the current program structure. They contend that it should not be eliminated prior to addressing foreign sugar subsidies that distort the world sugar market and thus pose a threat to efficient U.S. producers. Sugar users generally view the current program as overly prescriptive, which they argue has led to overly tight supplies and elevated prices in the domestic market. They advocate for providing USDA with greater program flexibility for managing domestic sugar supplies and allocating import quotas.

Program Payment Limits and Farm Size

Payment limits for the farm commodity programs, with the exception of the marketing assistance loan program, either set the maximum amount of farm program payments that a person can receive per year or set the maximum amount of income that an individual can earn and still remain eligible for program benefits (i.e., a means test). The payment limits issue is controversial, because it directly addresses questions about the size of farms that should be supported, whether payments should be proportional to production or limited per individual, and who should receive payments. Some policymakers want limits to be tightened in order to save money, to respond to general public concerns overpayments to large farms, and to reduce the possibility of encouraging expansion of large farms at the expense of small farms. Others say larger farms should not be penalized for the economies of size and efficiencies they have achieved. Crop insurance has no payment limits, a feature that some policymakers say makes crop insurance an attractive centerpiece of farm policy because it helps small and large farms alike, with neither apparently gaining at the expense of the other.

Farm Policy Alignment with U.S. Trade Commitments

Trade plays a critical role in the U.S. agricultural sector: Exports account for over 30% of U.S. farm sector gross earnings. As a WTO member, the United States has committed to abide by WTO rules and disciplines, including those that govern domestic farm policy. Because the United States plays such an important role in so many global agricultural markets, its farm policy is often subject to intense scrutiny, particularly for compliance with current WTO rules—as evidenced by the 2009 WTO challenge successfully brought by Brazil against U.S. cotton support programs.[32]

In particular, the United States faces pressure to minimize any "trade-distorting" incentives inherent in its farm safety net programs.

CBO projections suggest that the United States is unlikely to violate its WTO spending limit of $19.1 billion for nonexempt, trade-distorting amber box outlays. Perhaps more relevant to U.S. agricultural trade is the concern that, because the United States plays such a prominent role in most international markets for agricultural products, any distortion resulting from U.S. policy would be both visible and vulnerable to challenge under WTO rules. An unexpected period of extended low market prices in future years could generate substantial PLC and/or ARC-CO outlays and lead to a potential challenge, particularly if the current farm safety net structure is retained under a new farm bill.

Effectiveness of the Current Farm Safety Net

Industrial Hemp Provision in the 2014 Farm Bill

Industrial hemp is an agricultural commodity that is cultivated for a range of hemp-based goods, including foods and beverages, cosmetics and personal care products, nutritional supplements, fabrics and textiles, yarns and spun fibers, paper, construction/insulation materials, and other manufactured goods. The 2014 farm bill provided that certain research institutions and state departments of agriculture may grow industrial hemp as part of an agricultural pilot program if allowed under state laws (P.L. 113-79, §7606; 7 U.S.C. 5940). The provision was included as part of the research title of the farm bill. However, because industrial hemp is a variety of *Cannabis sativa*—the same plant species as marijuana—it is therefore subject to U.S. drug laws. Under current U.S. drug policy, all cannabis varieties, including industrial hemp, are considered Schedule I controlled substances under the Controlled Substances Act (21 U.S.C. §§801 et seq.) and the U.S. Drug Enforcement Administration (DEA) continues to control and regulate hemp production. Despite changes made by Congress in the 2014 farm bill, full implementation of the law's hemp provision has been limited given continued DEA actions regarding hemp production. In subsequent omnibus appropriations, Congress has blocked DEA and other federal law enforcement authorities from interfering with state agencies, hemp growers, and agricultural research. Appropriations bills have also blocked USDA from prohibiting the transportation, processing, sale, or use of industrial hemp that is grown or cultivated in accordance with the 2014 farm bill provision. Congress has continued to consider legislation to further advance industrial hemp and could further address these concerns in a new farm bill.

---

[32] This WTO case resulted in cotton's exclusion from eligibility for ARC and PLC in the 2014 farm bill.

Some producers have criticized farm safety net programs for being too slow to respond to disasters, for not being well integrated, or for not providing adequate risk protection. In contrast, long-time farm program critics question the need for any farm subsidies, contending that government funding could be better spent advancing environmental goals or improving productivity. Others cite economic arguments against the programs—that they distort production, capitalize benefits to the owners of the resources, encourage concentration of production, harm smaller domestic producers and farmers in lower-income foreign nations, and pay benefits to high-income recipients or when there are no losses.

SPECIALTY CROPS, CERTIFIED ORGANIC AND LOCAL FOODS

During the past few farm bill debates, a diverse set of agricultural producers—covering specialty crops, certified organic agriculture, and local and regional foods—have argued that their sectors should occupy a larger role in farm bill policy discussions and that benefits supporting major commodity producers should be extended to these producers in order to create "a broader, more equitable farm bill."[33] Producers in these sectors are not eligible for support under USDA's farm commodity revenue support programs, but these sectors are eligible for other types of USDA programs and support throughout several farm bill titles. These include, but are not limited to, programs in the nutrition, conservation, research, crop insurance, disaster assistance, rural development, and trade titles. Other federal agencies also play important roles in these sectors.

Specialty crops—defined as "fruits and vegetables, tree nuts, dried fruits, and horticulture and nursery crops (including floriculture)"[34]—comprise a major part of U.S. agriculture. In 2012, the value of farm-level specialty crop production totaled nearly $60 billion, representing about one- fourth of the value of U.S. crop production but only 3% of all harvested cropland acres. USDA reports that retail sales of fresh and processed fruits and vegetables for at-home consumption total nearly $100 billion annually.[35] Exports of U.S. specialty crops totaled about $26 billion in 2015.[36] In 2012, about 244,000 farming operations grew more than 350 types of fruit, vegetable, tree nut, flower, nursery, and other horticultural crops.[37] Specialty crop production is concentrated in California, Florida, Washington, Oregon, North Dakota, and Michigan, but every state has some commercial specialty crop production.

---

[33] See, for example, comments from the Specialty Crop Farm Bill Alliance.

[34] Defined in the Specialty Crops Competitiveness Act of 2004 (P.L. 108-465, Section 3), as amended. For more information, see CRS Report R44719, *Defining "Specialty Crops": A Fact Sheet*.

[35] As reported by AMS in "PACA—Your Partner in Produce." Reflects estimates for 2008.

[36] CRS estimate from data in the U.S. International Trade Commission's Trade DataWeb database. Includes fresh and processed fruits, vegetables, tree nuts, nursery plants, and processed goods such as wine, olive oil, fruit juice, coffee, and tea.

[37] NASS, *2012 Census of Agriculture*.

Agricultural products certified as "USDA organic" account for a small but growing share of the U.S. farming sector.[38] USDA reports that farm sales of certified organic products totaled $5.5 billion in 2014, spanning an array of plant and animal products.[39] Leading organic commodities based on farm value include milk, eggs, broiler chickens, lettuce, apples, meat products, grapes, corn for grain, hay, and spinach. In 2014, there were more than 14,000 organic farms and ranches, covering a total of 3.7 million acres, or about 1% of total U.S. cropland in farms. Production is concentrated in California, Florida, Washington, Pennsylvania, Oregon, Texas, and Wisconsin, but USDA reports organic production in each U.S. state. At the retail level, U.S. organic sales totaled $43.3 billion in 2015, representing roughly 5% of all food sales in the United States.[40] Exports of all U.S. organic products total about $2 billion annually.

In addition, a range of farm businesses are considered to be engaged in local food production. There is no established definition of what constitutes a "local food," but generally local food systems refer to agricultural production and marketing that occurs within a certain geographic proximity (between farmer and consumer) or that involves certain social or supply chain characteristics in producing food (such as small family farms, urban gardens, or farms using sustainable agriculture practices).[41] Sales of locally produced foods also comprise a small but growing part of U.S. agricultural sales. Though estimates vary, USDA reports that local food sales totaled an estimated $6.1 billion in 2012, reflecting sales from nearly 164,000 farmers selling locally marketed foods.[42] This represents 8% of U.S. farms and an estimated 1.5% of the value of total U.S. agricultural production.

Existing Farm Bill Provisions

The 2008 farm bill expanded support and funding for existing specialty crop and organic programs and created new incentives for producers under a new bill title, "Horticulture and Organic Agriculture." The 2014 farm bill reauthorized many of the existing farm bill provisions and increased spending on programs supporting specialty crops and certified organic agriculture, as well as local foods, as part of the

---

[38] The Organic Foods Production Act of 1990 and USDA's National Organic Program (NOP) regulations require that agricultural products labeled as "organic" originate from farms or handling operations certified by a state or private entity that has been accredited by USDA. OFPA was enacted as part of the 1990 farm bill (P.L. 101-624). NOP is a voluntary production and handling certification program administered by USDA. NOP regulations are at 7 C.F.R. 205.

[39] USDA, *2014 Organic Production Survey*, ACH 12-29, September 2015.

[40] Organic Trade Association (OTA), "U.S. Organic Sales Post New Record of $43.3 Billion in 2015," May 19, 2016.

[41] Such operations include direct-to-consumer marketing, farmers' markets, farm-to-school programs, community-supported agriculture, community gardens, school gardens, food hubs and market aggregators, kitchen incubators, and mobile slaughter units, among other types of operations.

[42] USDA, *Trends in U.S. Local and Regional Food Systems: Report to Congress*, APN-068, January 2015.

"Horticulture" title. When the 2014 farm bill was enacted, CBO estimated that mandatory outlays for programs authorized in the horticulture title would increase nearly $340 million over the next five years (FY2014-FY2018) compared with the previous five-year period.[43] Despite this increase, funding under this title still comprises a small share—less than one-half of 1%—of total mandatory farm bill spending. Across all farm bill titles, mandatory spending for specialty crops, organic agriculture, and local food systems was expected to average about $770 million annually (FY2014-FY2018).[44] Key programs include the Specialty Crop Block Grant Program (SCBGP), the Specialty Crop Research Initiative (SCRI), pest and disease prevention programs (including the so-called Section 10007 program), and nutrition programs targeting fruits and vegetables. The 2014 farm bill also provided for an additional roughly $300 million in average annual appropriations across related programs.

In general, the types of programs in which many of these groups share a common interest are USDA marketing and promotion programs (including rural development programs), domestic food and nutrition programs, research and cooperative extension programs, and conservation programs, among others. Although USDA has historically not provided direct support for specialty crops and organic production, over the decades Congress has authorized a wide range of programs in these areas that are viewed as facilitating the growth of and benefiting the economic health of these and related sectors.

Issues and Options

Despite some shared program interests and a shared farm bill title, there are often significant differences between U.S. specialty crop and organic producers in terms of their overall farm bill priorities and in the types of key farm bill programs each group supports. The U.S. horticulture sector is among the most diverse of U.S. farm sector groups, with advocates spanning a wide range of policy priorities.[45] The certified organic and the local foods sectors are even more diverse, with wide-ranging priorities.[46] Given the perception of the importance of fruits and vegetables within many varied policy arenas, including child nutrition and wellness, and continued calls for enhanced equity

---

[43] CBO cost estimate of the conference agreement on H.R. 2642, January 28, 2014. This estimate does not include costs for provisions in other farm bill titles benefitting specialty crop and organic producers.

[44] For more information, see CRS Report R43632, *Specialty Crop Provisions in the 2014 Farm Bill (P.L. 113-79)*.

[45] Among specialty crop growers, the principal groups promoting the sector's farm bill priorities are the Specialty Crop Farm Bill Alliance (SCFBA), the United Fresh Produce Association, the Produce Marketing Association, and the American Fruit and Vegetable Processors and Growers Coalition, as well as regional groups such as Western Growers.

[46] Representatives in the organic sector include the Organic Trade Association, the Organic Farming Research Foundation, the National Organic Coalition, the Organic Consumers Association, and the Organic Farmers Association. Interests among these groups and those representing local foods often overlap with other agricultural interests such as those of the National Sustainable Agriculture Coalition (NSAC) and the National Farmer Union, among other groups.

across farm sectors, the specialty crop industry is expected to call for continued expansion of funding for a range of existing USDA programs. Similarly, continued growth in both consumer demand and producer investment in the certified organic and locally produced food sectors is likely to drive calls for increasing support for these markets both within USDA and at the state and local levels. Such expansion proposals may draw resistance from more traditional agricultural producers as well as by more established program recipients within the fruit and vegetable sectors due to competition for limited funds.

Previously, farm bill recommendations by specialty crop interest groups (as well as some leading fruit and vegetable producing state agencies, such as California) spanned most farm bill titles.[47]

Most groups supported maintaining funding for each of the primary nutrition programs—such as the Fresh Fruit and Vegetable (Snack) Program, minimum purchase requirements under the Section 32 program, and the DOD Fresh program—and also called for changes to improve the nutritional status of U.S. food stamp recipients. They also recommended expanded funding for block grants, plant pest and disease programs, research programs (such as SCRI), and disaster assistance (including raising payment limitations on tree replacement). Within export promotion, these groups recommended maintaining funding for USDA's Market Access Program (MAP) and expanding the Technical Assistance for Specialty Crops (TASC) to address sanitary and phytosanitary and technical barriers to U.S. specialty crop exports. They also recommended that certain conservation programs be expanded to assist specialty crop producers and that AGI limitations not apply to conservation programs.[48] Finally, SCFBA recommended continued funding for the Value-Added Producer Grant Program and other changes to certain rural development title programs that affect farmworkers.

Farm bill recommendations promoted by the organic industry that could resurface in the next farm bill are focused on existing programs, including funding for the National Organic Program and the National Organic Certification Cost-Share Program and support for research under the Organic Agriculture Research and Extension Initiative (OREI) and the Organic Transitions Integrated Research Program (ORG).[49] Other priorities have included improving organic producers' access to USDA conservation programs and crop insurance, as well as addressing certain marketing issues, such as organic data collection at USDA and potential losses associated with contamination of organic crops from genetically engineered crops.

Many of the farm bill programs supporting specialty crops and organic agriculture are also supported by organizations promoting local and regional food systems. Some of

---

[47] See, for example, SCFBA's and United's recommendations for the 2014 farm bill, as well as recommendations by the state of California ("California and the Farm Bill," http://www.aginnovations.org/).

[48] See, for example, SCFBA policy positions dated July 8, 2015, and May 11, 2015 (http://www.unitedfresh.org/).

[49] See, for example, OTA and National Organic Coalition recommendations for the 2014 farm bill.

the leading programs for local food producers also include the Farmers Market and Local Food promotion programs, the Senior Farmers Market Nutrition Program, and also related policies and incentives under SNAP, such as the Food Insecurity Nutrition Incentives, support for Community Food Projects, and Farm to School provisions. These groups also generally promote several rural development programs, including the Rural Micro-Entrepreneur Assistance Program. They also promote grant and loan programs that broadly support strategic regional community and economic development as well as beginning and socially disadvantaged farmers and ranchers.

In anticipation of the 2018 farm bill reauthorization, the ranking member of the Senate Agriculture Committee, Senator Debbie Stabenow, introduced the Urban Agriculture Act of 2016 (S. 3420) in the 114th Congress. This bill proposed to expand existing farm programs and funding, as well as fund new programs and incentives, to promote urban agriculture by expanding provisions in several titles throughout the farm bill. Proposed provisions include expanded support for competitive grants and research initiatives supporting urban farming along with expanded risk management tools, among other provisions. When this bill was introduced, it was widely noted as being intended to become part of the 2018 farm bill and could be reintroduced in the 115th Congress.[50] In addition, in the 114th Congress, comprehensive legislation was introduced to address food waste and recovery in both the House (H.R. 4184) and Senate (S. 3108). These bills proposed to expand the mission and funding for several existing federal programs to cover a range of food waste efforts, including additional funds for loans and grants to support composting and energy projects. Other bills addressing food waste were also introduced in the 114th Congress, and the House Agriculture Committee held a hearing on the subject in May 2016. Accordingly, food waste efforts could be considered as part of the larger farm bill debate.

Animal Agriculture

Farm bills have traditionally not provided livestock and poultry producers with farm revenue support programs like those for major crops such as grains, oilseeds, and cotton. Instead, the livestock and poultry industries look to the federal government for leadership in protecting animal health; establishing transparent, science-based rules for trading animal products; resolving foreign trade disputes; and assuring that supplies of domestic and imported meat and poultry are safe, of high quality, and free from pests and diseases.

[50] Based on comments by Senator Stabenow reported in *Hagstrom Report*, "Stabenow Introduces Urban Ag Bill Before Big Conference," September 2016.

Existing Farm Bill Provisions

The "Miscellaneous" title of the 2014 farm bill contained eight provisions addressing livestock and poultry producers. Five provisions were related to animal health. These included funding and certification process changes for the Trichinae Certification Program and additional funding for three other programs: the (1) National Aquatic Animal Health Plan, (2) the National Animal Health Laboratory Network, and (3) the National Poultry Improvement Plan. It also included a sense of Congress provision that feral swine eradication be considered a high priority.

In addition, the last farm bill addressed both country-of-origin labeling (COOL) and USDA catfish inspection, which were originally in the 2008 farm bill. The 2014 farm bill directed USDA to conduct an economic analysis of the COOL rule that USDA wrote and amended to implement 2008 farm bill requirements. During the 2014 farm bill debate, the United States was in the midst of a WTO dispute settlement case over COOL with Canada and Mexico, and the WTO had determined that COOL violated U.S. WTO obligations. Congress repealed the beef and pork COOL provisions in December 2015. The 2014 farm bill also confirmed the catfish inspection provision that transferred catfish inspection from the Food and Drug Administration to USDA. It also defined catfish as "all fish of the order 'Siluriformes'" in order to require inspections of both domestic and imported catfish. USDA issued the final rule in December 2015 that went into effect in March 2016.

Finally, the farm bill provided funding for the National Sheep Industry Improvement Center, which works to enhance the sheep and goat industry. Aside from the animal-related provisions in the miscellaneous title, the 2014 farm bill's permanent reauthorization of disaster assistance programs was a key achievement for livestock and poultry producers. (See discussion in "Farm Safety Net Programs").

Issues and Options

In the upcoming farm bill debate, Congress is expected to consider extending support for the livestock and poultry sectors through reauthorizing and funding existing animal health programs, which protect the health of animals and the livelihood of producers. In particular, the outbreak of highly pathogenic avian influenza (HPAI) in 2014-2015 in U.S. laying hen flocks and the subsequent economic losses for producers and disruptions in trade for the entire poultry industry demonstrated the crucial role that USDA plays in animal health. Ongoing concerns about HPAI suggest that the livestock and poultry industries may be interested in engaging Congress on possible policies such as expanded indemnities or animal disease insurance that could aid producers affected by outbreaks.

The livestock industry would like USDA to develop a vaccine stockpile for foot-and-mouth disease (FMD). Congressional hearings in 2016 addressed FMD and preparedness at USDA's Animal and Plant Health Inspection Service (APHIS) in the event that it should ever be reintroduced into the United States.[51] The last U.S. FMD outbreak was in 1929. Another FMD outbreak would be devastating for U.S. livestock producers, with estimated annual losses of nearly $13 billion over 10 years, according to one study.[52] U.S. law does not allow for the domestic production of FMD vaccine. USDA stockpiles viral antigen concentrate (VAC) that is used to produce vaccine doses. USDA's current vaccine supplies, however, would be insufficient in the event of a large FMD outbreak. The livestock industry is calling for USDA to expand funding and capabilities to provide sufficient doses of vaccine if ever needed.

Expansion of feral swine eradication programs is another potential farm bill issue. Feral hogs were found in 39 states in 2016. By one estimate, feral swine cause $1 billion in damages to agriculture and another $1.5 billion to other parts of the U.S. economy in crop and natural resource destruction annually.[53] Feral swine are also a vector for animal disease. Congress appropriated $20 million to APHIS in 2014 for feral swine programs that are undertaken cooperatively with states and tribal nations. Congress could consider whether additional support for expanding existing funding and programs is merited.

During past farm bill debates, there has been interest is addressing consolidation and competition in the livestock and poultry sectors. USDA rules proposed by the Grain Inspection, Packers and Stockyards Administration (GIPSA) in 2010—partly finalized in 2011 and partly reproposed in 2016—continue to divide livestock and poultry producers, agricultural associations, and Members of Congress.[54] It is now up to the Trump Administration to decide whether to proceed with the GIPSA rules released by the Obama Administration in December 2016. Some farm and rancher groups and rural advocacy groups may look to the farm bill as an opportunity to propose new policies that support producers, especially contract growers.

Current law under the Animal Welfare Act (9 U.S.C. §2131 et seq.) requires minimum care standards for most types of warm-blooded animals bred for commercial sale, used in research, transported commercially, or exhibited to the public. Although farm animals are exempt, they are covered by other federal laws addressing humane transport and slaughter. Some members of the House and Senate Agriculture Committees

---

[51] U.S. Congress, House Committee on Homeland Security, Subcommittee on Emergency Preparedness, *Food for Thought: Efforts to Defend the Nation's Agriculture and Food*, 114th Cong., February 26, 2016, and U.S. Congress, Senate Committee on Agriculture, Nutrition, and Forestry, *A Review of the U.S. Livestock and Poultry Sectors: Marketplace Opportunities and Challenges*, 114th Cong., May 26, 2016. The United States has been free of FMD since 1929.

[52] Dermot Hayes et al., "Economy-Wide Impacts of a Foreign Animal Disease in the United States," Center for Agricultural and Rural Development, Working Paper 11-WP 525, November 2011.

[53] Chris Bennett, "Wild Pig Bomb Still Rocking Agriculture," *PorkNetwork*, January/February 2017, p. 24.

[54] See CRS Report R41673, *USDA's "GIPSA Rule" on Livestock and Poultry Marketing Practices*, and CRS Insight IN10638, *USDA Releases GIPSA Rules*.

have expressed a preference for farmers to continue to pursue voluntary approaches to farm animal welfare. Increased consumer interest in farm animal welfare, as well as interest among some Members of Congress, may lead to proposals addressing animal welfare on the farm. For example, since FY2007, horse slaughter has been debated each year during appropriations debates, and Congress has prohibited USDA's Food Safety Inspection Service (FSIS) from carrying out horse slaughter every year except FY2012-FY2014. In the 115th Congress, the Safeguard American Food Exports Act of 2017 (H.R. 113) proposed deeming horse meat as unfit for human consumption and banning the transport of horses to be slaughtered for human consumption. A new farm bill could be viewed as an avenue to permanently settle the annual appropriations debate on horse slaughter.

AGRICULTURAL CREDIT

The federal government has a long history of providing credit assistance to farmers. This intervention has been justified by many factors, including market failure due to imperfect knowledge of information between lenders and farmers, lack of competition in some rural lending markets, insufficient lending resources in rural areas, and the desire to targeted lending to disadvantaged groups.

The agricultural lender with the greatest connection to the federal government is the USDA Farm Service Agency (FSA). It issues direct loans to farmers who cannot qualify for regular commercial credit and guarantees the repayment of certain loans made by other lenders. FSA also has statutory mandates to target loans to beginning farmers and socially disadvantaged groups based primarily on race and gender. Of the $350 billion in total farm debt as of year-end 2015, FSA provides about 2% through direct loans and guarantees about another 4%-5%.

Another agricultural lender with a federal mandate is the Farm Credit System (FCS). FCS is a cooperatively owned and federally chartered private lender with a statutory mandate to serve only agriculture-related borrowers. FCS makes loans to creditworthy farmers. It is *not* a lender of last resort but it is a government-sponsored enterprise receiving tax benefits, among other preferences, in return for restrictions on its lending base. FCS accounts for about 40% of farm debt. A third agricultural lender created by federal statute is Farmer Mac, another government- sponsored enterprise that is privately held and provides a secondary market for agricultural loans.

The statutory authority for FSA, FCS, and Farmer Mac is permanent, but farm bills often make adjustments to eligibility criteria and the scope of operations.

Existing Farm Bill Provisions

The 2014 farm bill made relatively small policy changes to USDA and FCS farm lending programs. It eliminated term limits on USDA-guaranteed farm operating loans, gave USDA discretion to recognize alternative legal entities to qualify for farm loans, and allowed alternatives to meet a three-year farming experience requirement. It also increased the maximum size of down payment loans. It further increased the percentage of a conservation loan that can be guaranteed, added another lending priority for beginning farmers, and facilitated loans for the purchase of highly fractionated land in Indian reservations. The farm bill also stated that compensation decisions for FCS executives rests with FCS boards of directors.

Issues and Options

Credit issues are not expected to be a major part of a new farm bill, and changes that might occur are not expected to be particularly significant or comprehensive within the scope of agricultural credit statutes. Nonetheless, several issues could arise as legislation develops, including:

- Further targeting of FSA lending resources to beginning and socially disadvantaged farmers;
- Providing carve-outs for emerging or nontraditional parts of the agricultural industry, such as local or regional food systems, organic agriculture, and sustainable production, or providing financing for farmers, cooperatives, and/or food businesses that serve food deserts or finance urban agriculture; and
- Determining the scope of FCS and/or Farmer Mac lending activities, including the carve-outs mentioned above.

AGRICULTURAL RESEARCH

USDA was created in 1862 in part to support agricultural research in an expanding, agriculturally dependent country. USDA conducts intramural research at federal facilities with government- employed scientists and supports external research at universities and other facilities through competitive grants and formula-based funding. The breadth of contemporary USDA research spans traditional agricultural production techniques, organic and sustainable agriculture, bioenergy, nutrition needs and composition, food safety, animal and plant health, pest and disease management, economic decisionmaking, and other social sciences affecting consumers, farmers, and rural communities.

Four agencies carry out USDA's research and education activities, grouped together into the Research, Education, and Economics (REE) mission area. The Agricultural Research Service (ARS) is USDA's intramural science agency and conducts research on food and agriculture issues of national and regional importance. The National Institute of Food and Agriculture (NIFA) sponsors extramural research by distributing federal funds to land-grant universities and other outside partners for state- and regional-level research, education, and extension activities. The Economic Research Service (ERS) conducts economic and social science research about agriculture, rural development, food, commodity markets, and the environment. Finally, the National Agricultural Statistics Service (NASS) conducts the Census of Agriculture and provides official statistics on agricultural production and other relevant indicators about the farm sector.

Existing Farm Bill Provisions

The research title of the 2014 farm bill reauthorized funding for various USDA research activities through FY2018, subject to appropriations, and amended authority so that only competitive grants can be awarded under certain programs. Mandatory spending was increased for several programs, including the Specialty Crop Research Initiative (SCRI), the Organic Agricultural Research and Extension Initiative (OREI), and the Beginning Farmer and Rancher Development Program (BFRDP). It also provided mandatory funds to establish the Foundation for Food and Agriculture Research, a nonprofit corporation designed to accept private donations and award grants for collaborative public/private partnerships among USDA, academia, and the private sector.

Issues and Options

Several research programs mentioned above received mandatory funding in the 2014 farm bill but do not have a budget baseline that extends beyond FY2018.[55] If policymakers want to continue these programs in a new farm bill, they would need to pay for them with other offsets. These include $100 million over five years for both OREI and BFRDP and $200 million to establish the Foundation for Food and Agriculture Research ($200 million in FY2014).

USDA differs from most other federal science agencies in allocating more than half of its annual research appropriation to intramural research agencies, including ARS, ERS,

[55] CRS Report R44758, *Farm Bill Programs Without a Budget Baseline Beyond FY2018*.

and NASS. Coordinating intramural and extramural research objectives and activities continues to be a concern and could be considered as part of a new farm bill debate. Likewise, the appropriate split between formula funding and competitive funding for extramural research in NIFA remains a concern of various interests. Lastly, within the competitive grants programs, especially the flagship Agriculture and Food Research Initiative (AFRI), allocation and prioritization of funding among various research areas remains a concern. Interest groups that want more funding for their research needs and commodities may seek inclusion via farm bill legislation.

AGRICULTURAL TRADE AND EXPORT PROMOTION

The federal government provides support for U.S. agricultural exports through two types of programs: export market development and export credit guarantees. The 2014 farm bill repealed the Dairy Export Incentive Program, thereby eliminating the use of direct export subsidies for U.S. agricultural products. Legislative authorizations for agricultural trade programs are included in the trade title of the 2014 farm bill. USDA's export promotion programs are administered by USDA's Foreign Agricultural Service (FAS) and generally funded using mandatory monies. One of the larger programs, MAP, was targeted for cuts or elimination in a number of deficit reduction proposals but was retained intact in the 2014 farm bill.

Existing Farm Bill Provisions

Export market development programs—whose primary aim is to assist U.S. industry efforts to build, maintain, and expand overseas markets for U.S. agricultural products—include MAP, the Foreign Market Development Program (FMDP), the Emerging Markets Program (EMP), the Quality Samples Program (QSP), and TASC. The 2014 farm bill extended budget authority forthese programs through FY2018, making funding mandatory and thus not subject to annual appropriations.

The 2014 farm bill also reauthorized GSM-102, the FAS-administered short-term export credit guarantee program,[56] and the Facility Guarantee Program (FGP). Under these programs, the CCC provides payment guarantees for the commercial financing of U.S. agricultural exports. GSM-102 guarantees repayment of commercial financing by approved foreign banks, mainly of developing countries, for up to two years for the purchase of U.S. farm and food products. FGP guarantees financing of goods and

[56] GSM refers to the General Sales Manager, an official within FAS appointed by the FAS administrator charged with increasing exports and managing the programs that encourage foreign countries and companies to import U.S. farm products.

services exported from the United States to improve or establish agriculture-related facilities in emerging markets.

While the 2014 farm bill extended these programs largely intact, it did make several changes. To comply with a WTO decision in a cotton case won by Brazil, Congress made several changes to GSM-102. These changes included shortening the loan guarantee period from three years to two, repealing a requirement that the Secretary of Agriculture maximize the amount of credit guarantees available each year, and removing a provision that restricted the Secretary from adjusting program fees to fully cover the cost of operating the program. Congress also broadened the scope of TASC to fund projects that address technical barriers to trade beyond sanitary and phytosanitary measures.

At a more strategic level, the 2014 farm bill directed USDA to consult with the House and Senate Agriculture Committees and Appropriations Committees and then propose a plan to reorganize the international trade functions of USDA. The law directs that the plan establish an Under Secretary for Farm and Foreign Agricultural Affairs within USDA, a position that would require Senate confirmation. Currently, USDA's Under Secretary for Farm and Foreign Affairs oversees FAS and the export programs the agency administers, as well as several major domestic farm program areas. At a hearing of the Senate Agriculture Committee in September 2016, former USDA Secretary Vilsack said he intended to lay the groundwork for the next Administration to pursue this task.[57] At the beginning of 2017, however, USDA had not transmitted a reorganization plan to Congress.

Issues and Options

Federal support for agricultural export promotion invariably raises questions about the appropriateness of government support for private sector export promotion and the effectiveness and impact of these programs. Some have argued that MAP and FMDP are forms of corporate welfare in that they fund activities that private firms and industry groups could and should fund themselves. Other critics argue that the principal beneficiaries of export promotion programs are foreign consumers and that funds could be better spent, for example, on educating U.S. firms about how to export and on overcoming trade barriers.

Questions about whether export promotion programs are as effective as they could be, and whether new approaches to facilitating and promoting U.S. farm exports may be needed (or both), could be topics of discussion in a new farm bill, considering that the value of U.S. exports and farm income have both declined since the enactment of the previous farm bill. The eligibility of certain types of organizations and producer groups,

[57] Senate Agriculture Committee hearing of September 21, 2016.

and the levels of funding for various programs are likely topics of debate as policymakers consider farm bill trade programs. Congress could also revisit the unfinished business of its directive to reorganize the international trade functions of USDA under a new Under Secretary position with a unique focus on promoting U.S. farm and food exports. Other trade-related issues that are outside the context of the farm bill—but may arise in the debate around the trade title in view of lower farm export sales in recent years— may include various multilateral and bilateral trade negotiations that are generally supported by some U.S. agricultural groups.[58]

INTERNATIONAL FOOD AID AND ASSISTANCE

The United States has led global funding support for international food assistance for over 60 years.[59] These programs originated with blended goals to support the domestic agricultural safety net, agricultural trade goals, and the maritime industry in addition to supporting efforts to alleviate hunger abroad.[60] This blending of objectives is manifested through statutory requirements that most U.S. international food assistance be (1) based on the donation of U.S. agricultural commodities to be distributed as food or sold to generate funds for development programs[61] and (2) shipped primarily on U.S.-flag vessels.[62]

Two agencies implement the international food assistance programs authorized under the farm bill: the U.S. Agency for International Development (USAID), and FAS. USAID implements the largest program, Food for Peace Title II (Emergency and Private Assistance Programs), which averaged $1.8 billion in annual outlays from FY2006-FY2015. FAS implements all other international food assistance programs funded through the farm bill authorization, with total annual average outlays of $395 million per year from FY2006-FY2015.[63]

---

[58] For example, the U.S. International Trade Commission concluded that the proposed Trans-Pacific Partnership regional free-trade agreement between the United States and 11 Pacific-facing nations could have boosted U.S. farm and food exports (International Trade Commission, *Trans-Pacific Partnership Agreement: Likely Impact on the U.S. Economy and on Specific Industry Sectors*, publication no. 4067, May 2016).

[59] See for example http://www.wfp.org/fais/ for data on food aid donations over time.

[60] For more on the origins of U.S. international food assistance policies, see CRS Report R41072, *U.S. International Food Aid Programs: Background and Issues*.

[61] This applies to nearly all of the programs authorized through the farm bill—with some exceptions, including the Local and Regional Procurement Projects program and some uses of the 202(e) funds under Food for Peace Title II.

[62] The specific requirement is called agricultural cargo preference, the specifics of which have fluctuated several times. In 2012 the requirement was reduced from 75% to 50% of food aid cargo shipments, and it eliminated programs that offset the increased costs that they incur due to the cargo preference requirement.

[63] CRS calculations based on data available from International Food Aid Reports.

Existing Farm Bill Provisions

The United States provides U.S. agricultural commodities, procured by USDA, as the primary form of emergency and economic development assistance in response to food security problems in developing countries. The suite of programs that govern U.S. international food assistance was reauthorized in the trade title of the 2014 farm bill. Programs include (1) Food for Peace, (2) Food for Progress, (3) the McGovern-Dole International Food for Education and Child Nutrition Program, and (4) the Bill Emerson Humanitarian Trust. The Food for Peace Act's Title II, Emergency and Private Assistance Programs, is the primary vehicle for U.S. international food aid. Title II of Food for Peace is administered by USAID. Title II provides donations of U.S. agricultural commodities to respond to emergency food needs or to be used in development projects. All other food aid programs are administered by FAS. The 2014 farm bill also enacted modest flexibilities into the Food for Peace Act.[64]

The 2014 farm bill also made permanent the Local and Regional Food Aid Procurement Projects program (which was authorized in the 2008 farm bill as a temporary pilot program), but it also changed its funding from mandatory to discretionary, increasing the authorization from $60 million total during FY2009-FY2012 to $80 million per year, subject to annual appropriations. It also introduced additional reporting requirements on administrative costs, transportation, storage, and cost recovery of monetized food aid authorized through the farm bill.[65]

Issues and Options

U.S. international food assistance programs have evoked considerable debate on whether to relax, retain, or strengthen statutory requirements that affect implementation of the programs. The 115th Congress might continue these discussions or might consider new legislation that also addresses global hunger issues.

In previous Congresses, debate about U.S. international food assistance programs intensified during farm bill discussions and other legislative proposals.[66] Issues that Congress discussed included whether to alter requirements on where food aid is

---

[64] These changes include an increase in the amount and flexibility in use of cash funds (also referred to as 202(e) funds), which allows Food for Peace programs to use up to 20% of funds as cash for program administration, vouchers, or local and regional procurement. Other flexibilities include increases in authorizations to fund commodities at prepositioning sites (intermediate storage locations to reduce time lags when shipping commodities to destinations).

[65] USAID and USDA report this information in annual International Food Aid Reports.

[66] Legislative proposals to reduce requirements within U.S. international food assistance programs included, in the 113th Congress, S. 2421 (Food for Peace Reform Act of 2014), H.R. 1983 (Food Aid Reform Act), and H.Amdt. 190 to H.R. 1947 (Federal Agriculture Reform and Risk Management Act of 2013); in the 114th Congress, S. 525 (Food for Peace Reform Act of 2015) and S. 1252 (enacted as the Global Food Security Act of 2016, P.L. 114-195).

purchased, how it is transported, and the extent to which U.S. agricultural commodities must be sold (or "monetized") to support Food for Peace development programs. Proponents for increased flexibility argue that requirements on sourcing and transportation increase program expenses, and flexibility could allow U.S. international food assistance programs to benefit more people at no additional cost.[67] Supporters of the existing program mechanisms cite the value of leveraging the international programs to also support U.S. agriculture, shipping, and military readiness.[68]

The 2016 Global Food Security Act (P.L. 114-195) codified a new program—the Emergency Food Security Program (EFSP)—but did not alter programs that are authorized through the farm bill. The new EFSP operates without restrictions on sourcing or shipping—cash transfers are permissible. The Global Food Security Act mandated additional coordination efforts of all U.S. programs that address hunger internationally.[69] Authorizations for food aid programs under both the farm bill and the act expire after FY2018. The simultaneous expiry of these programs with similar goals and distinct reporting mechanisms may generate congressional discussion on how to coordinate oversight and reauthorization across both agricultural and foreign affairs jurisdictions. USAID's Office of Food for Peace implements EFSP, but the program does not operate with funding authorized through the Food for Peace Act. The program reports to the foreign affairs committees, not to the agricultural committees.

Food and Nutrition

Domestic food assistance programs reauthorized in the farm bill's nutrition title include the Supplemental Nutrition Assistance Program (SNAP, formerly the Food Stamp Program), the Emergency Food Assistance Program (TEFAP), the Commodity Supplemental Food Program (CSFP), the Food Distribution Program on Indian Reservations (FDPIR), and other programs administered by USDA's Food and Nutrition Service (FNS). According to CBO's projected costs at the time of enactment, the nutrition title makes up nearly 80% of spending under the 2014 farm bill (though subsequent estimates show that actual spending has been less than was projected at that time; see Table 1 and Figure 1). SNAP accounts for the vast majority of the spending in this title. At the time of enactment, the policy changes contained in the nutrition title of the 2014 farm bill were projected to save $8 billion relative to baseline spending over 10 years (FY2014- FY2023). The savings are primarily from changes to SNAP, but there are increasing investments in some areas.

---

[67] See for example discussion from USAID Office of Food for Peace at https://www.usaid.gov/foodaidreform.

[68] See, for example, letter to House Committee on Agriculture from a range of industries, March 21, 2013.

[69] USAID's government-wide U.S. Global Food Security Strategy was submitted to Congress in October 2016. See USAID, "U.S. Government Global Food Security Strategy 2017-2021."

Most farm bill domestic food assistance programs—except for CSFP, FDPIR, and the administrative cost component of TEFAP—are generally treated as mandatory spending for budget purposes. SNAP is open-ended mandatory spending and is funded through appropriations laws. As such, amending SNAP eligibility, benefits, or other program rules can have a budgetary impact, but the availability of appropriated funding also affects operations. Discretionary spending programs in the farm bill include CSFP, the administrative cost component of TEFAP, and a portion of FDPIR.

Typically, the Special Supplemental Nutrition Program for Women, Infants, and Children (WIC) and the child nutrition programs (National School Lunch Program, School Breakfast Program, Child and Adult Care Food Program, Summer Food Service Program, and others) are not reauthorized in the farm bill. These programs, located in the Child Nutrition Act of 1966 and the Richard B. Russell National School Lunch Act, were last reauthorized in 2010 in P.L. 111-296, the Healthy, Hunger-Free Kids Act of 2010. Despite efforts to complete the next child nutrition reauthorization during the 114th Congress, the legislation did not advance beyond committees.[70]

Program Design and Operation

The sections to follow provide program background and highlight some of the 2014 farm bill's major changes.

Supplemental Nutrition Assistance Program (SNAP)

Formerly known as the Food Stamp Program, SNAP provides benefits to eligible low-income households on electronic benefit transfer (EBT) cards.[71] Benefits can be exchanged for eligible foods at authorized retailers. In FY2016, an average of 44.2 million individuals in 21.8 million households participated in SNAP each month.[72] Federal spending for FY2016 totaled approximately $70.8 billion. The vast majority of the spending ($66.6 billion, 94%) was the cost of benefits themselves, which are 100% federally financed.

SNAP eligibility and benefits are calculated on a household basis. Financial eligibility is determined through a traditional or a categorical eligibility path. Under *traditional* eligibility, applicant households must meet gross income, net income, and asset tests. Specifically, household gross monthly income (all income as defined by SNAP law) must be at or below 130% of the federal poverty level, and household net

---

[70] See CRS In Focus IF10266, *An Introduction to Child Nutrition Reauthorization*, and CRS Report R44373, *Tracking the Next Child Nutrition Reauthorization: An Overview*.

[71] For more SNAP background, see CRS Report R42505, *Supplemental Nutrition Assistance Program (SNAP): A Primer on Eligibility and Benefits*.

[72] Administrative data from FNS as of December 9, 2016, available at https://www.fns.usda.gov/pd/supplemental-nutrition-assistance-program-snap.

monthly income (with SNAP-specified deductions subtracted) must be at 100% of the federal poverty level. The traditional asset rules are set at $2,000 per household (inflation adjusted). (Households that contain an elderly or disabled member have a higher asset limit and also do not have to meet the gross income test.) Under *categorical* eligibility, SNAP eligibility is automatically conveyed based upon the applicant's participation in other means-tested programs, namely Supplemental Security Income (SSI), Temporary Assistance for Needy Families (TANF), or General Assistance (GA). Because TANF is a broad-purpose block grant, the state option to extend SNAP eligibility to applicants that receive a TANF-funded benefit allows states to offer program eligibility under rules that vary from those discussed in this paragraph, including an elimination of the asset test ("broad-based categorical eligibility"). Applicants are also subject to nonfinancial rules, which include work- related requirements such as a time limit for Able-Bodied Adults Without Dependents (ABAWDs). If eligible for SNAP, an applicant household undergoes a calculation of its monthly benefit amount (or allotment) based on household size and any applicable SNAP deductions.

Although the nutrition title of the 2014 farm bill (P.L. 113-79) contains a number of provisions that changed aspects of SNAP, Congress retained most of SNAP's existing authorizing law.[73] The 2014 farm bill amended how Low-Income Home Energy Assistance Program (LIHEAP) payments are treated in the calculation of SNAP benefits, reducing benefit amounts in some states. The law included policies related to the SNAP Employment and Training (E&T) program, including a pilot project authority and related funding ($200 million over FY2014 and FY2015) for states to implement and for USDA to evaluate a variety of work programs for SNAP participants. Since SNAP provides benefits redeemable for SNAP-eligible foods at SNAP-eligible retailers, much of SNAP law pertains to retailer authorization and benefit issuance and redemption. The 2014 farm bill included changes to retailer and redemption provisions. The law now requires stores to stock more fresh foods, requires retailers to pay for their EBT machines, and provides additional funding for combatting trafficking (the sale of SNAP benefits).[74] The 2014 farm bill also includes $100 million in mandatory funding (over 10 years) for Food Insecurity Nutrition Incentive grants, which will support organizations that offer bonus incentives for SNAP purchases of fruits and vegetables.

The Emergency Food Assistance Program (TEFAP)

Under TEFAP, the federal government provides USDA-purchased commodity foods to states. This assistance supplements other sources of food aid for needy persons and is often provided in concert with food bank and homeless shelter projects as either food packages or meals. States make eligibility decisions for TEFAP assistance and choose local administering agencies.

---

[73] The 2014 farm bill amended SNAP's authorizing statute, the Food and Nutrition Act of 2008.

[74] See CRS Report R44650, *Updated Standards for SNAP-Authorized Retailers: Final Rule*.

National emergency provider and food bank networks (such as Feeding America) are also heavily involved. In addition to state allocations in entitlement commodities, each state receives a share of discretionary money to fund expenses of administration and distribution (e.g., storage, transportation) of the commodities. State entitlements to TEFAP commodities are supplemented with bonus commodities (about $305 million in FY2016) that USDA has acquired in its agriculture support programs.

The 2014 farm bill increased mandatory funding for TEFAP entitlement commodities. According to CBO's estimate (which accounts for inflation), the 2014 farm bill increases funding for TEFAP's entitlement commodities by $125 million over 5 years and $205 million over 10 years. The increases first took effect in FY2015 with an increase of $50 million above prior law. Among other changes, the 2014 law also requires funding for TEFAP to be available to be spent over a two-year period.

Commodity Supplemental Food Program

CSFP provides supplemental foods primarily to low-income elderly persons. For elderly participants, eligibility is limited to those with income below 130% of the federal poverty income guidelines. USDA purchases the foods and distributes them to grantees. CSFP grantees also receive funding for administrative costs. Commodities and administrative funding are generally apportioned by the number of persons served in the prior year. If new money is appropriated or if allocated "slots" are not used, new projects can be added. In FY2016, 47 states, the District of Columbia, and two Indian Tribal Organizations (ITOs) operated CSFP projects.

The 2014 farm bill changed CSFP's eligibility rules, phasing out eligibility for low-income pregnant, postpartum, and breastfeeding women, infants, and children. According to FY2016 FNS administrative data, nearly all of the over 585,000 program participants were elderly (defined as 60 years of age or older).

Other Farm Bill Programs

Programs in Lieu of SNAP

Puerto Rico, American Samoa, and the Commonwealth of the Northern Mariana Islands (CNMI) do not participate in the SNAP program. Instead, they receive a nutrition assistance block grant, under which they administer a nutrition assistance program with service delivery unique to each territory. Indian tribal organizations may choose to operate FDPIR instead of having the state offer SNAP benefits. The full cost of benefits and most administrative expenses are covered by the federal government. This option operates on over 250 Indian reservations in 22 states. The 2014 farm bill included policies related to the programs in lieu of SNAP. For instance, it required certain feasibility studies of the food assistance programs in Puerto Rico and CNMI.

Senior Farmers' Market Nutrition Program (SFMNP)

Under the SFMNP, low-income seniors receive vouchers that they can redeem at farmers' markets and roadside stands for fresh produce. The 2014 farm bill maintained mandatory funding at $20.6 million per year.

School and Institution Food Programs

As discussed above, the school meals programs are reauthorized in legislation separate from the farm bill. However, the 2014 farm bill did include several provisions and resources that pertain to the child nutrition programs, in particular the USDA commodity foods served in the school meal programs. Related policies include:

- Processing of USDA commodities. The 2014 law extended the authority for USDA to enter into reprocessing agreements with private companies to process commodity foods. The law also included a new provision that allowed USDA to contract with processors and retain title to those foods while processing.
- USDA purchases of fresh fruits and vegetables; farm to school. The 2014 law continued the requirement that $50 million of USDA's additional acquisitions of fruits and vegetables be fresh fruit and vegetables. The law also created a pilot grant program that would allow eight states to use this funding for their own local sourcing of fresh fruits and vegetables.
- Pulse crop pilot program. The new law included the Senate bill's proposal to create a pilot project to purchase pulse crops (dry beans, dry peas, lentils, and chickpeas) and pulse crop products for schools. Up to $10 million in appropriations was authorized.
- Fresh Fruit and Vegetable ("snack") Program. This program was permanently authorized and funded in the 2008 farm bill, but in 2014 a pilot was authorized to test and evaluate providing fruit and vegetable snacks in other forms.

Community Food Projects

In the 1996 farm bill (Federal Agriculture Improvement and Reform Act of 1996, P.L. 104-127), Congress established a program of assistance for community food projects intended to promote innovative local self-help initiatives to meet nutrition and farm needs. The 2014 farm bill made some amendments to the grant program and increased mandatory funding from $5 million per year to $9 million per year (beginning FY2015).

Issues and Options

As discussed earlier, the 2014 farm bill was formulated and enacted amid contentious debate that centered on SNAP spending, eligibility and benefit rules, and inclusion of certain programs in the farm bill. It is possible that some of the controversial policies included in House-passed bills but not in the enacted law will be debated again in the 115th Congress's consideration of the next nutrition title. The Trump Administration may affect how and what issues are discussed in the next reauthorization. Developments in the 114th Congress—namely the findings from the bipartisan congressional commission, the National Commission on Hunger,[75] and the House Committee on Agriculture's 114th Congress hearing series, "Past, Present, and Future of SNAP"[76]—may also preview future issues and options. It is also possible that SNAP, as the lion's share of the farm bill's mandatory spending, will be part of budgetary decisionmaking for the bill as a whole. The sections to follow briefly discuss examples of SNAP issues that came up during the last farm bill or have come up since that time.

SNAP Categorical Eligibility, Asset Limits

In current law, SNAP eligibility is available to applicants that already receive benefits from low- income programs, including SSI, TANF,[77] and state-financed GA programs. As of August 2016, 42 states adopted the "broad-based" categorical eligibility option, which gives states increased flexibility with the income and asset limits. Because of this "broad-based" option, most states are assessing applicants' eligibility without conducting an assessment of their assets. As these policies are considered, possibly in a new farm bill, so may be the role of asset tests in general.

Work-Related Rules in SNAP

SNAP law has rules on employment or work-related activities for able-bodied, nonelderly adult participants.[78] Some rules apply in all states that operate SNAP—for example, requiring unemployed program participants to register for work and accept a suitable job if offered one. However, some requirements can vary by state, depending on how each state designs its own SNAP Employment and Training Program (E&T)—for example, whether a work registrant's E&T participation is voluntary or mandatory.

In addition to the nationwide and state-specific work eligibility rules, SNAP law has a time limit for ABAWDs who are not working a minimum of 20 hours per week. If such

---

[75] This congressional commission was created by the FY2014 appropriations law, P.L. 113-76, "to provide policy recommendations to Congress and the USDA Secretary to more effectively use existing programs and funds of the Department of Agriculture to combat domestic hunger and food insecurity." National Commission on Hunger, *Freedom from Hunger: An Achievable Goal for the United States of America*, 2015, https://hungercommission.rti.org/.

[76] For a summary of these findings from the hearing, see Chairman K. Michael Conaway, *Past, Present, and Future of SNAP: Hearing Series Findings: 114th Congress*, House Committee on Agriculture, December 7, 2016.

[77] See additional resource on these programs: CRS Report RL32279, *Primer on Disability Benefits: Social Security Disability Insurance (SSDI) and Supplemental Security Income (SSI)*, and CRS Report RL32760, *The Temporary Assistance for Needy Families (TANF) Block Grant: Responses to Frequently Asked Questions*.

[78] A longer explanation of these rules is located in CRS Report R42505, *Supplemental Nutrition Assistance Program (SNAP): A Primer on Eligibility and Benefits*. Discussion of related House and Senate 2014 farm bill proposals is located in CRS Report R43332, *SNAP and Related Nutrition Provisions of the 2014 Farm Bill (P.L. 113-79)*.

individuals do not work the required number of hours, they can receive no more than three months of benefits over a 36-month period. SNAP law also authorizes waivers (tied to job availability in a state or portions of a state) and exemptions from the time limit. Some controversy has developed in recent years, including the years of the 2014 farm bill's formulation, because the vast majority of states had statewide waivers from enforcing the time limit. Currently, fewer states are eligible for those statewide waivers, and the time limit is becoming more prevalent. Participants are increasingly being time-limited off benefits, and there are anecdotal reports of food banks experiencing increased demand as a result.[79]

A new farm bill may consider work-related rules. As mentioned earlier, the 2014 law ultimately authorized and funded E&T pilot programs in 10 states; each pilot is participating in a rigorous evaluation. It is possible that a new farm bill could propose changes to work-related rules based on (likely interim) findings from the evaluation of the 2014 farm bill's pilot programs and/or political and ideological positions around work requirements.[80]

SNAP-Eligible Foods, Retailer Standards

For decades, policymakers and the general public have debated what SNAP benefits should be allowed to purchase and whether further restrictions would promote better eating habits. Under current law, SNAP benefits can buy most foods for household consumption sold at SNAP- authorized retailers. In recent months, FNS released a study of SNAP participants' foods purchased, and the House Committee on Agriculture held a hearing on SNAP-eligible foods.[81] A new farm bill may revisit rules around eligible foods or eligible retailers or may propose policy options to promote healthier eating for SNAP participants.[82] The current definition of SNAP-eligible foods is in federal law.[83] If states or localities wish to implement SNAP-eligible foods policies different than this definition—for instance, one restricting sugar-sweetened beverage purchases—they must apply to USDA for permission to run demonstration projects. Over the years, some states have sought permission to restrict foods from SNAP purchase, but USDA has not yet approved one.[84] The last two farm bills expanded federal funding to provide and test

---

[79] See FNS, "SNAP: Able-Bodied Adults Without Dependents (ABAWDs)," https://www.fns.usda.gov/snap/. See, for example, Ashley McGowan, "SNAP Food Assistance Cuts Coming to Pima County: 500k-1 Million to Lose Benefits Across U.S.," *Tucson Sentinel*, April 1, 2016.

[80] For a discussion of time limits and work requirements across several public benefit programs, see CRS Report R43400, *Work Requirements, Time Limits, and Work Incentives in TANF, SNAP, and Housing Assistance*.

[81] FNS study (conducted by Impaq International) published November 2016. See also U.S. Congress, House Committee on Agriculture, *Pros and Cons of Restricting SNAP Purchases*, 115th Cong., 1st sess., February 16, 2017.

[82] For more information, see CRS Report R42505, *Supplemental Nutrition Assistance Program (SNAP): A Primer on Eligibility and Benefits*, and CRS Report R44650, *Updated Standards for SNAP-Authorized Retailers: Final Rule*.

[83] Section 3(k) of the Food and Nutrition Act of 2008 (codified at 7 U.S.C. 2012(k)).

[84] See, for example, Patrick McGeehan, "U.S. Rejects Mayor's Plan to Ban Use of Food Stamps to Buy Soda," *New York Times*, August 19, 2011.

incentives for SNAP participants' purchases of fruits and vegetables. The 2008 farm bill authorized and funded the "Healthy Incentives Pilot." The 2014 farm bill authorized and funded the Food Insecurity Nutrition Incentive grant program. It is possible that a new farm bill could further support incentive-based approaches.

The 2014 farm bill required significant changes to the inventory requirements for SNAP- authorized retailers. The changes to stocking requirements will go into effect in May 2017 for new applicant stores and January 2018 for currently authorized stores. Retailers' experiences under the new rules may impact development of a new farm bill.

CONSERVATION AND ENVIRONMENT

The conservation title of the farm bill generally contains a number of reauthorizations, amendments, and new programs that encourage farmers and ranchers to voluntarily implement resource-conserving practices on private land. Starting in 1985, farm bills have greatly broadened the range of topics considered to be conservation. While the number of programs has increased and techniques to address resource problems continue to emerge, the basic approach has remained unchanged: financial and technical assistance supported by education and research programs.

Existing Farm Bill Provisions

USDA currently administers a number of conservation programs that assist private landowners with natural resource concerns. These programs provide technical and financial assistance to willing landowners in exchange for the implementation of resource-conserving practices. Some of these programs focus on improving or restoring resources that have been degraded, while others create conditions to limit degradation in the future. In most cases, conservation programs have multiple resource conserving goals related to soil, water, and wildlife. Since 1985, each succeeding farm bill has expanded the range of natural resource problems to be addressed as well as the number of conservation programs and level of funding. The 2014 farm bill reauthorized, repealed, consolidated, and amended a number of conservation programs. Generally, farm bill conservation programs can be grouped into the following categories based on similarities: working land programs, land retirement programs, easement programs, conservation compliance programs, and other programs and overarching provisions (see text box below). Most of these programs are authorized to receive mandatory funding (i.e., they do not require an annual appropriation) and include authorities that expire with other farm bill programs at the end of FY2018. Other types of conservation programs—such as watershed programs, emergency land rehabilitation programs, and technical assistance—

are authorized in other nonfarm bill legislation. Most of these programs have permanent authorities and receive appropriations annually through the discretionary appropriations process. These programs are not generally addressed in the context of a farm bill unless amendments to the program are proposed.

Issues and Options

Budget and Baseline

USDA Farm Bill Conservation Programs and Provisions

Working lands programs are typically classified as programs that allow private land to remain in production while implementing various conservation practices to address natural resource concerns specific to the area.

- Environmental Quality Incentives Program (EQIP), Conservation Stewardship Program (CSP), and Agricultural Management Assistance (AMA).

Land retirement programs provide federal payments to private agricultural landowners for temporary changes in land use and management to achieve environmental benefits. Generally requires removing land from production or to a less intensive use.

- Conservation Reserve Program (CRP)—includes the Conservation Reserve Enhancement Program (CREP), Farmable Wetland Program, and Transition Incentives Program (TIP).

Easement programs impose a permanent or long-term land-use restriction that is voluntarily placed on the land in exchange for a government payment.

- Agricultural Conservation Easement Program (including agricultural land easements and wetland reserve easements) and Healthy Forests Reserve Program (HFRP).

Conservation compliance prohibits a producer from receiving select federal farm program benefits (including conservation assistance and crop insurance) when conservation program requirements for highly erodible lands and wetlands are not met.

- Highly erodible land conservation (Sodbuster), wetland conservation (Swampbuster), and Sodsaver.

Other conservation programs and provisions include Conservation Innovation Grants, Grassroots Source Water Protection Program, Regional Conservation Partnership Program (RCPP), Voluntary Public Access, and Habitat Incentive Program.

The conservation title is one of the larger nonnutrition titles of the farm bill, accounting for 6% of the total projected 2014 farm bill, or $58 billion of the total $956 billion in 10-year mandatory funding authorized (FY2014-FY2023). Current budgetary constraints continue to drive the debate on conservation in a new farm bill. Similar to the conditions during debate on the 2014 farm bill, the current farm bill debate may be driven in part by demand for fiscal restraint. Ultimately the 2014 farm bill reduced the conservation title by $3.97 billion over 10 years, or 24% of the total $16.5 billion in savings. In addition to a reduction in mandatory authorization, the conservation title continues to be affected by budgetary dynamics such as sequestration and reductions through annual appropriations.[85] It remains uncertain what impact these reductions will have on a new farm bill's baseline.[86] While most producers are in favor of conservation programs, it is unclear how much of a reduction in other farm program spending they would be willing to support to expand or maintain conservation efforts.

Program Backlog

Arguments for expanding conservation in earlier farm bills proved particularly persuasive when documentation was presented of large backlogs of interested and eligible producers that were unable to enroll because of a lack of funds. Debate on a new farm bill could see similar arguments, as demand to participate in many of the conservation programs exceeds the available program dollars several times over. For example, in FY2015 (most recent data available), the working lands programs funded 27% of the applications received for CSP, 31% of the applications received for EQIP, and 12% of the applications received for AMA.[87] The FY2016 CRP general sign-up resulted in 1.9 million acres offered for enrollment and 411,000 acres accepted (22%).[88] The acceptance rate was even lower for the CRP grasslands enrollment, which had over 1 million acres offered and 101,000 accepted acres (10%).[89] Easements under ACEP also faced a limited acceptance rate, with agricultural land easements enrolling 26% of applications and wetland reserve easements accepting 38% of offers in FY2015 (most recent data available). The new RCPP also experienced high demand, accepting 88 of the 147 projects proposed (60%) in FY2017 and 84 of the 265 project proposed (32%) in FY2016. Large, ongoing backlogs could provide a case for additional funding, while other policy mechanisms could be proposed to reduce demand.

---

[85] See CRS In Focus IF10041, *Reductions to Mandatory Agricultural Conservation Programs in Appropriations Law*.

[86] For more information, see CRS Report R44758, *Farm Bill Programs Without a Budget Baseline Beyond FY2018*.

[87] NRCS, *FY2017 President's Budget Request*, February 2016.

[88] FSA, *49th CRP Signup Results,* https://www.fsa.usda.gov/Assets/USDA-FSA-Public/usdafiles/Conservation/Excel/su49state0524.xlsx.

[89] FSA, *Grassland Ranking Period 200 Results—Offered and Acceptable Acres*, https://www.fsa.usda.gov/ Assets/USDA-FSA-Public/usdafiles/Conservation/Excel/200 GrasslandsOfferedAcceptable.xlsx.

Working Lands or Land Retirement

Land retirement programs (e.g., CRP) provide producers with financial incentives to temporarily remove from production and restore environmentally sensitive land. In contrast, working lands programs (e.g., EQIP) allow land to remain in production and provide producers with financial incentives to adopt resource-conserving practices. Over time, high commodity prices, changing land rental rates, and new conservation technologies have led to a shift in farm bill conservation policy toward an increased focus on conservation working lands programs. Some of this shift has already occurred in the last decade and was continued in the 2014 farm bill as the percentage of mandatory program funding for land retirement programs has declined relative to working lands programs. With lower commodity prices, a new farm bill could shift this focus again, potentially increasing funding for land retirement programs. Most conservation and wildlife organizations support both land retirement and working lands programs, but the appropriate "mix" continues to be debated. With any proposal, it is likely that environmental interests will not support a reduction in one without an increase in the other.

Targeting and Partnerships

Interest is increasing in programs that partner with state and local communities to target conservation funding to local areas of concern. These partnership programs leverage private funding with federal funding to multiply the level of assistance in a select area. A number of these partnership programs were repealed in the 2014 farm bill and replaced with the new Regional Conservation Partnership Program (RCPP). The program receives $100 million annually in mandatory funding and redirects 7% of the funding from other programs—EQIP, ACEP, CSP, and HFRP—to partnership agreements. Now in its fourth year of project selection, RCPP has received considerable interest (see backlog discussion above). Some praise the program's ability to leverage nonfederal funding and incorporate the use of other state and local partners in a targeted effort. Others question whether the program redirects funds to areas with the greatest established support rather than those with the greatest resource concerns.

Compliance Requirements

The 1985 farm bill created the highly erodible lands (HEL) conservation and wetland conservation compliance programs, which tied various farm program benefits to conservation standards.[90] The provision has since been amended numerous times to remove certain benefits and add others. Most recently, the 2014 farm bill added crop insurance premium subsidies as a program benefit that could be denied if conservation standards were not met. In 2015, USDA issued a requirement that to remain eligible for

---

[90] For additional information, see CRS Report R42459, *Conservation Compliance and U.S. Farm Policy*.

crop insurance premium subsidies, producers must certify their compliance with the conservation compliance provisions through a standard form. Following the 2015 deadline, USDA reported a 98.2% certification rate, suggesting that those not certified were likely no longer farming or had filed forms with discrepancies that may still be reconciled.[91] Despite this high compliance rate, many view the conservation compliance requirements as burdensome, and they continue to be unpopular among producer groups. Since its introduction in the 1985 farm bill, conservation compliance has remained a controversial issue, and debate will likely continue.

Environmental Regulation

Farm bill conservation programs are a voluntary federal policy to address environmental impacts related to agriculture. Another way for the federal government to address environmental impacts is through regulation. Increasingly, conservation programs are called upon to prevent or reduce the need for environmental regulation. While a new farm bill debate will not likely focus specifically on environmental regulations—because most environmental law originates outside the House and Senate Agriculture Committees—debate could focus on strengthening the voluntary response to environmental issues through conservation programs. This, in turn, could influence the funding debate and the portion of the overall farm bill budget made available for conservation programs.

RURAL DEVELOPMENT

Since 1973, omnibus farm bills have included a rural development title. How to create and support new competitive advantage in rural areas so these areas can better compete in a global economic environment is a key issue framing current debates about the future of rural America. While the search for new sources of rural economic development is part of the policy equation, also increasingly appreciated is the need to develop new approaches for federal assistance to rural areas that go beyond the largely piecemeal programming that has long characterized rural economic development policy.

The rural development title of farm bills generally provides assistance for rural business creation and expansion and also rural infrastructure with traditional assistance for housing, electrical generation and transmission, broadband, water and wastewater, and economic and institutional capacity in local communities. In the past several farm bills, policymakers have also supported innovative and alternative business development (e.g., bioenergy, value-added production, local food production) and innovative mechanisms to finance it (e.g., the Rural Microentrepreneur Assistance Program).

[91] USDA, "Record Number of Farmers and Ranchers Certified Under 2014 Farm Bill Conservation Compliance," press release, July 10, 2015.

Support for such alternative approaches is expected to continue as policymakers recognize the great diversity among rural communities, with some rural areas growing and prospering and others falling further behind as their primary industries (including agriculture) decline and population outmigration continues, particularly among younger, educated residents.

Existing Farm Bill Provisions

The rural development title of the 2014 farm bill generally reauthorized or amended long- standing programs under the Consolidated Farm and Rural Development Act (P.L. 92-419) and the Rural Electrification Act of 1937. New programs are also authorized under these statutes.

Concerns about how effectively USDA targets its rural development loan and grant assistance have been a recurring consideration for policymakers and rural development practitioners. The general concern is that rural development funding may not be targeted as well or as effectively as it could be. The 2014 farm bill directed USDA to begin collecting data regarding economic activities created through its rural development grants and loans and to measure the short- and long-term viability of award recipients. It also directed USDA to report to Congress every two years on rural employment generation, new business start-ups, and any increased local revenue.

The 2014 farm bill authorized a new Strategic Economic and Community Development initiative to support economic development plans on a multi-jurisdictional basis, giving priority to certain projects and reserving 10% of available appropriations for community facilities, rural utilities, and rural business, among other types of operations. The bill created other rural development programs and/or modified or reauthorized other existing programs. It authorized the Rural Energy Savings Program to provide loans to utility districts and Rural Utility Service borrowers to assist rural households and small businesses in implementing energy efficiency measures. It also authorized the Rural Business Development Grants program, merging the general functions of two grant programs—the Rural Business Enterprise and the Rural Business Opportunity grant programs—which were terminated. It also reauthorized loans and loan guarantees under the Business and Industry Guaranteed Loan Program for locally or regionally produced agricultural food products—those products that travel less than 400 miles between production and marketing—and targeted low-income areas without access to fresh fruits and vegetables. Priority is given to projects benefitting underserved communities (i.e., those with limited access to affordable, healthy foods and with high rates of poverty or food insecurity). Grants were also authorized to fund technical assistance and training.

In addition to these programs, the rural development title includes other provisions to reauthorize and/or amend a wide variety of loan and grant programs that provide further assistance in four key areas: (1) broadband and telecommunications, (2) rural water and wastewater infrastructure, (3) business and community development, and (4) regional development. Each of these programs has authorized discretionary spending subject to annual appropriations, with the exception of one mandatory spending authorization of $150 million for reducing the backlog of pending water and wastewater applications.

The 2014 farm bill also modified the definition of *rural area* for the Housing Act of 1949. The provision increased the maximum eligible population threshold to 35,000 from 25,000 and permits any rural area that was eligible in the 1990, 2000, and 2010 censuses to remain eligible for Rural Housing Service programs until the 2020 decennial census.

Issues and Options

Some policymakers contend that current farm policies, which rely heavily on commodity support for a few production sectors, play a lesser role in the vitality of most rural areas. Rural manufacturing, which tends to be lower-skilled and lower-waged, continues to lose out to foreign competition. While transformation to a service economy continues in rural America, service employment in many rural areas also tends to be in lower-wage personal services rather than business and producer services.

Economic development efforts in some areas have targeted entrepreneurial strategies and microenterprise development, including new markets for value-added agricultural products. Rather than simply seeking to attract relocating businesses, these approaches attempt to capitalize on a particular area's distinctive social, economic, and environmental assets and advantages to build endogenously on existing local and regional strengths. Developing a regional entrepreneurial culture seems to be an important approach in these efforts.

The mixed success of these and past efforts, as helpful to rural areas as they may be, suggests to many rural development experts and policymakers that the current structure of federal assistance to rural areas needs to be reexamined. For example, regularly tweaking the definition of *rural* to determine eligibility for certain programs seems unlikely to produce significantly improved economic development outcomes. Some contend that greater emphasis on the socioeconomic relations between rural communities and urban areas within a regional context could lay the foundation for more successful rural (and regional) development outcomes. While both the 2008 and 2014 farm bills provided a greater emphasis on regional efforts, some policymakers believe that redesigning existing programs to better target regional efforts could yield positive results. To that end, the 2014 farm bill authorized a new data collecting activity to assess the effectiveness of federal development assistance to rural businesses.

Application processes for program loans and grants can be a barrier for many rural projects, especially those in smaller, poorer rural areas. The way assistance is currently provided (mostly through direct and guaranteed loans) has limitations because it is often driven by individual projects rather than integrated into an overall development strategy. Many rural communities may benefit from technical assistance support for strategic planning. The Obama Administration saw interagency coordination among federal agencies that target rural areas (e.g., Department of Housing and Urban Development, Department of Health and Human Services) as in need of significant improvement.[92]

These are not so much new concerns about federal assistance to rural areas as they are continuing issues identified by rural development experts and rural policymakers. In the current budget environment, it may be difficult to advance substantively new approaches to rural development in a new farm bill. However, with many in Congress concerned that current federal approaches to rural development need to be reexamined and programs better targeted to overall development strategies, a new farm bill is likely the major legislative vehicle to address these issues.

ENERGY

Commercial interest in renewable energy, mainly ethanol and biodiesel production, expanded rapidly with the enactment of the Renewable Fuel Standard (RFS) and in response to a strong rise in domestic and international fuel prices. Many policymakers view agriculture-based biofuels as a catalyst for rural economic development, an important source of demand for agricultural production, and a home-grown response to lowering U.S. dependence on imports of foreign energy. USDA renewable energy programs have been used to incentivize adoption of renewable energy projects including solar, wind, and anaerobic digesters. Initially, the primary focus of these programs was to promote U.S. biofuels production and use—including cornstarch-based ethanol, soybean-based biodiesel, and cellulosic ethanol—but over time their focus has shifted toward promoting renewable power, biomass-based products, and efforts to bring biomass-based fuel, such as cellulosic ethanol, and other advanced renewable fuels to market.

Many of the federal programs that currently support renewable energy production are outside the purview of USDA and have legislative origins outside of the farm bill. The 2002 farm bill (Farm Security and Rural Investment Act of 2002, P.L. 107-171) was the first omnibus farm bill to explicitly include an energy title. The energy title authorized grants, loans, and loan guarantees to foster research on agriculture-based renewable energy, share development risk, and promote the adoption of renewable energy systems. The 2002 farm bill was followed by two major energy bills (the Energy Policy Act of

[92] On June 9, 2011, the White House issued an executive order to create a new White House Rural Council, which will focus on job training, credit access, regional networks, expansion of health technology, broadband, and other economic development concerns. The council will be led by USDA and include the Departments of the Treasury, Defense, Justice, Interior, Commerce, Labor, Health and Human Services, Housing and Urban Development, Transportation, Energy, Education, Veterans Affairs, and Homeland Security.

2005, P.L. 109-58; and the Energy Independence and Security Act of 2007, P.L. 110-140), which established and expanded the RFS along with several other renewable energy programs.

Existing Farm Bill Provisions

The 2014 farm bill built on the 2008 farm bill, which had refocused earlier biofuels policy initiatives in favor of non-corn feedstocks, especially cellulosic-based feedstocks. This was in response to growing concerns about the emerging spillover effects of increased corn use for ethanol production. Like the 2002 and 2008 farm bills, the 2014 farm bill contained a distinct energy title that extended most of the existing bioenergy programs. In reauthorizing these programs, Congress significantly reduced mandatory funding, which was lowered to $694 million (FY2014-FY2018) from $1 billion under the 2008 farm bill. Discretionary funding authorization was also reduced to $765 million from $1.1 billion under the 2008 farm bill. Subsequent to the enactment of the 2014 farm bill, Congress has rescinded or reduced funding for a number of these programs through annual appropriations bills. Congress has also generally refrained from providing discretionary funding for these programs, with the exception of limited funds it has appropriated for the Rural Energy for America Program (REAP) and the Sun Grant Initiative. While most of the farm bill energy programs are authorized in the energy title, several programs are contained in other titles.

Among significant changes to these programs that were ushered in by the 2014 farm bill, Congress made a number of substantive changes to BCAP, including lowering rates for establishment and matching payments, altering eligibility requirements, and sharply curbing the previously open-ended availability of funding. The 2014 law also precluded the use of REAP funding for retail energy dispensers (such as blender pumps) and repealed the Forest Biomass for Energy Program and the Agricultural Bioenergy Feedstock and Energy Efficiency Research and Extension Initiative, in addition to several bioenergy-related studies. The Rural Business- Cooperative Service within USDA's Rural Development Agency administers the major grant, loan, and loan guarantee programs—BAP, RAP, and REAP. In contrast, FSA administers BCAP, and NIFA administers BRDI.

Issues and Options

Among the farm bill's bioenergy programs, only REAP is authorized beyond FY2018, as the law provides mandatory funding for REAP for FY2014 and each fiscal year thereafter. Mandatory baseline funding authority for several other bioenergy programs expires prior to FY2018, including RAP (after FY2014), BAP (FY2016), and

BRDI (FY2017). An upcoming farm bill could provide an opportunity for Congress to consider the ongoing utility of these programs in light of budgetary constraints. For instance, mandatory funding for BCAP, which was authorized at "such sums as necessary" in the 2008 farm bill, was limited to $25 million annually under the 2014 farm bill. Since then, Congress has further limited funding for BCAP through annual appropriations laws, most recently limiting it to $3 million for FY2016.

Most of these programs were conceived in a prior era when oil prices were higher, the United States was more dependent on imported energy, and new techniques for extracting tight oil deposits and shale gas (such as directional drilling and hydraulic fracturing) were not being deployed widely enough to bring onto the market transformational quantities of domestic oil and gas. These changes largely occurred after the 2008 farm bill was enacted. At the same time, biofuels and renewable energy may have tangible advantages in that they are not derived from finite resources, can offer environmental benefits compared with traditional energy alternatives, and can provide an economic benefit to rural America. These are among the considerations that Congress could weigh as it considers the direction of energy policy and the role of a new farm bill in defining the opportunities the agricultural sector and rural America may have in contributing to the country's energy future.

FORESTRY

Existing Farm Bill Provisions

One-third of the land area in the United States is forestland (766 million acres).[93] These lands provide wood for lumber, plywood, paper, and other materials, as well as a host of ecological services, including recreation, clean water, wildlife habitat, and more. The federal government owns one-third of the forestland in the United States (238 million acres), and nonindustrial private landowners (private, noncorporate entities that do not own wood processing facilities) own 298 million acres (39%).[94]

The Forest Service is the principal federal forest management agency, managing 19% of all U.S. forestlands (145 million acres). In addition to administering the National Forest System (NFS),[95] the Forest Service provides technical and financial assistance—primarily through state forestry agencies—to nonfederal landowners. The Forest Service

[93] S. N. Oswalt et al., *Forest Resources of the United States, 2012*, General Technical Report WO-91, October 2014.

[94] The remaining 230 million acres are owned by states, other public entities, and private corporate landowners (e.g., timber investment trusts).

[95] The 193 million acre NFS includes 145 million acres of forestland and 48 million acres of grasslands and woodlands.

also conducts research to advance the science of forestry and engages in international forestry assistance and research efforts.

Past farm bills have contained forestry provisions or a separate forestry title. Although many forestry provisions are permanently authorized, a new farm bill would allow Congress to modify programs to support assistance to nonfederal forest owners, forest research, and the management of federal forests. The forestry title of the 2014 farm bill repealed, modified, created, and reauthorized several forestry programs.[96] For example, the 2014 farm bill permanently authorized stewardship contracting and extended the good neighbor authority nationwide.[97] A new farm bill may modify existing programs and possibly establish new options for forestry research, management of federal lands, and assistance to nonfederal forest owners.

Issues and Options

Among the issues that might be considered in a new farm bill's forestry title are expanded wildfire protection, support of woody biomass for energy, and additional controls to address invasive species.

The threat of wildfires to forests, communities, and homes seems to have grown. The 2002 farm bill authorized a new community wildfire protection program, but the program has been funded only as part of state fire assistance. New programs to enhance wildfire protection on both federal and nonfederal lands might be considered in a new farm bill.

Interest in producing energy from woody biomass and other renewable sources (as discussed above) derives from both supply and demand. Supply could come from efforts to reduce wildfire threats and to control invasive species. Demand is likely to be driven by state and federal requirements for renewable transportation fuels and possibly for electricity production. Many of the energy programs face budgetary challenges, and a new farm bill might extend, expand, alter, or terminate these programs or possibly replace them with alternative approaches.

Invasive species, typically exotic plants and animals, are increasingly displacing or harming native plants and animals in the United States and worldwide. Invasive species have been described as one of the four major threats to the nation's forests and rangelands. Options and opportunities to prevent and control the spread of invasive species, especially forest pests and especially on private forestlands, might be a farm bill issue.

---

[96] For more information, see CRS Report R43431, *Forestry Provisions in the 2014 Farm Bill (P.L. 113-79).*

[97] Stewardship contracting authorizes the Forest Service (and Bureau of Land Management in the Department of the Interior) to enter in to dual service and timber sale contracts for up to 10 years to achieve certain land management goals. The good neighbor authority allows the two agencies to enter into agreements authorizing state agencies to conduct watershed restoration and protection projects on neighboring national forest land.

Appendix. Titles and Subtitles of the 2014 Farm Bill (Agricultural Act of 2014, P.L. 113-79)

I. Commodities
- A. Repeals and Reforms
- B. Marketing Loans
- C. Sugar
- D. Dairy

II. Conservation
- A. Conservation Reserve Program
- B. Conservation Stewardship Program
- C. Environmental Quality Incentives Program
- D. Agricultural Conservation Easement Program
- E. Regional Conservation Partnership Program
- F. Other Conservation Programs
- G. Funding and Administration
- H. Repeal of Superseded Program Authorities and Transitional Provisions; Technical Amendments

III. Trade
- A. Food for Peace Act
- B. Agricultural Trade Act of 1978
- C. Other Agricultural Trade Laws

IV. Nutrition
- A. Supplemental Nutrition Assistance Program
- B. Commodity Distribution Programs
- C. Miscellaneous

V. Credit
- A. Farm Ownership Loans
- B. Operating Loans
- C. Emergency Loans
- D. Administrative Provisions
- E. Miscellaneous

VI. Rural Development
- A. Consolidated Farm and Rural Development Act
- B. Rural Electrification Act of 1936
- C. Miscellaneous

VII. Research, Extension and Related Matters
- A. National Agricultural Research, Extension, and Teaching Policy Act of 1977
- B. Food, Agriculture, Conservation, and Trade Act of 1990
- C. Agricultural Research, Extension, and Education Reform Act of 1998

In: The Farm Bill: Review, Background, and the WTO
Editor: Katie M. Harrison
ISBN: 978-1-53615-272-2
© 2019 Nova Science Publishers, Inc.

Chapter 3

AGRICULTURE IN THE WTO: RULES AND LIMITS ON U.S. DOMESTIC SUPPORT*

Randy Schnepf

SUMMARY

Omnibus U.S. farm legislation—referred to as the farm bill—has typically been renewed every five or six years. Farm income and commodity price support programs have been a part of U.S. farm bills since the 1930s. Each successive farm bill usually involves some modification or replacement of existing farm programs. A key question likely to be asked of every new farm proposal or program is how it will affect U.S. commitments under the World Trade Organization's (WTO's) Agreement on Agriculture (AoA) and its Agreement on Subsidies and Countervailing Measures (SCM).

The United States is currently committed, under the AoA, to spend no more than $19.1 billion annually on those domestic farm support programs most likely to distort trade—referred to as amber box programs and measured by the Aggregate Measure of Support (AMS). The AoA spells out the rules for countries to determine whether their policies—for any given year—are potentially trade distorting and how to calculate the costs.

The most recent U.S. notification to the WTO of domestic support outlays (made on May 1, 2018) is for the 2015 crop year. To date, the United States has never exceeded its $19.1 billion amber box spending limit. However, this has been achieved in some years (1999, 2000, and 2001) through judicious use of the *de minimis* exclusion described below.

An additional consideration for WTO compliance—the SCM rules governing adverse market effects resulting from a farm program—comes into play when a domestic

* This is an edited, reformatted and augmented version of Congressional Research Service Publication No. R45305, Updated September 6, 2018.

farm policy effect spills over into international markets. The SCM details rules for determining when a subsidy is "prohibited" (e.g., certain export- and import-substitution subsidies) and when it is "actionable" (e.g., certain domestic support policies that incentivize overproduction and result in significant market distortion—whether as lower market prices or altered trade patterns). Because the United States is a major producer, consumer, exporter, and/or importer of most major agricultural commodities, the SCM is relevant for most major U.S. agricultural products. As a result, if a particular U.S. farm program is deemed to result in market distortion that adversely affects other WTO members—even if it is within agreed-upon AoA spending limits—then that program may be subject to challenge under the WTO dispute settlement procedures.

Designing farm programs that comply with WTO rules can avoid potential trade disputes. Based on AoA and SCM rules, U.S. domestic agricultural support can be evaluated against five specific successive questions to determine how it is classified under the WTO rules, whether total support is within WTO limits, and whether a specific program fully complies with WTO rules:

- Can a program's support outlays be excluded from the AMS total by being placed in the green box of minimally distorting programs?
- Can a program's support outlays be excluded from the AMS total by being placed in the blue box of production-limiting programs?
- If amber, will support be less than 5% of production value (either product-specific or non-product-specific) thus qualifying for the *de minimis* exclusion?
- Does the total, remaining annual AMS exceed the $19.1 billion amber box limit?
- Even if a program is found to be fully compliant with the AoA rules and limits, does its support result in price or trade distortion in international markets? If so, then it may be subject to challenge under SCM rules.

INTRODUCTION

Trade plays a critical role in the U.S. agricultural sector. The U.S. Department of Agriculture (USDA) estimates that exports account for about 20% of total U.S. agricultural production.[1] Furthermore, given the substantial volume of its agricultural exports, the United States plays a significant role in many international agricultural markets. As a result, U.S. farm policy is often subject to intense scrutiny both for compliance with current World Trade Organization (WTO) rules and for its potential to diminish the breadth or impede the success of future multilateral negotiations. In part, this is because a farm bill locks in U.S. policy behavior for an extended period of time during which the United States would be unable to accept any new restrictions on its domestic support programs.

Farm income and commodity support programs have been a part of U.S. farm legislation since the 1930s.[2] Today, these support programs are authorized as part of omnibus U.S. farm legislation—referred to as the farm bill—which has typically been

[1] CRS Report R45117, *U.S. Farm Income Outlook for 2018*.

[2] See CRS Report R43448, *Farm Commodity Provisions in the 2014 Farm Bill (P.L. 113-79)*.

renewed every five or six years. Each successive farm bill usually involves some modification or replacement of existing farm programs. The current omnibus farm bill, the Agricultural Act of 2014 (P.L. 113-79; the 2014 farm bill), which was signed into law on February 7, 2014, made several substantial changes to the previous farm safety net of the 2008 farm bill.[3] The commodity programs of the 2014 farm bill became operational with the 2014 crop year. They are scheduled to expire on September 30, 2018, or with the 2018 crop year. Ultimately, the current farm bill will either be (1) replaced with new legislation, (2) temporarily extended, or (3) allowed to lapse and replaced with "permanent law"—a set of essentially mothballed provisions for the farm commodity programs that date from the 1930s and 1940s.[4]

WTO Commitments May Influence Policy Choices

A potential major constraint affecting U.S. agricultural policy choices is the set of commitments made as part of membership in the WTO.[5] The WTO has three basic functions: (1) administering existing agreements, including those governing agriculture and trade;[6] (2) serving as a negotiating forum for new trade liberalization; and (3) providing a mechanism to settle trade disputes among members.[7] With respect to disciplines governing domestic agricultural support, two WTO agreements are paramount—the Agreement on Agriculture (AoA)[8] and the Agreement on Subsidies and Countervailing Measures (SCM).[9]

The AoA sets country-specific aggregate spending limits on the most market-distorting policies. It also defines very general rules covering trade among member countries. In general, domestic policies or programs found to be in violation of WTO rules may be subject to challenge by another WTO member under the WTO dispute settlement process. If a WTO challenge is successful, the WTO remedy would likely imply the elimination, alteration, or amendment by Congress of the program in question to bring it into compliance. Since most governing provisions over U.S. farm programs are statutory, new legislation could be required to implement even minor changes to achieve

---

[3] CRS Report R43076, *The 2014 Farm Bill (P.L. 113-79): Summary and Side-by-Side.*

[4] For example, see CRS Report R42442, *Expiration and Extension of the 2008 Farm Bill.*

[5] The WTO is a global rules-based, member-driven organization dealing with the rules of trade between nations. As of July 29, 2016, the WTO included 164 members. See CRS In Focus IF10002, *The World Trade Organization.*

[6] For a complete list of WTO agreements and their text, see WTO, *The Legal Texts* (Cambridge University Press and World Trade Organization, 1999), https://www.wto.org/english/docs_ e/legal_e/legal_e.htm.

[7] See CRS In Focus IF10436, *Dispute Settlement in the World Trade Organization: Key Legal Concepts.*

[8] See CRS Report RL32916, *Agriculture in the WTO: Policy Commitments Made Under the Agreement on Agriculture.*

[9] See CRS Report RS22522, *Potential Challenges to U.S. Farm Subsidies in the WTO: A Brief Overview.*

compliance.[10] As a result, designing farm programs that comply with WTO rules can avoid potential trade disputes.

This report provides a brief overview of the WTO commitments that are most relevant for U.S. domestic farm policy. A key question that many policymakers ask of virtually every new farm proposal is how it will affect U.S. commitments under the WTO. The answer depends not only on cost but also on the proposal's design and objectives, as described below.

Agreement on Agriculture (AoA)

Under the AoA, WTO member countries agreed to general rules regarding disciplines on domestic subsidies (as well as on export subsidies and market access). The AoA's goal was to provide a framework for the leading members of the WTO to make changes in their domestic farm policies to facilitate more open trade.

Domestic Support Categorization

The WTO's AoA categorizes and restricts agricultural domestic support programs according to their potential to distort commercial markets. Whenever a program payment influences a producer's behavior, it has the potential to distort markets (i.e., to alter the supply of a commodity) from the equilibrium that would otherwise exist in the absence of the program's influence. Those outlays that have the greatest potential to distort agricultural markets—referred to as amber box subsidies—are subject to spending limits.[11] In contrast, more benign outlays (i.e., those that cause less or minimal market distortion) are exempted from spending limits under green box, blue box, *de minimis*, or special and differential treatment exemptions.[12]

The AoA contains detailed rules and procedures to guide countries in determining how to classify its programs in terms of which are most likely to distort production and trade; in calculating their annual cost, measured by the Aggregate Measure of Support (AMS) index;[13] and in reporting the total cost to the WTO. Specifically, the WTO uses a traffic light analogy to group programs:

---

[10] For example, see CRS Report RL32571, *Brazil's WTO Case Against the U.S. Cotton Program.*

[11] These spending and subsidy commitments are detailed in each member's country schedule. For more information, see CRS Report RL32916, *Agriculture in the WTO: Policy Commitments Made Under the Agreement on Agriculture.*

[12] WTO special and differential treatment exemptions are reserved for "developing" countries and are thus not relevant for evaluating U.S. domestic farm policy.

[13] The AoA, Part I, Article 1(a), defines AMS as the annual level of support, expressed in monetary terms, provided for an agricultural product in favor of the producers of the basic agricultural product or non-product-specific support provided in favor of agricultural producers in general other than support provided under programs that qualify for exemption as described in the remainder of this report.

- *Green box* programs are minimally or non-trade distorting and not subject to any spending limits.
- *Blue box* programs are described as production-limiting. They have payments that are based on either a fixed area or yield or a fixed number of livestock and are made on less than 85% of base production. As such, blue box programs are also not subject to any payment limits.
- *Amber box* programs are the most market-distorting programs and are subject to a strict aggregate, annual spending limit. The United States is subject to a spending limit of $19.1 billion in amber box outlays subject to certain *de minimis* exemptions.[14]
- *De minimis exemptions* are domestic support spending that is sufficiently small—relative to either the value of a specific product or total production—to be deemed benign. *De minimis* exemptions are limited by 5% of the value of production—either total or product-specific.[15]
- *Prohibited (i.e., red box)* programs include certain types of export and import subsidies and nontariff trade barriers that are not explicitly included in a country's WTO schedule or identified in the WTO legal texts.[16]

This chapter describes the AoA classifications in more detail below in the section titled "Questions for Evaluating WTO Compliance of Domestic Farm Spending."

Domestic Support Notification

To provide for monitoring and compliance of WTO policy commitments, each WTO member country is expected to routinely submit notification reports on the implementation of its various commitments. The WTO's Committee on Agriculture has the duty of reviewing progress in the implementation of individual member commitments based on member notifications. Furthermore, the WTO posts the notifications on its official website for all members to review.[17] The most recent U.S. notification to the WTO of domestic support outlays (made on May 1, 2018) is for the 2015 crop year.

---

[14] For developed member countries, the AMS was to be reduced from a 1986-1988 base period average by 20% in six equal annual installments during 1995-2000. For the United States, the initial 1986-88 AMS base was $23.879 billion. This was lowered to $19.103 billion by 2000, where it has been fixed ever since.

[15] General domestic support (not specific to any one commodity, such as rural infrastructure or extension) that is below 5% of the value of total agricultural production is deemed sufficiently benign that it does not have to be included in the amber box. Similarly, support for a specific commodity (such as sugar or dairy price support, marketing loan benefits, commodity storage payments, etc.) that is below 5% of that commodity's value of production is deemed sufficiently benign that it does not have to be included in the amber box.

[16] The term *red box* is not actually used by the WTO but is included here to complete the traffic light analogy.

[17] WTO, "WTO Documents Online," https://docs.wto.org/dol2fe/Pages/FE_Search/FE_S_S003. aspx.

Agreement on Subsidies and Countervailing Measures (SCM)

To the extent that domestic farm policy effects spill over into international markets, U.S. farm programs are also subject to certain rules under the Agreement on Subsidies and Countervailing Measures (SCM).[18] The SCM details rules for determining when a subsidy is "prohibited" (as in the case of certain export- and import-substitution subsidies) and when it is "actionable" (as in the case of certain domestic support policies that incentivize overproduction and result in significant market distortion—whether as lower market prices or altered trade patterns).[19]

The key aspect of SCM commitments is the degree to which a domestic support program engenders market distortion. Based on precedent from past WTO decisions, several criteria are important in establishing whether a subsidy could result in significant market distortions:

- The subsidy constitutes a substantial share of farmer returns or covers a substantial share of production costs.
- The subsidized commodity is important to world markets because it forms a large share of either world production or world trade.
- A causal relationship exists between the subsidy and adverse effects in the relevant market.

The SCM evaluates the "market distortion" of a program or policy in terms of its measurable market effects on the international trade and/or market price for the affected commodity:

- Did the subsidy displace or impede the import of a like product into the subsidizing member's domestic market?
- Did the subsidy displace or impede the exports of a like product by another WTO member country other than the subsidizing member?
- Did the subsidy (via overproduction and resultant export of the surplus) result in significant price suppression, price undercutting, or lost sales in the relevant commodity's international market?
- Did the subsidy result in an increase in the world market share of the subsidizing member?

---

[18] For details, see CRS Report RS22522, *Potential Challenges to U.S. Farm Subsidies in the WTO: A Brief Overview*.

[19] Part II: Prohibited Subsidies, Articles 3-4, and Part III: Actionable Subsidies, Articles 5-7, ASCM, WTO Legal Texts, http://www.wto.org/english/docs_e/legal_e/legal_e.htm.

For any farm program challenged under the SCM, a WTO dispute settlement panel reviews the relevant trade and market data and makes a determination of whether the particular program challenged resulted in a significant market distortion.[20]

Under WTO rules, challenged subsidies that are found to be prohibited by a WTO dispute settlement panel must be stopped or withdrawn "without delay" in accordance with a timetable laid out by the panel. Otherwise the member nation bringing the challenge may take appropriate countermeasures. Similarly, actionable subsidies, if successfully challenged, must be withdrawn or altered so as to minimize or eliminate the distorting aspect of the subsidy, again as laid out by a WTO panel or as negotiated between the two disputing parties.

WTO Dispute Settlement Understanding (DSU)

The WTO Understanding on Rules and Procedures Governing the Settlement of Disputes (DSU) provides a means for WTO members to resolve disputes arising under WTO agreements. WTO members must first attempt to settle their dispute through consultations, but if these fail, the member initiating the dispute may request that a panel examine and report on its complaint. The DSU provides for Appellate Body review of panel reports, panels to determine if a defending member has complied with an adverse WTO decision by the established deadline in a case, and possible retaliation if the defending member has failed to do so.

Since the WTO was established in 1995, 564 complaints have been filed under the DSU, with nearly one-half (272) involving the United States as a complainant or defendant.[21] The Office of the United States Trade Representative represents the United States in WTO disputes.[22]

Questions for Evaluating WTO Compliance of Domestic Farm Spending

The United States is currently committed, under the AoA, to spend no more than \$19.1 billion per year on amber box trade-distorting support. The WTO's AoA

---

[20] The final interpretation of *significant* is left to a WTO panel. However, two notable trade economists suggest that economic and statistical modeling can be used to show causal linkages between specific agricultural support policies and prejudicial market effects as measured by market share, quantity displacement, or price suppression. Richard H. Steinberg and Timothy E. Josling, "When the Peace Ends: The Vulnerability of EC and US Agricultural Subsidies to WTO Legal Challenge," *Journal of International Economic Law*, vol. 6, no. 2 (July 2003), pp. 369-417.

[21] WTO dispute settlement data as of August 15, 2018, https://www.wto.org/english/tratop_e/ dispu_e/dispu_e.htm.

[22] See CRS Report RS20088, *Dispute Settlement in the World Trade Organization (WTO): An Overview*.

procedures for classifying and counting trade-distorting support are somewhat complex. However, four questions might be asked to determine whether a particular farm measure will cause total U.S. domestic support to be above or below the $19.1 billion annual AMS limit. A subsequent fifth question may be asked to ascertain whether AoA-compliant outlays are also SCM-compliant.

1. Can the measure be classified as a "green box" policy—one presumed to have the least potential for distorting production and trade and therefore not counted as part of the AMS?
2. Can it be classified as a "blue box" policy—that is, a production-limiting program that receives a special exemption and therefore is also not counted as part of the AMS?
3. If it is a potentially trade-distorting "amber box" policy, can support still be excluded from the AMS calculation under the so-called 5% de minimis exemption (explained later in more detail) because total support is no more than 5% of either:
    - the value of total annual production if the support is non-product specific, or
    - the value of annual production of a particular commodity if the support is specific to that commodity?
4. If such support exceeds the de minimis 5% threshold (and thus cannot be exempted), when it is added to all other forms of non-exempt amber box support is total U.S. AMS still beneath the $19.1 billion limit?
5. If a program is fully compliant with the AoA rules and limits, does its support result in price or trade distortion in international markets that, in turn, cause adverse effects upon another WTO member? If so, then it may be subject to challenge under SCM rules.

Question 1: Can This Measure Be Placed in the Green Box?

No limits are placed on green box spending, since it is considered to be minimally or non-trade distorting (*Figure 1*). To qualify for exemption in the green box, a program must meet two general criteria, as well as a set of policy-specific criteria relative to the different types of agriculture-related programs.[23] The two general criteria are the following:

1. It must be a publicly funded government program (defined to include either outlays or forgone revenue) that does not involve transfers from consumers.

---

[23] The so-called green box is actually Annex 2 of the AoA, *WTO Legal Texts*.

2. It must not have the effect of providing price support to producers.

In addition, every green-box-qualifying program must comply with at least one of the following criteria and conditions specific to the program itself:

- *A "general service"* benefitting the agricultural or rural community in general cannot involve direct payments to producers or processors. Such programs can include research; pest and disease control; training, extension, or advisory services; inspection services, including for health, safety, grading, or standardization; marketing and promotion services, including information advice and promotion (but not spending for unspecified purposes that sellers could use to provide price discounts or other economic benefits to purchasers); and generally available infrastructure such as utility, transportation, or port facilities, water supply facilities, or other capital works construction.
- Public acquisition (at current market prices) and *stockholding of products for food security* must be integral to a nationally legislated food security program and be financially transparent.
- *Domestic food aid* is to be based upon clearly defined eligibility and nutritional criteria, be financially transparent, and involve government food purchases at current market prices.
- *"Decoupled" income support* is to use clearly defined eligibility criteria in a specified, fixed base period; not be related in any way after the base period to (a) domestic or world prices, (b) type or volume of crop or livestock production, or (c) factors of production; and, further, not be contingent on any production in exchange for payments.
- Government financial participation in an income *insurance or income safety net program* shall define eligibility as agricultural income loss exceeding 30% of average gross income (or equivalent in net income terms) in the preceding three-year period (or preceding five-year period, excluding the highest and lowest years—the so-called Olympic average), with such payment compensating for less than 70% of the income loss in year of eligibility and payments based solely on income, not production, price, or inputs. Total annual payments under this and natural disaster relief (see next paragraph) cannot exceed 100% of a producer's total loss.
- Payments (whether direct or through government crop insurance) for *natural disaster relief* are to use eligibility based on formal government recognition of the disaster. Payments are to be determined by a production loss exceeding 30% of production in the preceding three-year (or five-year Olympic average) period; they are to apply only to losses of income, livestock, land, or other production factors; and they cannot exceed the total replacement cost or require specific

future production. Total annual payments under this and the income insurance or safety net measure cannot exceed 100% of a producer's total loss.

- *Structural adjustment through producer retirement* shall tie eligibility to clearly defined criteria in programs to facilitate producers' "total and permanent" retirement from agricultural production or their movement into nonagricultural activities.
- *Structural adjustment through resource retirement* shall be determined through clearly defined programs designed to remove land, livestock, or other resources from marketable production with payments (a) conditioned on land being retired for at least three years and on livestock being permanently disposed, (b) not contingent upon any alternative specified use of such resources involving marketing agricultural production, and (c) not related to production type/quantity or to prices of products using remaining productive resources.
- *Structural adjustment provided through investment aids* must be determined by clearly defined criteria for programs assisting financial or physical restructuring of a producer's operations in response to objectively demonstrated structural disadvantages (and may also be based on a clearly defined program for "re-privatization" of agricultural land). The amount of payments (a) cannot be tied to type/volume of production or to prices in any year after the base period, (b) shall be provided only for a time period needed for realization of the investment in respect of which they are provided, (c) cannot be contingent on the required production of designated products (except to require participants not to produce a designated product), and (d) must be limited to the amount required to compensate for the structural disadvantage.
- *Environmental program payments* must have eligibility determined as part of a clearly defined government environmental or conservation program and must be dependent upon meeting specific program conditions, including conditions related to production methods or inputs. Payments must be limited to the extra costs (or loss of income) involved with program compliance.
- *Regional assistance program payments* shall be limited to producers in a clearly designated, contiguous geographic region with definable economic and administrative identity that are considered to be disadvantaged based on objective, clearly defined criteria in the law or regulation that indicate that the region's difficulties are more than temporary. Such payments in any year (a) shall not be related to or based on type/volume of production in any year after the base period (other than to reduce production) or to prices after the base period; (b) where related to production factors, must be made at a degressive rate above a threshold level of the factor concerned; and (c) must be limited to the extra costs or income loss involved in agriculture in the prescribed area.

In summary, the above measures are eligible for placement in the green box (i.e., exempted from AMS) so long as they (1) meet general criteria one and two above and (2) additionally comply with any criteria specific to the type of measure itself. If these conditions are satisfied, no further steps are necessary—the measure is exempt. *However, if not, then the next step is to determine whether it qualifies for the blue box exemption.*

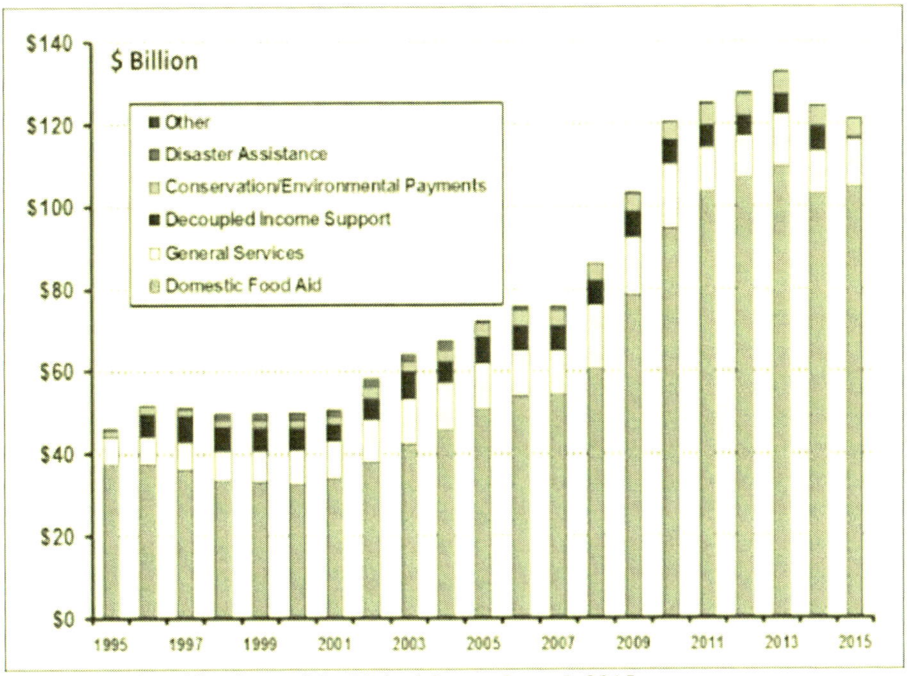

Source: WTO, annual notifications of the United States through 2015.

Note: Until 2008, crop insurance subsidies were calculated as "net indemnities" (equal to indemnities paid minus producer-paid premium) and notified as non-product-specific AMS. In 2008, USDA began notifying certain crop insurance outlays—including administrative costs, delivery-cost reimbursements, and underwriting losses—as green box "General Services," while notifying federal premium subsidies as non-product-specific AMS. In 2012, USDA again changed its notification strategy to notify federal premium subsidies as crop-specific AMS.

Figure 1. U.S. Annual Green Box Notifications by Category.

Question 2: Can This Measure Be Placed in the Blue Box?

No limits are placed on blue box spending, in part because it contains safeguards to prevent program incentives from expanding production. To qualify for exemption in the blue box,[24] a program must be a direct payment under a production-limiting program[25] and must also either:

---

[24] AoA, *WTO Legal Texts*, Article 6.5.

- be based on fixed areas and yields,
- be made on 85% or less of the base level of production, or
- if livestock payments, be made on a fixed number of head.

If these conditions are satisfied, the measure is exempt. *However, if not, then it is considered to be an amber box policy, and the next step is to determine whether spending is above or below the 5%* de minimis *rate.*

Question 3: If Amber, Will Support Exceed 5% of Production Value?

The AoA states that developed country members (including the United States), when calculating their total AMS, do not have to count the value of amber box programs whose total cost is small (or benign) relative to the value of either a specific commodity, if the program is commodity-specific, or the value of total production if the program is not commodity-specific.[26] In other words, "amber box" (i.e., potentially trade-distorting) policies may be excluded under the following two *de minimis* exclusions:

- *Product-specific domestic support*, whereby it does not exceed 5% of the member's "total value of production of a basic agricultural product during the relevant year." Support provided through all of the measures specific to a product—not just a single measure in question—is tallied to determine whether the 5% level is exceeded. For example, the value of the 2015 U.S. corn crop was $49.3 billion, and 5% of that was $2.467 billion.[27] This compares with corn-specific AMS outlays of $2.362 billion. Since it is below the 5% product-specific *de minimis* threshold, the entire $2.362 billion was exempted from inclusion under the AMS limit for the marketing year 2015. In contrast, U.S. sugar support of $1.525 billion for 2015 easily exceeded its 5% product-specific *de minimis* of $133.2 million (based on total sugar value of $2.7 billion) and, therefore, was counted against the AMS limit.
- *Non-product-specific domestic support*, whereby it does not exceed 5% of the "value of the member's total agricultural production." All non-product-specific

[25] An example of a production-limiting program is the now-abandoned U.S. target-price, deficiency-payment program that linked payments to land set-aside requirements. The target-price, deficiency-payment program was first established under the 1973 farm bill (the Agricultural and Consumer Protection Act of 1973; P.L. 93-86) and was terminated by the 1996 farm bill (The Federal Agriculture Improvement and Reform Act of 1996; P.L. 104-127). As a result, the United States only notified blue box payments under this program for 1995.

[26] AoA, *WTO Legal Texts*, Article 6.4.

[27] Data are from the U.S. notification to the WTO Committee on Agriculture, domestic support commitments (Table DS:1 and the relevant supporting tables) for the marketing year 2015, G/AG/N/USA/121, May 1, 2018.

support is tallied to determine whether the 5% level is exceeded. For example, the value of 2015 U.S. agricultural production was notified to the WTO as $372.7 billion.[28] The 5% threshold for non-product-specific support was $18.6 billion. The United States notified outlays of $8.2 billion for non-product-specific support in 2015. As a result, the entire $8.2 billion was exempted from inclusion under the AMS limit.

These provisions are known as the so-called *de minimis* clause. *If the cost of any particular measure effectively boosts the total support above 5%, then all such support (not just the portion of support in excess of 5%) must be counted toward the U.S. total annual AMS.*

Question 4: Does Total Annual AMS Now Exceed $19.1 Billion?

Finally, all support that does not qualify for an exemption is added for the year. If total U.S. AMS does not exceed $19.1 billion, the WTO commitment is met (*Figure 2*). Through 2015, the most recent year for which the United States has made notifications to the WTO, the United States has never exceeded its $19.1 billion amber box spending limit. The closest approach was in 1999, when the United States notified a total AMS of $16.862 billion. However, the *de minimis* exemptions have been instrumental in helping the United States avoid exceeding its amber box limit in 1999, 2000, and 2001, when total AMS outlays prior to exemptions were $24.3 billion, $24.2 billion, and $21.5 billion, respectively (*Figure 3*).

The 2014 farm bill includes a provision, Section 1601(d), that serves as a safety trigger for USDA to adjust program outlays (subject to notification being given to both the House and Senate agriculture committees) in such a way as to avoid breaching the AMS limit.

Question 5: Does Domestic Support Result in Significant Market Distortion in International Markets?

An additional consideration for WTO compliance—the SCM rules governing adverse market effects resulting from a domestic farm support program—comes into play when a domestic farm policy effect spills over into international markets. This is particularly relevant for the United States because it is a major producer, consumer, exporter, and/or

[28] WTO Committee on Agriculture, domestic support commitments for the marketing year 2015.

importer of most major agricultural commodities—but especially of temperate field crops (which are the main beneficiaries of U.S. farm program support). If a particular U.S. farm program is deemed to result in market distortion that adversely affects other WTO members—even if it is compliant with all AoA commitments and agreed-upon spending limits—then that program may be subject to challenge under the WTO dispute settlement procedures. (Brazil's WTO case against U.S. cotton programs is a prime example of this.)[29]

CONCLUSION

The AoA's structure of varying spending limits across the amber, blue, and green boxes is intentional. By leaving no constraint on spending in the green box while imposing limits on amber box spending, the WTO implicitly encourages countries to design their domestic farm support programs to be green box compliant.[30]

Negotiations to further reform agricultural trade within the context of the WTO—referred to as the Doha Round of multilateral trade negotiations—began in 2001.[31] In 2009, negotiations hit an impasse but resumed in 2011 when ministers agreed to concentrate on topics where progress was most likely to be made.[32] They are not expected to be completed in the near future.

As U.S. lawmakers consider policy options for agriculture, other countries will likely be evaluating not only whether, in their view, these options will comply with the U.S. commitments under the AoA but also how they reflect on the U.S. negotiating position in WTO multilateral talks. The U.S. objective, in the past, has been for the negotiations to result in substantial reductions in trade-distorting support and for stronger rules that ensure that all production-related support is subject to discipline (to avoid costly and time-consuming challenges via the WTO Dispute Settlement process)[33] while still preserving criteria-based "green box" policies that can support agriculture in ways that minimize trade distortions. At the same time, Congress might seek domestic farm policy measures that it can justify as AoA- and SCM-compliant.

[29] CRS Report R43336, The WTO Brazil-U.S. Cotton Case.

[30] Carl Zulauf and David Orden, *U.S. Farm Policy and Risk Assistance: The Competing Senate and House Agriculture Committee Bills of July 2012*, International Centre for Trade and Sustainable Development, http://www.ictsd.org.

[31] For more information, see CRS Report RS22927, *WTO Doha Round: Implications for U.S. Agriculture*.

[32] WTO, Agriculture Negotiations (as of August 24, 2018), https://www.wto.org/english/tratop_e/agric_e/negoti_e.htm.

[33] As exemplified by the recent U.S. challenge of China's domestic support for agricultural producers. WTO, Dispute Settlement cases, DS511: China—Domestic Support for Agricultural Producers, first initiated by the United States on September 13, 2016, https://www.wto.org/english/tratop_e/dispu_e/cases_e/ds511_e.htm.

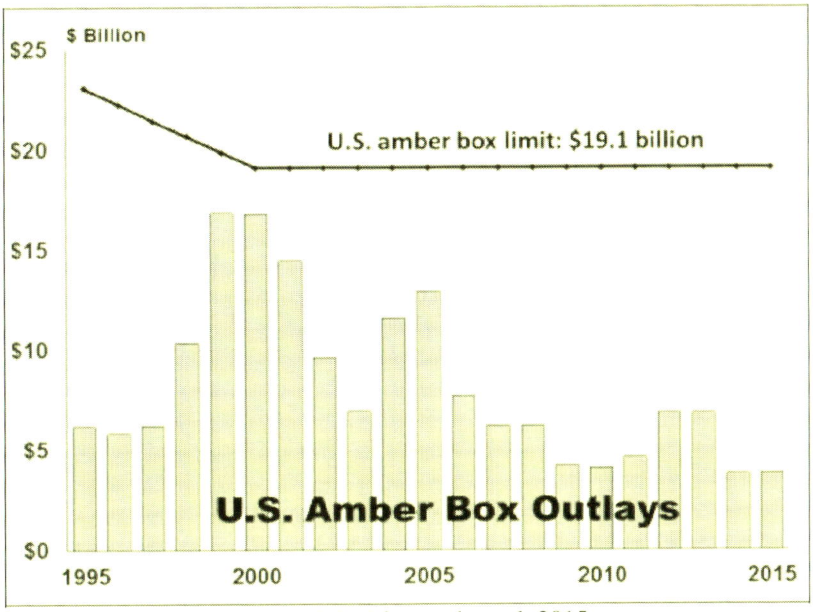

Source: WTO, annual notifications of the United States through 2015.

Figure 2. U.S. Amber Box Outlays Subject to AMS Spending Limit.

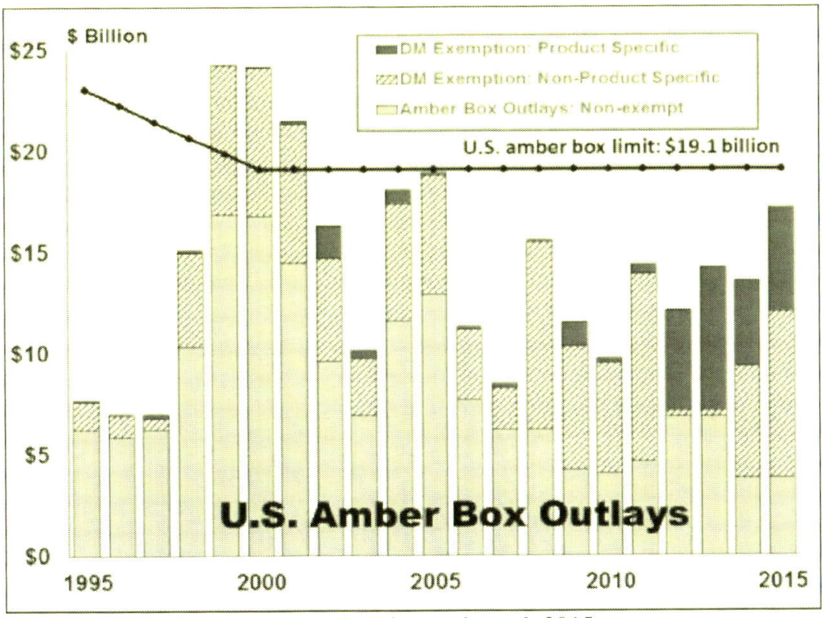

Source: WTO, annual notifications of the United States through 2015.

Note: In the initial WTO agreement, "developed" countries made AMS reduction commitments from a 1986-1988 base period average by 20% in six equal installments during 1995-2000. Amber box spending limits have been fixed since 2000 at $19.1 billion.

Figure 3. U.S. Amber Box Outlays Including Exemptions.

INDEX

A

B

C

G

H

I

L

M

N

O

P

R

S

T

U

V

W

The Supplemental Nutrition Assistance Program (SNAP): Benefits, Eligibility, and Provisions in the 2014 Farm Bill

Editor: Samuel C. Ward

Series: Hunger and Poverty: Causes, Impacts and Eradication

Book Description: The Supplemental Nutrition Assistance Program (SNAP), formerly called the Food Stamp Program, is designed primarily to increase the food purchasing power of eligible low-income households to help them buy a nutritionally adequate low-cost diet. This book describes the rules related to eligibility for SNAP benefits as well as the rules for benefits and their redemption. In addition, this book discusses categorical eligibility and some of the issues raised by it.

Hardcover ISBN: 978-1-63483-730-9
Retail Price: $140

Agriculture, Food, and Food Security: Some Contemporary Global Issues

Editor: Clinton Lloyd Beckford, Ph.D.

Series: Agriculture Issues and Policies

Book Description: *Agriculture, Food and Food Security: Some Global Perspectives* is an edited collection of scholarly work. The book looks at agriculture and food in a framework of enhancing food security.

Hardcover ISBN: 978-1-53613-483-4
Retail Price: $160